A PORTRAIT OF THE *ISRAELI SOLDIER*

**Recent Titles in
Contributions in Military Studies**

History of the Art of War: Within the Framework of Political History, The Modern Era
Hans Delbrück; Walter J. Renfroe, Jr., translator

In Peace and War: Interpretations of American Naval History, 1775–1984. A Second Edition
Kenneth J. Hagan, editor

America's Forgotten Wars: The Counterrevolutionary Past and Lessons for the Future
Sam C. Sarkesian

The Heights of Courage: A Tank Leader's War on the Golan
Avigdor Kahalani

The Tainted War: Culture and Identity in Vietnam War Narratives
Lloyd B. Lewis

Shaping a Maritime Empire: The Commercial and Diplomatic Role of the American Navy, 1829–1861
John H. Schroeder

The American Occupation of Austria: Planning and Early Years
Donald R. Whitnah and Edgar L. Erickson

Crusade in Nuremburg: Military Occupation, 1945–1949
Boyd L. Dastrup

The Dogma of the Battle of Annihilation: The Theories of Clausewitz and Schlieffen and Their Impact on the German Conduct of Two World Wars
Jehuda L. Wallach

Jailed for Peace: The History of American Draft Law Violators, 1658–1985
Stephen M. Kohn

Against All Enemies: Interpretations of American Military History from Colonial Times to the Present
Kenneth J. Hagan and William R. Roberts

Citizen Sailors in a Changing Society: Policy Issues for Manning the United States Naval Reserve
Edited by Louis A. Zurcher, Milton L. Boykin, and Hardy L. Merritt

Strategic Nuclear War: What the Superpowers Target and Why
William C. Martel and Paul L. Savage

Soviet Military Psychiatry: The Theory and Practice of Coping with Battle Stress
Richard A Gabriel

A PORTRAIT OF THE *ISRAELI SOLDIER*

——————— REUVEN GAL

Contributions in Military Studies, Number 52

Greenwood Press
New York • Westport, Connecticut • London

Library of Congress Cataloging-in-Publication Data

Gal, Reuven, 1942-
  A portrait of the Israeli soldier.

  (Contributions in military studies, ISSN 0883-6884 ; no. 52)
  Bibliography: p.
  Includes index.
  1. Sociology, Military—Israel. 2. Israel—Armed Forces. I. Title. II. Series.
  UA853.I8G27 1986   355'.0095694   85-27170
  ISBN 0-313-24315-8 (lib. bdg. : alk. paper)

Copyright © 1986 by Reuven Gal

All rights reserved. No portion of this book may be reproduced, by any process or technique, without the express written consent of the publisher.

Library of Congress Catalog Card Number: 85-27170
ISBN: 0-313-24315-8
ISSN: 0883-6884

First published in 1986

Greenwood Press, Inc.
88 Post Road West, Westport, Connecticut 06881

∞

The paper used in this book complies with the Permanent Paper Standard issued by the National Information Standards Organization (Z39.48-1984).

10 9 8 7 6 5 4 3 2 1

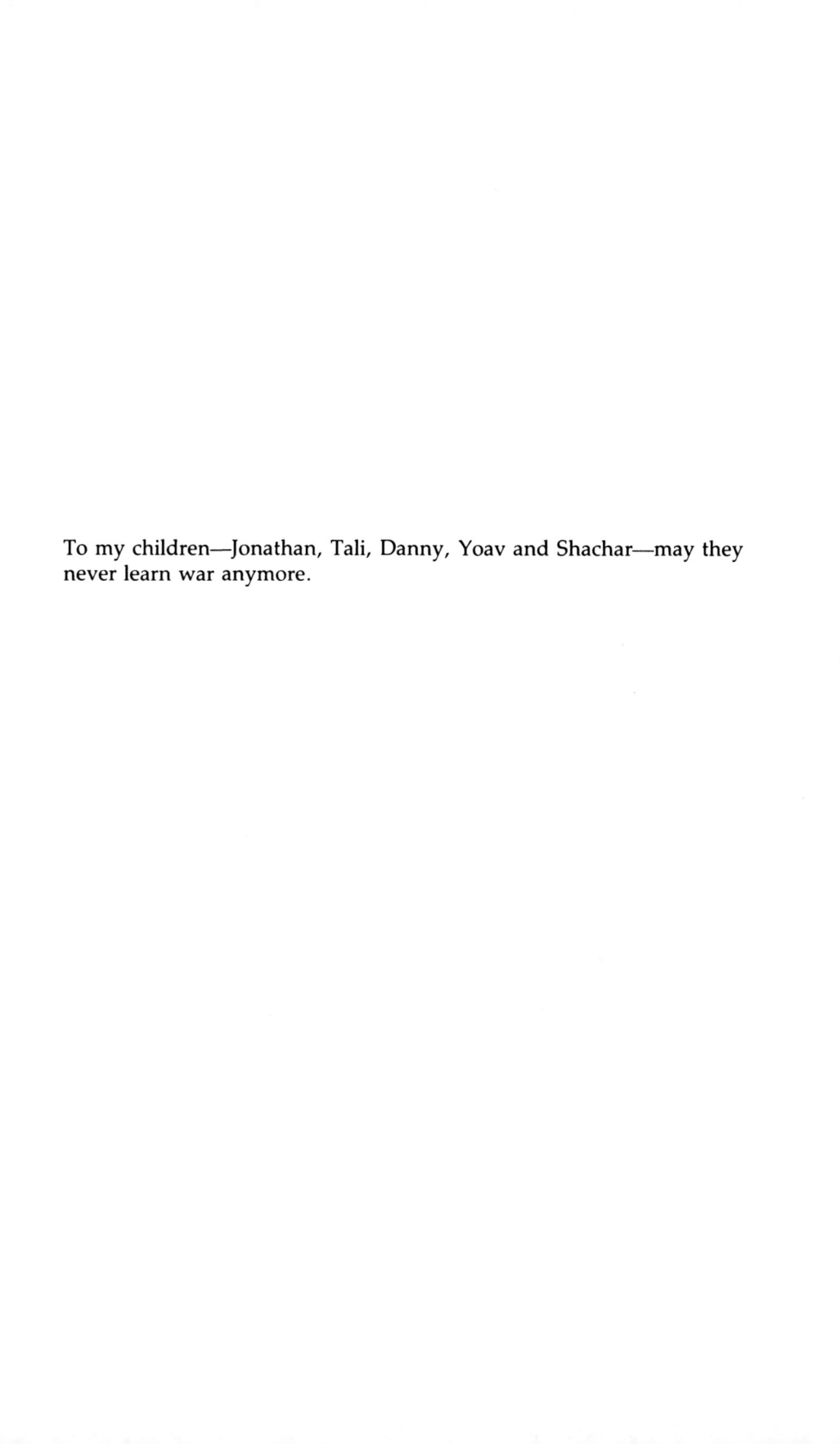

To my children—Jonathan, Tali, Danny, Yoav and Shachar—may they never learn war anymore.

Contents

Illustrations	ix
Figures	xi
Tables	xiii
Preface	xv
1. Historical Background	1
2. Military Service in Israel	30
3. Women in the IDF	46
4. Motivation for Military Service	58
5. The Selection, Classification and Placement Process	76
6. The First Steps: Induction and Basic Training	97
7. The Leadership Corps	115
8. The Fighting Spirit	143
9. Senior Leadership	166
10. Heroism: The Roots of Bravery	190
11. Battle Stress and Combat Reactions	209
12. Military Norms and Ethics	231
13. Fault Lines	246
Bibliography	259
Index	269

Illustrations

Following page 142. All photographs are from the IDF Spokesman.

1. An Israeli tank on parade.
2. A squad leader (corporal) checking his men's weapons.
3. Night river crossing.
4. A tank crew, belonging to one of the "Yeshivot companies," taking their prayers during a lull in training.
5. Practicing "carrying the wounded."
6. Basic training: the trainees and their instructor.
7. Instructing a fresh group of conscripts in "Bakum" (Induction Base).
8. IDF female soldiers in the Artillery School.
9. Paratrooper trainees receive their personal weapon during a night ceremony near the Wailing Wall, Jerusalem.
10. A group of "miluimmniks" (reservists).
11. Impromptu command briefing in the field. (Sitting on the Jeep is Major General "Yanoush" Ben-Gal.)
12. "Nahal" commanders during training lull.
13. An Infantry unit reviewing a just-completed exercise. (Lieutenant General Moshe Levi is sitting on the left.)
14. Aboard a naval gunboat.
15. Two Israeli combat pilots on their way to their aircraft.
16. Air Force air traffic controllers.

17. IDF soldiers in Kiriat Shmona (a town in Upper Galilee) after massive PLO bombardment.
18. Infantry troops patrolling in Lebanon.
19. IDF soldiers upon return from night operation in Lebanon.
20. An Israeli soldier feeding PLO POWs.

Figures

2.1 Order to Report for Registration at District Recruiting
    Offices   31
5.1 Distribution of Ranks by Kaba (Quality Group) Scores   82
8.1 Correlations Between Morale and Other Variables   152
8.2 Level of Confidence in Commanders   156
11.1 Percentage of Soldiers Involved in Physical (Wounded)
     and Psychiatric Casualties by Day of Combat   214

Tables

1.1	Israeli and Arab Air Losses During the Six Day War	20
1.2	IDF Total Manpower Strength in 1973 and 1983	23
3.1	Sample of IDF Specialties and Frequency of Preference by Chen Conscripts	51
4.1	Responses on the 1980 Preinduction Survey	62
4.2	Percentage of Conscripts Expressing their Willingness to Serve in Volunteer (V) or Non-Volunteer (NV) Units/Corps in the IDF	64
4.3	Israeli Ministers of Defence since the Establishment of the State of Israel	71
5.1	Range of Validity Coefficients (Pearson correlation) and Multiple Correlation Coefficient (MCC) of the Kaba and Its Components	80
7.1	Percentage of Soldiers (in Each of Four Main Ground Combat Corps) Referring to Various Levels of Command as Their "Direct Commander"	133
7.2	IDF Casualties (KIA and WIA) by Ranks in the Lebanon War	138
9.1	The 1984 IDF General Staff Members	168
9.2	Israeli Chiefs of Staff: 1948 to 1983	172
9.3	1973 Yom Kippur War and 1982 Lebanon War Fatalities and Bravery Awards	177
10.1	Distribution of Medal Recipients According to Types of Military Service	196
10.2	Distribution of Medal Recipients According to Branch of Service	197
10.3	Distribution of Medal Recipients According to Military Rank	197

10.4	Distribution According to Age Groups of Medal Group and Control Group	199
10.5	Distribution by Countries of Birth and Origin of Medal and Control Groups	200
10.6	Means of Indices of Military Background	201
10.7	Mean Scores of Personality Evaluations	202
10.8	Distribution of Medal and Citation Recipients Following the Lebanon War According to Military Rank	205
11.1	Number and Proportion of Fatalities in Israel's Six Wars	210
11.2	Distribution of Psychiatric and Physical (Wounded) Casualties by Military Assignment	215
11.3	Distribution of Psychiatric and Physical Casualties by Kaba Scores	216
11.4	Unit-Related Factors as Experienced by Two Groups of Combat Soldiers	217

Preface

This book is about the Israeli soldier—an entity that, in reality, does not exist. Obviously, there is no such figure, and proposing a portrait of *the* Israeli soldier is, granted, risking vast generalization. Not only are there universal differences among individuals, in the Israeli case there are enormous differences between the young generations and the not-so-young (though still serving) generations; between Sabras (Israeli natives) and non-Sabras; between Sepharadim (and the many ethnic groups among them) and the Ashkenazim (and their diversities); between kibbutznicks and city kids. Even within the Israeli Defence Forces (IDF), one may easily note major differences among corps, branches and units. The Israeli Air Force, for example, has its own norms, character and esprit de corps; the Navy carries its own lore. And within the ground forces the Armor troops and their officers are distinctly different from the Infantry soldiers and their leaders. Even within the Infantry corps, the "Golani" brigade esprit is quite remote from that of the paratroopers, to mention only one example.

Yet, this book is about the Israeli soldier, because beyond all these distinct characteristics there are some common features shared by almost all of them. These common features pertain to the basic attitudes, norms, feelings and perceptions that the majority of Israeli soldiers—conscripts, reservists and regulars alike—all have with regard to the IDF. These features pertain to the basic motivation of the Israelis to serve in their military and to fight their wars. They pertain to the structure and nature of leadership within the IDF, which is so different from most other military organizations. And they also pertain to the essential ingredients of the fighting spirit which have made the Israeli soldier victorious throughout all the wars.

In an attempt to minimize overgeneralizations, this book focuses, throughout its chapters, on the Israeli ground forces—indeed, portraying primarily (though not exclusively) the Israeli soldier rather than his counterparts, the sailors or pilots. It also emphasizes the fighting elements, the combat units among the ground forces. This was done deliberately for several reasons. First, the ground forces are the clear majority of the Israeli armed forces. Second, the IDF is traditionally dominated by the "green suits" and the Army's fighting spirit (all of Israel's Chiefs of Staff, for example, have always been Army officers). And third, it is the line units (again, predominantly ground units) and combat issues that are always given the highest priorities in the IDF and set the standards and norms for the rest of it. Hence the focus in this book on those units and these issues, although perhaps narrowing the scope of analysis, nonetheless, magnifies its core.

Another risk of erroneous generalization stems from the lack of time perspective. The Israeli soldier portrayed in this book is from the period between the 1973 Yom Kippur War and the post–1982 Lebanon War. Any attempt to delineate trends or changes occurring during this period within the IDF is liable to be either outdated or too early to assess. While not a history book, this volume attempts to analyze processes and structures. The insufficient historical perspective certainly made this not an easy task.

Finally, this book is not free of biases. I served twenty-three years in this army, admittedly not without personal involvement. Such an experience cannot leave one—even the most rigorous scholar—completely unbiased. I confess this openly, though I hope that my bias did not result in any inaccuracies. The personal involvement, however, hopefully enabled me to have a closer familiarity and a better understanding of some of the inside aspects of the subject matter. With this, I believe, I make my amends for the biases.

A Portrait of the Israeli Soldier was harbored for a long time within me. In its final format, however, this book owes a great deal to many. Eugene Weiner, a dear friend, was the first to encourage me on this endeavor. Rick Gabriel, a colleague and a friend, and Jim Sabin have been supportive all along. My friends and colleagues in the Department of Behavioral Sciences in the IDF not only provided the needed help, but their direct contribution is apparent throughout the pages of this book. The IDF Spokesman was very helpful and provided all of the photographs in this volume. And helpful as well were various members of the Chief Education Corps' Office and the *Bamahane* Editorial Office.

However, the main burden of my writing was suffered by my colleagues in the Department of Military Psychiatry, Walter Reed Army Institute of Research (WRAIR), Washington, D.C. Special thanks are due to David Marlowe, the Department Chief, who never ceased to provide his idiosyncratic encouragement. Joseph Rothberg, Rick Manning and Larry Ingraham were extremely helpful in so many ways. So were others in WRAIR. For these unique two years in Washington, D.C., I owe my deep gratitude to the National Research Council (of the National Academy of Science) and the Division of Neuropsychiatry, WRAIR.

Linette Sparacino deserves a special award for combating the *Israeli Soldier* throughout its entire creation. Her assistance in editing, typing, arranging and rearranging the material was beyond any appreciation.

My whole family bore with me throughout this long endeavor. But more than anyone else I am grateful to my woman of valor, Ivria. Without her this book would have never seen light.

A PORTRAIT OF THE *ISRAELI SOLDIER*

1
HISTORICAL BACKGROUND

The Israeli soldier—an image taken for granted as an inseparable part of contemporary Israeli society—is, in fact, a historical oddity. Jews, throughout their two millenium of Diaspora, were never viewed as warriors; neither was Zionism, the nineteenth-century renewed Jewish nationalistic ideology, ever a martial movement. The development of the modern Israeli military has been the result of a multitude of historical necessities combined with contemporary social, political and cultural forces. Together they gradually formed and shaped the current profile of the Israeli soldier.

At the same time, the Israeli military has had its own impact upon the shape of the modern State of Israel, in its political, economic, social and cultural aspects. In the mind of the average Israeli it is impossible to separate the Israeli military from the history and characteristics of modern Israel.

In order to better understand the unique nature and characteristics of the Israeli Defence Forces (IDF), one has to have fuller knowledge of its origins. As in any psychological case analysis, the process begins with basic background information including details about ancestors and critical events which might have influenced the conception itself.

The Israeli Defence Force was formally established on May 26, 1948, just twelve days after the birth of the new State of Israel and in the midst of the War of Independence. Officially named "Zvah Haganah LeIsrael"[1] it quickly became known as "Zahal" (its acronym which is pronounced "tsahal"). Thus was created the first official army in an independent Jewish state in over 2,000 years. The roots of the IDF, however, begin at the turn of the twentieth century.

This chapter is a review of the most significant of these roots as they have influenced the development of the IDF. It does not pretend to be a complete historical analysis.[2] Rather, it will attempt to illuminate those events, processes and figures in the history of the IDF that have played a major role in shaping and molding the portrait of the Israeli soldier.

The Prestate Phase

In September 1907, a group of ten young Jewish pioneers, recent immigrants from Russia to Palestine, met secretly in the town of Jaffa with their leader, an intense Russian Jew named Israel Shochat. This group of young men and women had been strongly influenced by the socialistic revolutionary movement of Tsarist Russia and had abandoned their religious background as Eastern European Jews upon immigrating to Palestine. Inspired by the decree of Theodor Herzl, the founder of modern Zionism, they were committed to create "a publicly recognized, legally secured home in Palestine for the Jewish people." The young Shochat now argued that it would be impossible to achieve the Zionist ideal unless Jews were prepared to undertake their own self-defense.

The result of that secret meeting was the foundation of the first society of armed Jewish watchmen. Though unlawful under the Turkish rule, these young militants were ready to assume any guard duties for the miniature Jewish settlements starting to be built in the wild land that was Palestine. The society was named Bar-Giora, after a Jewish leader who fought against the Romans in A.D. 70 in a war which had seen the destruction of the last sovereign state of the Jews.

The secret society was soon replaced by an open movement which changed its name to "Hashomer" (the watchman). Its members—all volunteers of exceptional motivation and quality—became the elite of the small Jewish community in Palestine. In their ideology they were committed to three major goals: self-defense, the promotion of modern Zionism and socialism. Before finally disbanding during the World War I years, these founders of the future Israeli armed forces had demonstrated that Jews could be daring fighters, capable of forcibly protecting Jewish lives and property.

During World War I many of the young Zionists who were later to become leaders of the emerging state volunteered to the Jewish Legion, part of the British Army. Here they gained military experience and earned high praise from General Allenby for their dedication.

As the war ended, the Jewish Legion was discharged, and Palestine became a British Mandate. In the following years it became quite evident that the restless Arab population of Palestine was not ready to tolerate the growing Jewish community. Furthermore, it soon became clear that the British Army was not overly concerned with protecting the Jewish settlements from Arab attacks. During the years 1920–21 several such attacks on Jewish communities in Jerusalem and Jaffa resulted in the murder of many Jews. Later, in 1929, nearly 150 men, women and children were brutally murdered in Hebron, Jerusalem, Jaffa and elsewhere by uncontrolled Arab mobs. The obvious need for self-defense could no longer be ignored.

The formation of the Haganah (literally translated as "defense") in 1920 was the response of the Jewish community in Palestine to the Arab threats. This clandestine Jewish self-defense, paramilitary organization was the precursor of the IDF. The Labor-Zionists who founded and manned the Haganah perceived their martial responsibilities as more than just protecting the entire community of Palestine Jewry. They viewed it as an inseparable part of a wider ideal of reconstructing Jewish life in the Land of Israel, based on humanistic-socialistic principles of justice, righteousness and social solidarity. Along with their commitment to stand armed against any hostile attacks, they also saw their mission as that of creating "a new society of farmers and workers who would subdue the land by the sweat of their brow."

For the student of the Israeli military it is important to note that the Haganah emerged from a strong pacifist background. Even in the face of continuing Arab riots and murderous attacks, the Labor-Zionist leaders of the Haganah strongly opposed the use of force except for self-defense. This self-restraint policy, based on both moral principle "to keep your weapon clean" (later to develop into one of the IDF's most important slogans—"tohar haneshek" or purity of arms) and on a political need to gain favorable British public opinion, was, nevertheless, objected to by many Haganah extremists who felt that this approach was morally naive and tactically inept. Yet, one has to remember that the Haganah was not solely a military organization. Composed predominantly of a cultural elite of idealistic intellectuals, it was also the nucleus of the political administration of the nation to emerge.

Thus, from its early days the Haganah was involved in nation-building affairs. Its first large-scale operation was the organization of illegal immigration of Jewish refugees into Palestine. Without bloodshed the Haganah rescued thousands of families whose lives were threatened in pre-Nazi Europe or in increasingly anti-Jewish Muslim countries. Likewise, in response to Arab gang attacks on Jews in Palestine, the Haganah's retaliation was not by counterattack or personal violence, but by erecting, overnight, new Jewish settlements—"the Tower and Stockade Settlements"—thus providing additional strength to the development of the new nation.

The increasing Arab violence and attacks in the early 1930s, and the inability of the British authorities to provide effective protection for the Jewish community, resulted in the formation of full-time, authorized Jewish auxilliary guards. Named the Jewish Settlement Police (JSP), they were trained, armed and paid by the British Mandate authorities. Most of the JSP members were, in fact, members of the Haganah which thus acquired a legal cover for its continued growth in arms and personnel.[3]

As would reoccur throughout the later phases of IDF history, a small elite unit emerged, in 1937, from the JSP and Haganah forces. This new unit was an unconventionally trained force capable of being quickly mobilized whenever and wherever needed. Known as "Fosh" (from the Hebrew abbreviation for "field companies"), these special companies were trained under the extraordinary leadership of Yitzhak Sadeh. Sadeh, virtually idolized by his men, was a robust yet romantic immigrant from Russia who had served as a combat officer in the Red Army. By 1938 Sadeh's volunteer force was a thousand strong and served as an exemplary spearhead for the entire Haganah forces.

Another critical and unexpected development occurred with the appearance on the scene of a brilliant, eccentric young British officer, Orde Wingate. He had been assigned by the British Army to Palestine in order to halt the repeated damage inflicted by Arab guerrillas on the British-owned oil pipeline going to the Haifa refineries. Captain (later General) Wingate, a Protestant Christian raised in the Bible-reading tradition of the Non-Conformist sects and also a passionate believer in the Zionist revival, responded to the challenge in an unconventional way. He formed a mixed Jewish-English counterguerrilla unit, known as Special Night Squads (SNS), to protect this vital pipeline. However, in his biblical vision and with the love he felt for the peoples of the Bible, he saw the SNS as the Jewish Army in embryo and thus dedicated himself to the task of cooperating with the Jewish underground army.

With Wingate's combat approach of applying daring tactics while carrying the battle into the enemy's territory, and Sadeh's dynamic and assertive leadership, the Haganah tradition of defensive strategy began to give way to a more "active defense" policy, which was later to become the very essence of the IDF fighting spirit.

> Yigal Allon, himself a legendary figure in the IDF's history (who later became the commander of the Palmach), was a devoted pupil of both Yitzhak Sadeh (called "the Old Man" by his comrades in the Haganah) and Orde Wingate (known as "the Friend"). In his book, *The Making of Israel's Army*, Allon devoted a long chapter to the influence of these two leaders. He saw in Sadeh "a military genius of world calibre [sic], one of the greatest commanders in Jewish history, the father of modern warfare, the teacher of most young Israeli commanders, including myself." With regard to "the Friend," Allon noted that the "appearance of Wingate, with his extraordinary Zionist ardour inspired by the Bible, his unconventional military gifts and his outstanding courage, was an event of historic importance for the Haganah."
>
> Despite their charismatic similarities there were polar differences

between them: "Wingate was proud and self-contained; Sadeh, also proud, was open and warm. Wingate was lean and ascetic, Sadeh, burly, a professional wrestler, a lover of life, full of vitality. Wingate was born into the tradition of the English Dissenters and Puritans, more religious than emotional. Sadeh was a product of the winds of change that blew through the Jewish world, and of the great Russian Revolution in particular." However, concludes Allon, "both of them were far-sighted men, fashioning their revolutionary military doctrines in obedience to the imperatives of the present with the distant past—the heroic tales of the Scriptures—as their primary model. . . . By teaching the Haganah units to patrol remote fields, plantations and roads, to ambush enemy paths, and to carry out raids against enemy bases which helped to check the enemy's initiative, they effectively pulled the Haganah out of its trenches and barbed wire into the open field, making it adopt a more active kind of defence."[4] (P. 10)

It is particularly illuminating to list the main principles of Wingate's leadership and tactical approach, which left their mark on the doctrines and tactics of the Haganah and later the IDF. These characteristic principles included leadership based on personal example; purposeful yet meticulous discipline, always focused on the practical and operational aspects; careful planning before any operation to assure that every man in the unit understood the basis and purpose of the plan; full delegation of authority to subordinate commanders, always allowing improvisation in accordance with the changing conditions of battle; concentration of forces on the major objective, while at the same time skillfully managing to fragment and scatter the forces when needed; the exploitation of surprise, mobility and night maneuvers; and finally, the emphasis on the ideological motivation of the troops.[5]

The late 1930s witnessed the renewal of Arab riots and guerrilla attacks on Jewish communities. The self-restrained policy, still dominant with the Haganah headquarters authorities, was met with severe objections, especially from the non-socialist Revisionists. This radical right fragment disdained both the socialist domination of the Haganah and what they regarded as its overcautious policy. The controversy finally caused the formation of yet another illegal, more activist group, the National Military Organization (in Hebrew "Irgun Zvai Leumi"), popularly known as the "Irgun." The surreptitious leader of the Irgun was a young man named Menachem Begin, who forty years later, as Israel's Prime Minister, signed the first peace treaty with an Arab country. In 1939 a split within the Irgun further created the small "Lehi" group[6]—an even more radical militant group known as the Stern gang, after their leader, Yair Stern.

Though the Irgun had a few hundred active members and the Lehi no more than a few dozen,[7] these two radical groups initiated a number of offensive reprisals against both Arab and British forces. At the same time they also challenged the Haganah's sole dominance in the area of the Jewish defense. Indeed, their impact was most evident in their forcing the Haganah into a more aggressive defense policy.

On the eve of World War II the Jewish community in Palestine was quite confident in its ability to protect itself. The Haganah had grown significantly, both in size and strength. Its membership now included every able Jewish man and woman. Better weapons had been acquired and better training provided. Controlled by the two elected bodies of Palestine Jewry, the Haganah was still, however, primarily a part-time, voluntary militia, organized in local units but based at geographically strategic points. Though not yet capable of deploying a battalion as a tactical unit (companies being the highest tactical formations), the Haganah was nonetheless emerging "as a modern militia, an army in the making."[8]

At the outbreak of World War II, the Jews in Palestine allied themselves with the British in fighting against Nazism. More than 100,000 men and women registered as volunteers with the British authorities. The British, out of fear of annoying the hostile Arabs, initially assigned these volunteers only to non-combat duties (especially in the North African theatre), labeling them "Palestinians." Only toward the end of the war did the British agree to form the Jewish Brigade, which saw action on the North Italian front. Many leaders and members of the future IDF received their first formal military experience in these units.

With the advancement of the Axis powers in the Western Desert (in North Africa) and with most able-bodied young Jews already serving in the British forces, the Haganah high command decided, in May 1941, to organize a mobile field force for the defense of the remaining Jews in Palestine in the event of any further progress by the Nazi forces. Called "Palmach" (the initials of the Hebrew words for "striking companies"), this force became a distinctly elite unit, known for its bravery, enterprising in its military capabilities and unique in its social bondings and moral codes. In 1941, when the Haganah prepared for a last-ditch stand against the advancing German forces, the Palmach units were considered to be their last resort.

> In mid–1941, the Jews in Palestine felt trapped. From the north they were threatened by Vichy-controlled Syria and Lebanon, with Turkey also ready to join the Axis powers; from the south, by Rommel's African Corps which already threatened Egypt; and from the east by the entire community of Arab nations which was leaning toward joining forces with Berlin and Rome. These impending threats, coupled with the

possibility of being abandoned by the Allies, left the Jewish community in Palestine facing the threat of extinction by two enemies—the Germans and the Arabs. The Haganah—and its newly born striking force, the Palmach—was determined to save as many Jewish lives as possible. If they failed, they were determined "to die fighting rather than in the crematorium."[9]

With this determination, a highly imaginative plan was devised. The whole of Mount Carmel (in the northern part of what is now Israel) and its surrounding areas would be turned into "a huge, well fortified escape fortress for all the Jews in Palestine (numbering just over half a million): a kind of modern Massada."[10]

While this Mount Carmel plan fortunately was never used, its formulation shaped (as much as it also reflected) the decisive spirit of the founding fathers of the Israeli military.

The Palmach was not just another chapter in the history of Israel's military. Nor was it just another fragment of the Haganah. The Palmach became, in fact, the "heart and brain" of the Haganah, serving as an active laboratory for the future Army, where most of the fundamental military doctrines were developed. It further served as a training ground for many of the future leaders of the IDF. Moreover, it became an inspirational model within the Jewish community, guiding their resistance against threat and oppression. Under the extraordinary leadership of Yitzhak Sadeh, its first commander, the Palmach training methods were quite unconventional. It emphasized individual responsibility and leaders' independency of action. Even squad leaders were trained and indoctrinated to be independent commanders rather than subordinate NCOs. Group morale and cohesion, inventive tactics and daring leadership were all emphasized in order to compensate for the Palmach's small size and lack of adequate weapons.

A creative solution to the Palmach's critical lack of resources was provided by the left-wing kibbutz movement which adopted the Palmach units. Stationed in many kibbutzim across the country, Palmach members divided their time and energy between farm work and military training. Though not entirely kibbutznicks themselves, Palmach members were strongly influenced by the socialistic-collectivistic ideas of the kibbutz ideology. In fact, starting from the Hashomer period, throughout the Fosh and the Palmach, the same ideas (and many of the same individuals) underlying the unique kibbutzim concept also dominated the development of the Israeli armed forces. In later years, with the formation of the IDF and the disbanding of the Palmach, the volunteer "Nahal" units within the IDF represented the continuation of the Palmach spirit.

As the Palmach gained strength and stability, it soon developed its own reserve system—the first one in any of the Jewish military organizations. This was the seed for the future IDF's reserve corps. The rank and file of the Palmach were released after two years of active service and placed in a reserve unit. Section and squad commanders served for a period of three years, and for junior officers it was four years. With regard to company commanders and above, the period was individually determined by the commander of the Palmach.[11] Palmach reservists were called up for active duty for a few weeks during each year, to go through training and exercises and even occasionally to participate in a combat operation.

Gunther E. Rothenberg, a professor of military history and himself a World War II veteran of both the British Army and the U.S. Air Force, made the following observation:

"Essentially the Palmach, with about one-fifth of its members girls who participated in all actions, constituted a left-wing 'youth movement in arms,' with its own egalitarian style, defiant both of bourgeois values and of external discipline as exemplified by the British Army. ... Unrecognized, unpaid, often short even of elementary necessities, the Palmach compensated by developing a collective personality of its own. It proudly considered itself more than just a military unit, but a living communal elite, a 'fellowship of fighters' as Sadeh once expressed it. ... Its uniforms, if they can be so called, were khaki shirts and shorts, with the shirt commonly worn outside, supplemented by stocking caps and sweaters. The commanders were young. ... Rank conferred no privileges. There were no badges of distinction, all lived under the same conditions, ate the same food, and did the same work. The only special right accorded to commanders was that they were expected to lead during an attack and stay behind to cover a retreat—a concept that became embedded in the ethos of the Israeli Army."[12] (P. 30)

In 1945 a new and younger commander of the Palmach replaced the aging Yitzhak Sadeh: Yigal Allon, then twenty-eight years old and a disciple of Sadeh, became the first native-born (Sabra) to command a Jewish corps. His close colleague and another devoted pupil of Sadeh—Moshe Dayan—was soon to also fulfill a key role in the history of the Israeli military. Many others who were later to become prominent leaders of the IDF also began their military training and indoctrination as members of the Palmach. Among them were Yitzhak Rabin (later an IDF Chief of Staff and Prime Minister), Haim Bar-Lev (later to become another IDF Chief of Staff and a minister in Israel's government) and David ("Dado") Elazar (Chief of Staff during the Yom Kippur War).

At the end of World War II both the "official" military groups of the Haganah and Palmach and the two independent groups of the Irgun and Lehi concentrated on the task of aiding the thousands of survivors of the Nazi concentration camps to enter Palestine, which had now become the only home for these Jews. The British limited this flow of immigration and even turned many escaping refugee boats back to Europe. The Jewish resistance to the British role became increasingly aggressive with their rising demand for the formal establishment of an independent Jewish state.

The Independence War and the Birth of the IDF

The long-held desire for an independent Jewish state was finally realized. On November 29, 1947, the U.N. General Assembly approved the partition of Palestine into two independent states, one Jewish and one Arab. The British government, which did not approve the partition plan, decided to end the Mandate rule and to withdraw from Palestine within six months. These two decisions immediately ignited a severe armed struggle between the Arabs and Jews. The existence of the soon-to-be-Jewish state was threatened before it had even become a reality.

The entire Jewish population at this time was about 650,000. The Haganah, Palmach, Irgun and Lehi fractions combined had the capability of deploying a force of approximately 50,000[13] men and women, of which only about 15,000 were actual combat troops. The Palmach air wing had eleven light, one-engine aircraft, with a handful of pilots (half of them veterans of the British Royal Air Force). Its naval section was manned by a total of 350 sailors with a few boats.[14] These scattered forces formed the basis of the Israeli Defence Forces when it was created in 1948.

On May 14, 1948, the last British soldier left Palestine (except for a small enclave in the harbor of Haifa). On that same day five Arab military forces—made up of 10,000 Egyptians, 6,000 Jordanians, 4,000 Iraqis, 4,000 Syrians, and 1,500 Lebanese (plus smaller contingents from Saudi Arabia, Yemen and Morocco)—invaded Palestine to help their Palestinian brothers "regain the land." On that same day the establishment of the State of Israel was declared in Tel-Aviv in the midst of an aerial bombardment. The War of Independence was at its height when the official formation of the Israeli Defence Forces took place twelve days later, on May 26, 1948. On that date the three smaller fractions of the prestate defense forces—the Palmach, the Irgun and the Lehi—were all formally absorbed (not without agony and bitterness!) into the new organization of the official Israeli military forces. The Haganah, quite naturally, became the infrastructure for this new defense organization.

Thus the IDF came into existence under fire, which became a very significant characteristic of its spirit. Its entire development—in size, equipment, doctrine and spirit—was dictated by its actively engaged enemies and Israel's actual combat needs. The heritage of the Haganah, Palmach, Irgun and Lehi, as well as that of its predecessors—the Hashomer, the Fosh and SNS—was multifaceted. This heritage provided the structure (unified military, based on territorial sovereignty), leadership (a highly trained and dedicated cadre of combat-experienced commanders at all levels), and fighting spirit (a close-knit bond between unit members which emphasized a morale level and a code of conduct as intense and competent as their military skills) of the new IDF. It also instilled a vital sense of purposefulness and a deeply rooted democratic loyalty within its members.

In this newly born IDF, the initial deficiencies in numbers, weaponry and training were compensated for by dedication and motivation, intelligence and improvisation. These, eventually, came to personify the Israeli soldier.

This chapter is not the place to recapitulate the War of Independence. The war, which lasted almost a year and a half, ended in June 1949 with the signing of the last of four armistice agreements between Israel and its adversaries. It cost the Israelis over 6,000 lives (approximately 1 percent of the total Jewish population of Israel at that time)[15] and essentially exhausted its entire military force. But the new State of Israel persevered. In fact, the armistices of 1949 left Israel with a larger territory than was originally designated by the U.N.'s 1947 partition resolution. Even so, the total area was only 7,993 square miles (about the size of New Jersey). Furthermore, the new borders were formed by the armistice lines, not dictated by strategic concerns, and thus provided only minimal protection for the country's growing population.

The War of Independence, nevertheless, had done more than just preserve the newly born state. It also molded the scattered elements of the prestate defense forces into an integrated, self-assured military organization, which then became the dominant military factor in the Middle East. In retrospect, many of the combat norms and standards of the IDF were born in that period of the Independence War. While that war was not characterized by a multitude of noted senior commanders (with the exception of a few individuals such as Yigal Allon), its real heroes were the commanders at the battalion and company levels. Many of the future generals of the IDF—who would achieve spectacular victories in the wars to come—first served as platoon leaders and company and battalion commanders during the 1948 war. From there they brought with them the fundamental characteristics of decisiveness, purposefulness, leadership by personal example, utilization of night warfare and surprise attacks, and ability to improvise—in short, all those characteristics which enabled them to turn Israel's first war into a critical victory.

Between 1949 and 1956

Much of the shaping of the infant IDF in the years following the Independence War was due to David Ben-Gurion—the powerful and decisive first Prime Minister and (concurrently) Minister of Defence of Israel. With his charismatic personality he forcefully navigated the transitions required to transform an underground militia force into a regular army. Realizing that security would continue to be Israel's major concern, Ben-Gurion and the new Chief of Staff of the IDF, Major General Yigael Yadin, wrestled with the problem of how to create a standing army of sufficient strength to defend the country and yet not be so large as to become a heavy drain on Israel's limited manpower. Their solution was a military organization made up of three components: (1) a permanent ("Keva") service—a relatively small cadre of career officers and non-commissioned officers (NCOs); (2) a compulsory ("Hova") service, composed of drafted conscripts; and (3) a large body of standing reserves ("miluimm") including all those completing their compulsory service.

Molded partially after the Swiss model of reserve service and partially after the Haganah's own experience, the Israeli system became quite exceptional in that the reserve forces were its most important operational components, rather than just being an appendage to the regular forces.[16]

Under Yadin's leadership the new IDF was organized into a formal structure, which, for the most part, prevails today. There were three territorial commands (North, Central and South) and a unified General Staff.[17] Its Chief of Staff, also the only lieutenant general in the IDF, reported directly to the Minister of Defence. The other senior officers on the General Staff were named Aluf (major general), Tat Aluf (brigadier general, introduced only after the Six Day War), and Aluf Mishne (colonel)—all Hebrew terms taken from the Bible.

During its first years, and based on lessons learned from the War of Independence, the IDF's main strategical and tactical doctrines were formulated for years to come. Faced with a series of geopolitical constraints (such as a small standing army, lack of strategic depth, numerical inferiority and limited resources), the IDF developed its major deployment premises, which in fact continue to guide the Israeli military. These major premises were as follows: First, since the surrounding Arab states still threatened to ultimately annihilate the new Jewish nation, Israel had to quickly develop an extremely effective and overtly aggressive military which would serve as a powerful deterrence against such intentions. Second, such deterrence notwithstanding, in order to overcome the lack of strategic depth and its attendant short warning period, the IDF had to develop an efficient intelligence service, functioning almost faultlessly to minimize the possibility of surprise attack. Third, in order to avoid enemy penetration of its own narrow territory, it became imperative that Israel always attack first. Thus its military had to be constantly ready and capable of preempting a first strike and of carrying the war to the enemy's land. Fourth, since the main strength of Israel's military was dependent on reserve forces, it was critical that the IDF always keep its reserve units in full strength and with combat-ready equipment. This necessitated the capability to assemble and mobilize these units within a few hours to the front lines. Furthermore, it meant the Israeli Air Force had to be able to secure clear skies in order for such a massive mobilization to occur without enemy disruption. Fifth, from the very beginning Israel's size coupled with its tenuous economy dictated a "fast-war doctrine." Israel simply could not allow its wars to continue for any length of time or, particularly, to develop into a prolonged war of attrition. Therefore, the IDF's plans and tactics were always geared toward brief, fierce and decisive wars.

Finally, since it was evident that the IDF was becoming the largest single consumer of national resources and the predominant state institution, it naturally followed that it would also carry out a multitude of nation-building functions. This was, in fact, one of Ben-Gurion's most dominant presumptions in molding the IDF as a "people's military."

The following are the words of Ben-Gurion in describing the IDF as he saw it:

"Basically, our Army, Navy, Air Force—all of which operate under unified command . . . are a voluntary association of citizens profoundly oriented towards civilian life. They have dedicated themselves temporarily to national security in our country's great need. . . .

"The Israel Defence Forces . . . have [also] played a formidable part in integrating the different immigrant groups into our community. They have introduced thousands of young women and men to a life of pioneer farm settlement. They have proved themselves a great instrument for education. . . .

"We abhor war and military things as ends in themselves. Nevertheless, the IDF is a source of deep national pride. . . . Were we able to throw down our weapons—and how gladly we should do so—to live in peace with our neighbours, we would still continue to depend on the dynamic represented today by the IDF to fulfill a vast assignment of national development. Not with bullets but with bulldozers and the other constructive tools of modern civilization."[18] (Pp. 66–105)

During the first few years following the end of the War of Independence, the IDF suffered through its "childhood diseases." On the one hand the IDF faced the ongoing replacement of some of its best former Palmach and Haganah combatants. The new cohorts were much less committed conscripts who had come from the waves of immigrants pouring into Israel in the early 1950s. At the same time the IDF was confronted with the intensification of Arab incursions and Fedayeen ("self-sacrificers") attacks on Israeli settlements. The reorganizing infant Army had to quickly come up with effective treatments for these diseases. Some of the cures that emerged were instituted personally by Moshe Dayan, the thirty-eight-year-old newly appointed (late 1953) Chief of Staff. A devoted student of Sadeh and Wingate and himself a maverick leader, Dayan set out to greatly sharpen the teeth of the IDF. In addition to the expansion of the IDF's Intelligence corps and Air Force (but with much less support for the Navy and Armor corps), Dayan put his full weight behind developing a tough and aggressive core of commando fighters who would become the spearhead of the IDF's ground forces. The joint 101-paratroop unit,[19] commanded by Major Ariel Sharon, was assigned to lead the reprisal raids against Arab military installations from which the most recent attacks had been launched. These reprisal raids were adopted by the IDF as part of its policy for responding to frequent Arab strikes. Small as the unit was, its utilization and further development of Fosh and SNS tactics, based on flexibility, speed and surprise, long-range raids, and, above all, night tactics, nonetheless had a great impact on the IDF. These tactics all became, with Dayan's encouragement, standards for all IDF combat units.

Above all, however, Dayan's main credit in the IDF's history is his influence on what became the characteristic leadership style of Israeli officers. Being himself impatient with committees and formalities, Dayan insisted on officers who were fighting leaders rather than managers in uniforms. "Officers," he asserted, "do not *send* their men into battle; they *lead* them into battle." To spread the "paratroopers' spirit" in the IDF as a whole, Dayan required that every officer (including himself) undergo jump training. He further enforced a manpower policy by which career officers were to retire in their forties to make way in the IDF's upper echelons for younger officers. Thus, under Dayan's leadership the IDF formed and refined the distinct fighting characteristics long held by the Israeli soldier.

The Sinai Campaign

The Sinai campaign of 1956 was the first test of this newly formed military and also the first introduction to the world of what the IDF had achieved since its formation, a mere seven years earlier. In concert with

British and French forces (whose major objectives were related to the Suez Canal), the Israelis launched an offensive against the growing Soviet-erected Egyptian arsenal in Sinai. Along with the closing of both the Suez Canal and the Gulf of Aqaba to Israeli ships, and the continuing Fedayeen attacks supported by Egypt, this arsenal had become a critical threat to Israel's existence.

Using an operational plan that reflected Israel's strategic premises, the IDF initiated a fast-moving campaign, designed to be staged solely on the enemy's soil and to utilize surprise tactics and a circumventive approach. The operation began by dropping a paratrooper battalion near the Mitla Pass in western Sinai. The IDF mechanized and armored columns (composed mostly of reservists) soon joined up with the paratroopers, and together, in one hundred hours of operation, they reached the banks of the Suez Canal. It took fewer than four additional days for the IDF to completely conquer the Sinai peninsula which is three times the size of Israel itself. In the process the IDF destroyed an Egyptian force equal to about two divisions, with the loss of only 170 Israeli soldiers.

The Sinai campaign was, in many respects, an astounding success: a rapid and secretive mobilization of massive reserve forces quickly deployed with swift penetration and daring maneuvers, combined with a classic utilization of the indirect approach.[20] The IDF's field commanders demonstrated a great degree of flexibility, improvisation and daring. IDF officers at all levels led their troops from the front, thus proving in combat the standard of personal example, notwithstanding the toll in losses.

However, this campaign was not without its shortcomings. The reserve call-up was not fully accomplished prior to the deployment of units. Poor logistical preparations were manifested in many mechanical and maintenance difficulties. Command and control were excessively loose (partly because of Dayan's insistence on personally staying in the field most of the time). And, finally, coordination among components of ground forces suffered many difficulties.

The lessons of the Sinai campaign brought about a stronger emphasis on combined operations, especially between armored forces and the Air Force. The armored corps was significantly strengthened and became the spearhead of all ground forces. The Air Force, too, emerged from this campaign with an increased priority and quickly developed into a deadly striking force. However, no major modifications were required with regard to the human component of the post-Sinai IDF. The Israeli soldiers of the mid–1950s not only passed their first test of fire since the War of Independence, they also demonstrated their ability to decisively defend Israel in any wars to come.

The Six Day War

The first few years after the Sinai campaign were relatively quiet. The Israeli military used that period to prepare for any future threat. Indeed, tranquility did not last long. On Israel's nineteenth Independence Day a massive Egyptian force began mobilizing in the Sinai peninsula (returned to Egyptian control in 1957). Its strength was estimated at 95,000 men and nearly 1,000 tanks. On May 16, 1967, Cairo's official radio announced that "Egypt is now ready for a total war that will put an end to Israel." Soon thereafter Egyptian President Nasser demanded the complete withdrawal of all U.N. forces in the Sinai, and a few days later he declared the Straits of Tiran (at the entrance to the Aqaba Gulf) closed to all Israeli ships. With Jordan and Syria also mobilizing their forces, Israel was once again faced with a critical threat to its existence.

Much of the Israeli government's quandary as to whether to strike first with a preemptive attack, wait passively until the enemy attacked first, or seek, in vain, international intervention was possible because of Israel's confidence in its military capacity. Most senior military commanders fervently believed that the IDF could sustain a three-front engagement against surrounding enemy forces amounting to almost 330,000 troops, more than 2,300 tanks and about 680 aircraft.[21] Not surprisingly, the IDF's commanders, led by Chief of Staff Yitzhak Rabin, lobbied the government to take an offensive approach. Indeed, their confidence in their troops was unswerving.

The final Israeli decision was made clear on the morning of June 5: within three hours, in an extremely high-risk offense, the Israeli Air Force destroyed most of Egypt's combat aircraft, radar stations and military airfields. Similar damage was inflicted on the Syrian and Jordanian air forces. The fate of the Six Day War was already determined within these first few hours.

Since the details of the Six Day War have been described in so many publications, suffice it to say that with Israel's air supremacy firmly established, the ground forces consequently launched their offensive, fighting almost simultaneously in all three fronts. By the end of the six days of combat the IDF controlled the entire Sinai peninsula. They had also defeated the Syrians and Jordanians and thus captured the Golan Heights and the West Bank with the unification of the city of Jerusalem as the highlight of the war. The victory, moreover, was achieved with relatively low Israeli casualties—689 killed and 2,563 wounded[22]—less than .03 percent of the nation's total population and almost one-tenth of Israeli losses in the Independence War.

The IDF successes in the Six Day War were primarily because of the human factor. Strong combat motivation, high morale, daring leadership and decisive actions characterized the operations of the air, sea and ground forces. The Armor battles in the Sinai and Golan Heights, as well as some of the Infantry battles (such as the ones fought in Jerusalem and again in the Golan Heights) were marked by extraordinary courage on the part of both troops and commanders. The committed leadership and personal example demonstrated by these Israeli officers was reflected in the fact that a disproportionately high number (23 percent) of all IDF casualties in the war were officers.[23]

The personal ingredient, indeed, had to be more significant in this war than the material. The armored "Ugdot" divisions, deployed for the first time in the 1967 war, were equipped with a bizzare stock of tanks ranging from modern Pattons and Centurions to obsolete World War II Shermans and AMX-13 light tank destroyers. Troops were delivered by means of old U.S. surplus M-3 half tracks, civilian buses and delivery vans.

Likewise the Israeli Navy was poorly equipped. It consisted of a few old torpedo boats, two surplus British Z-class destroyers and two S-class World War II submarines. At the time of the Six Day War the Israeli Navy did not have any missile boats to confront the eighteen Egyptian Komar and Osa (Soviet-made) missile boats.

Though the Air Force was relatively well equipped with quality aircraft (with 286 French Mirages, Super-Mysteres, Mysteres and Ouragans) it was certainly outnumbered by the 682 Arab aircraft it faced (Egypt alone had 431).

The Six Day War essentially was won by a new generation of soldiers and young officers, many of them Sabras (native born), who had been trained by the post–1948 Israeli military. However, the senior officer corps was still composed of members of the prestate generation who had acquired their early combat experience within the Palmach and Haganah lines. For example, Chief Air Force Commander, General Mordechai ("Motti") Hod, who was the architect of the ingenious air attack on the first morning of the war, was one of the score of Palmach pilots who flew the one-engine Messerschmitt (S–199) fighters in the early days of the Independence War. The Southern, Central and Northern Commanders—generals Gavish, Narkis and Elazar ("Dado")—were also Palmach or Haganah veterans of the Independence War as were all the other General Staff officers in the Six Day War. A few weeks before the war broke out, Moshe Dayan, another founder of the Israeli military, was appointed to the position of Defence Minister. And commanding this efficient war machine was the forty-four-year-old, ex-Palmach commander, Lt. General Yitzhak Rabin.

Two weeks after the war ended, at a ceremony on Mount Scopus in Jerusalem, General Rabin was awarded an honorary degree of Doctor of Philosophy from the Hebrew University, in recognition of his services to the nation and those of the entire IDF in the recent victory.

His address on that occasion, summarizing what he believed was the secret of Israel's achievement, became a milestone in Israel's military lore. It included the following excerpts:

"I am filled with reverence as I stand here before the teachers of our generation, in this ancient, magnificent place overlooking our eternal capital and the sacred sites of our nation's earliest history. . . .

"I consider myself to be here solely as the representative of the whole Israel Defence Army: of the thousands of officers and tens of thousands of soldiers who brought the victory of the Six Day War to the State of Israel.

"It may well be asked why the University should have been moved to bestow the degree of honorary Doctor of Philosophy upon a soldier in recognition of his war services. What have soldiers to do with the academic world which stands for the life of civilization and culture? . . . The answer, I think, is that in this honour which you have conferred through me upon my fellow soldiers you choose to express your appreciation of the special character of the Israel Defence Army, which is itself an expression of the distinctiveness of the Jewish people as a whole. . . . The University is conferring on us an honorary degree . . . in recognition of the Army's moral and spiritual force as shown, precisely, in active combat. For we are all here in this place only by virtue of the hard-fought war which, though forced upon us, was transformed into a victory that has astounded the world. . . .

"All these things have their origin in the spirit and their end in the spirit. Our soldiers prevailed not by the strength of their weapons but by their sense of mission, by their consciousness of the justice of their cause, by a deep love of their country, and by their understanding of the heavy task laid upon them: to ensure the existence of our people in their homeland, and to affirm, even at the cost of their lives, the right of the Jewish people to live its life in its own state, free, independent, and in peace."[24] (Pp. 298–300, 302)

The 1967 war's outcome validated most of the doctrines and ethos that the IDF believed in and according to which it had prepared itself. Above all, the war verified the Israeli advantage in command and leadership at all levels. Trevor Dupuy, a noted military historian who has analyzed all Arab-Israeli wars, credited the Israeli victory first of all to the flexibility, aggressiveness and dynamic behavior of the Israeli leaders from the company to top command level. Second, he praised the Israeli fighting doctrines and their executions; and, third, he asserted that the

Israelis had more successfully adapted the modern weapons and sophisticated equipment available to them.[25]

However, the definitive victory was so overwhelming to the Israeli military that it resulted in frequent denial of obvious problems. For example, the Israelis downplayed the fact that their success on the ground was all possible because of the lack of air threat to them. They further overemphasized the role of their armored forces in their victory and thus in the future would concentrate their buildup around tanks to the detriment of the infantry and artillery.[26] More than anything else, the Israeli commanders tended to credit the victory to their own ingenuity rather than at least partially acknowledging the enemy's poor performance. Overconfidence on the part of the Israeli soldier began in those carnivallike days after the Six Day War.

By the end of the 1967 war, the people of Israel truly believed that any military threat to their survival in the near future had ceased and that an ultimate peace with their neighboring nations was close. They expected the "telephone call" from Egypt or Jordan offering peace at any moment. Part of that expectation stemmed from the self-perception that they had proven themselves to be so militarily strong that they had crushed the Arabs' hope of ever beating them. It also had to do with the national relief that Israel was no longer such a small and "squinched" state. The Six Day War had enlarged Israel's territory fourfold. The borders were now moved away from its civilian centers, leaving a critical strategic depth in the North, South and West. With these new territories, however, Israel also became responsible for more than a million additional civilians, mostly Palestinians, who lived in the Judaea and Samaria (West Bank) area, the Gaza strip, Sinai and the Golan Heights. These populations presented political, social and cultural problems to Israel as a whole. However, the task of administering these territories was given solely to the IDF. This new arena, that of forcefully occupying Palestinian populated areas, now created unsought challenges for the Israeli soldier.

The War of Attrition

The euphoric atmosphere of triumph and expansion that evolved in Israel after the Six Day War soon evaporated. Chances for immediate peace were drastically reduced with the Arab summit conference in Khartoum in August 1967. At this conference the response of the Arab countries to their recent defeat was reflected in their decision to pursue a policy of "no peace, no recognition and no negotiation" with Israel. On the military front, also, the situation deteriorated rapidly. Less than a month after the Six Day War cease-fire, the first combat confrontation between Israeli and Egyptian forces took place along the Suez Canal. In

October of the same year Egyptian missile boats hit and sank the Israeli destroyer *Eilat* in international waters off Port Said. This was the beginning of the War of Attrition, an entrenched, immobile, yet fierce war, which lasted for three years. Though most intensely fought along the Suez Canal, the War of Attrition also had frontiers in the Golan Heights (against the Syrians) and along the Jordan River (against the Jordanians). This steady war was dominated by heavy exchanges of artillery barrages and air strikes as well as local, short-range ground raids. Israel's insistence, on the one hand, on keeping all positions gained in 1967 and, on the other hand, extreme sensitivity to loss of soldiers' lives forced the IDF, for the first time in its history, into defensive warfare which precluded it from utilizing its normal offensive style. The heavy Bar-Lev Line of fortifications built by the Israelis along the Suez Canal (and numerous similar strongholds in the Golan Heights and the Jordan Valley) exemplify this unprecedented change in the IDF's tactics.

Paradoxically, the consequences of the victorious Six Day War and Israel's new borders increased rather than lightened military demands on Israeli society. The War of Attrition forced the IDF to maintain a larger standing army along its new frontiers. In order to alleviate manpower shortages, conscript service was extended from thirty to thirty-six months; more women were inducted into the military; reserve units were called for active duty for longer periods; and many reserve officers were called back for regular (Keva) service.[27]

Between July 1967 and August 1970, Israeli troops along the Suez Canal, in the Golan Heights and along the Jordanian border experienced virtually non-stop attacks, ambushes, raids and artillery fire. Also, during this period guerrilla and terrorist attacks (launched most frequently from Jordan) against Israeli civilian targets became frequent. It was during this period, too, that commercial airplanes (either Israeli or servicing Israel) began to be hijacked by various Palestinian terrorist organizations, thus signaling the beginning of a new international wave of terrorism.

Israel's military reaction during the War of Attrition was swift, retaliatory, and frequently surprising. Trying to avoid a defensive-reactive response, the IDF again used the indirect approach. Long-range strikes (more than 200 miles from the nearest Israeli point) were launched by Israeli fighter aircraft; airborne and armor raids were conducted across the Gulf of Suez. Similar, though less frequent, assaults were made along the Syrian and Jordanian fronts. In the face of the growing number of Soviet-made (and most frequently Soviet-operated) anti-aircraft systems on the Egyptian side of the canal, the Israelis relied upon their personnel quality edge. This was exemplified in the overall outcome of air-to-air confrontations: throughout the three years of the War of Attrition, the Israeli Air Force lost only two fighters (the French-made Mirage) in "dog-

Table 1.1
Israeli and Arab Air Losses During the Six Day War

	Air-to-air	Ground-to-air	Total
Israeli Air Force losses	2	25	27
Arab losses	125	37	162

fights" compared to over sixty MiG–21s, the best Soviet-made fighter at that time, lost by the Egyptian Air Force.[28] The overall kill ratios from aerial combat between July 1967 and May 1973 are presented in Table 1.1.[29]

The War of Attrition ended with a cease-fire imposed by the Soviets and Americans in August 1970. Though it did not weaken the Israeli hold on all the positions it had won in the Six Day War, it left the IDF licking its wounds: almost 600 Israeli soldiers had been killed and 2,000 wounded during that period. Israel's great sensitivity to its human losses was painfully apparent. Yet, at the same time, within the military the self-complacency of the post–1967 era continued. The prosperity that characterized the Israeli economy at that time, as well as the expanding military budget, all joined to generate a lax and casual attitude among the IDF senior officers. Furthermore, the impasse that was the War of Attrition left the IDF with no definite assessment regarding the effectiveness of its defensive strategy (e.g., the Bar-Lev line) against future attacks. This combination of complacent attitude and strategic ambiguity would cost bitterly three years later at the outbreak of the Yom Kippur War.

The Yom Kippur War

The IDF's conclusive victory in the Six Day War did not bring with it the anticipated peace. Nor did its persevering resistance during the War of Attrition dissuade the Arab nations from attempting yet another trial to achieve their often-stated desire of obliterating Israel.

In the early afternoon of October 6, 1973, on the Jewish holiest Day of Atonement (Yom Kippur), Egyptian and Syrian forces launched a surprise and well-coordinated attack along the Suez Canal and the Golan Heights. Within a few hours the Egyptian Army successfully crossed the canal, overrunning the Bar-Lev strongholds, while Syrian armored columns roared toward the heart of Israel's northern region, the Upper Galilee. A trimmed force of Israeli standing army troops was desperately trying to stop these massive attacking forces while most of Israel's citizens were still confined to their homes and synagogues on this day of prayer and fasting. A few hours later many of these same civilians were with their reserve units fighting for their lives in Israel's most bitter war.

> The impact of this startling military attack on the Israeli population can only be understood in light of its history and current state of mind. Once again, as during the War of Independence and in the anticipatory period prior to the Six Day War, the people of Israel faced a genuine threat to their very existence. Perhaps most indicative of this was the sense of shock felt by those Israelis who were Holocaust survivors. For them the 1973 Yom Kippur attack was a return to the trauma of the near-death experience they had gone through thirty years earlier.[30]

The Israeli Army was caught off guard by the Yom Kippur War. The IDF's Intelligence corps had discounted the possibility that the Arabs would initiate an all-out war with Israel. The standing forces in the Sinai and the Golan Heights were quite relaxed and overly self-confident.[31] Support troops servicing the military depots for the reserve combat units had been just as lax, if not neglectful, as the regular forces. Uncertainties and indecision led to the delayed mobilization of the IDF to its full strength, while the massive Egyptian and Syrian forces penetrated the Israeli lines.

During the first few days of the Yom Kippur War the Israeli situation was quite desperate—as they were suffering high casualty rates and were unable to wage effective counterattacks. It was the psychological impact of the surprise attack combined with the enormous gap in quantities between them and their adversaries that left the Israelis temporarily paralyzed, in sharp contrast to their usual military prowess.

The turning point in the Sinai frontier (which felt the effects of that paralysis more than the Northern command) came only on October 14, more than a week after the onset of the war. On that day the Israelis managed to successfully repulse a major Egyptian attack[32] which not only improved the Israeli tactical situation but, more importantly, re-elevated morale and self-confidence—an essential ingredient in the IDF's fighting spirit.[33] Once the Israeli forces regained their familiar zest, the counterattack across the Suez Canal followed shortly. When the final cease-fire came, on October 24, the Israelis had recaptured all their positions in the Sinai, plus hundreds of square miles of Egyptian territory west of the Canal, and had surrounded the entire Egyptian 3rd Army (about 45,000 men).

In the northern frontier, where geostrategic depth is much less, the IDF had turned to a counterattack strategy from the very beginning of the battles. While heroic defensive battles were still being fought by the original regular forces at some points along this front, at other points the just-mobilized reserve forces had already pushed the fight into Syrian territory. In six days of relentless fighting, the advanced Israeli units were within twenty-five miles of Damascus.

Despite the remarkable recovery of the IDF from initial surprise and defeat to an unequivocal victory, the Yom Kippur War nonetheless made the Israelis realize that their gallant military was not altogether invincible. In the course of averting a disaster, the IDF paid a toll of 2,680 dead and about 7,000 wounded. This loss rate (when adjusted for population-size differences) is more than thirty times the American loss rate in World War II. The impact of such a loss on a population of a tiny state (less than 3 million Jewish population in 1973) was enormous. Furthermore, if the 1967 war left the Israelis with the illusion that their superiority over the Arabs was unquestionable, the Yom Kippur War not only brought an end to that illusion, but it also demonstrated that overconfidence could develop into a weakness. Coming under increasing public pressure to scrutinize the "blunder of October"[34] and not to leave the lessons of the Yom Kippur War unlearned, the IDF would undergo some massive changes in the following years.

Perhaps the most important lesson was the realization that courage, devotion and decisiveness might not be enough any longer against the growing Arab military forces. Besides the political implications of such a realization, for the IDF it meant that in addition to maintaining its qualitative edge, it must also expand to achieve a quantitative comparability.

Between 1973 and 1982

Immediately after the Yom Kippur War, the IDF began an enormous expansion—in manpower, equipment and complexity. In less than ten years (when in 1982 it was again called upon to wage a large-scale war, this time in Lebanon), the IDF had evolved into a larger, more heavily equipped, more mobile and more complex force than the military which had fought in 1973. Some of the following figures are indicative. From a total of ten Armor brigades in 1973, the IDF expanded to thirty-three such brigades, thus establishing eleven combat-ready divisions (Ugdot). In 1973 the IDF had three artillery brigades; by 1982 they had fifteen such brigades. The total mobilization capability of the IDF in 1973 was estimated to be around 300,000. In 1982 this number had been raised to 500,000—an increase of almost 70 percent.[35] Table 1.2 delineates the manpower changes between the years 1973 and 1982.[36]

One may wonder how the IDF managed to locate additional manpower resources, particularly since a full draft system (with few exemptions) was already in operation in 1973. Starting in 1974 the IDF began to recruit conscripts from categories which had not been previously used.

Table 1.2
IDF Total Manpower Strength in 1973 and 1983

	July 1973	July 1983
Permanent Corps	30,000	51,700
Conscripts	85,000	120,300
Reserves	180,000	326,000
Total Mobilization (within 72 hours)	~300,000	~500,000

This included individuals with a low level of education in addition to those with adjustment problems (including some with a minor police record). More and more women were inducted and channeled into combat-support specialties to free more men for combat roles. In reserve units manpower rosters were scrupulously combed to locate individuals who could be reassigned from non-combat to combat positions. And finally the permanent (Keva) core of the IDF was augmented by more than 70 percent. The major objective was to create as many combat formations (mostly in terms of brigades) as the overall population pool of Israel could produce. The new IDF doctrine regarding the quantity-quality balance now sought as many, albeit small, units as possible.[37]

The massive buildup in the years following the Yom Kippur War brought the IDF's total strength to almost half a million, a sixth of Israel's total population. In a practical sense this means that almost every family in Israel has at least one member serving in one form or another of military service. More often than not, a family will have two or more representatives in the IDF. More than ever before, the IDF is now a citizen's army, and the Israeli soldier a reflection of Israel's population.

This unprecedented growth did not come to the IDF without bringing its share of problems. While increasing significantly the number of combat-ready regiments, growth also created many difficulties: the increase in quantity (coming especially from low-quality conscript categories) by necessity resulted in an overall decrease in the average quality. The pace of promotion was hastened, and time in assignment was shortened to the point, sometimes, of allowing inexperienced officers to assume command prematurely. (This was due not only to the expansion but also to the critical shortage of officers after the Yom Kippur War, in which almost 1,300 officers were either killed or wounded.)

Other problems resulting from the IDF's growth in size, equipment and complexity involved difficulties in command, control and communication; increasing centralization; and, consequently, increasing bureaucratization. The IDF began to develop the normal diseases of any large and complex organization. The sense of intimacy and personal familiarity that always used to characterize the officers' corps generally diminished. In the years following the Yom Kippur War, the military machine that is the IDF did indeed become more professional and perhaps even more effective. But the price it paid was increasing bureaucratization, careerism and technical dependency.

Along with the obvious effects that the Yom Kippur War had on the military came some unexpected political developments. Within four years of this war, President Sadat of Egypt arrived in Israel in November 1977 and thus began a process which led to the first peace treaty between Israel and an Arab country. However, another frontier remained as troublesome after 1973 as it had been before. Terrorist attacks by the Palestinian Liberation Organization (PLO) continued to disrupt life in Israel. Frequent artillery attacks from across the border, airplane hijackings, raids into Israeli villages, and killing and kidnapping civilians became almost daily events in Israel. The Israeli policy against these atrocities was without compromise. The IDF was called time and again to strike PLO positions in retaliation to forcefully rescue school children, bus passengers or hijacked Israeli air passengers. In no case did the IDF or the Israeli government ever concede to the demands of the terrorists.

The most famous and dramatic of all these operations was the raid on the Entebbe airport. On June 27, 1976, a group of four terrorists (two Palestinians and two Germans) hijacked an Air France plane en route from Tel-Aviv to Paris, with 256 passengers and 12 crew members. The airplane was forced to land in Entebbe, Uganda. All 105 passengers identified as being Jewish and Israeli were held hostage in the Entebbe airport (the non-Jewish passengers were freed by the hijackers). The Israeli government refused to bow to the terrorists' demands and, encouraged by the IDF authorities, decided to launch a military rescue operation. It took four C–130 Hercules transports and several Boeing passenger jets to carry a number of IDF elite units on a surreptitious seven-hour flight to Entebbe. Fifty-seven minutes later, the first Hercules took off with its cargo of disbelieving former hostages. Only one Israeli soldier was killed: Lt. Colonel Jonathan Netanyahu, who had commanded the assault force.

The Entebbe rescue, subsequently called "Operation Jonathan," was one of the most audacious military operations ever performed in history.

Its objectives were not to conquer or destroy. Rather it was waged to rescue the lives of innocent Jews and Israelis, victims of merciless terrorists. To the Israelis it proved once again that the IDF is their only shield between survival and death.

The Lebanon War

The most recent chapter in the IDF's history (as of the mid–1980s) is the 1982 War in Lebanon. It is too recent, however, to call it history. Certainly the impact on the IDF of "Operation Peace for Galilee" (as it was named in Israel) and the subsequent occupation of Lebanon is too early to be assessed. The Lebanon War, however, was a different war for Israel.

Since September 1970 (the "Black September" of the Palestinian terrorist groups) when the PLO guerrillas and their leader, Yaser Arafat, were forcefully expelled from Jordan, they had concentrated their forces in Lebanon, a state too weak and torn apart to resist the PLO incursion. From Lebanon, the PLO and its various splinter groups launched repeated terrorist attacks on Israeli and Jewish targets, both in Israel and Europe. The most disruptive of these attacks came from the Lebanese-based PLO units who almost daily fired Soviet-made Katyusha barrage-rockets on Israeli civilian settlements across the northern region of Israel.

The initial attempts by the IDF to deal with these harassments involved using artillery and air strikes, but soon it became apparent that these measures were inadequate against the elusive PLO. In March 1978 the IDF launched a limited ground operation into the southern part of Lebanon, in an attempt to destroy the PLO's infrastructure in that area. The "Litani Operation" (in reference to the Litani River which marked the farthest line of the Israeli advancement, some fifteen miles into Lebanon), though "well prepared and executed,"[38] did not bring an end to the PLO's activities from Lebanon. After the IDF withdrawal in June 1978 and despite the U.N. forces deployed in southern Lebanon (UNFIL), the PLO attacks were not only renewed but escalated. In summer of 1981, for example, PLO artillery barrages on thirty-three settlements in the Galilee lasted for ten days and were so devastating that many inhabitants were forced to flee their homes.

On June 6, 1982, the IDF once again crossed the border into Lebanon, this time with greater forces and the goal of totally eliminating PLO terrorists from Lebanon. The Syrian presence inside Lebanon forced the Israeli units to engage them also. Thus two separate campaigns, in fact, were conducted simultaneously by the IDF.

After two weeks of fierce, though quite circumspect, fighting, the Israeli forces controlled the entire southern half of Lebanon, inflicting upon the PLO some 1,000 fatalities and capturing approximately 7,000 of their forces along with a vast warehouse of military supplies. The remaining PLO terrorists were evacuated from Beirut by sea. In the course of engaging the Syrian forces in the Bekka Valley, the Israeli Air Force destroyed eighty-seven Syrian fighter aircraft, five helicopters and nineteen of the newest generation of Soviet-made SAM (surface-to-air missile) batteries. During these operations Israel lost only two fighter aircraft and two helicopters.[39]

However, the bitter price Israel paid in this war was in its casualties. During the major fighting in Lebanon these reached 340 dead and over 2,000 wounded. A great many of these casualties were due to the IDF's restricted use of heavy fire in order to avoid casualties among the civilian population (which inadvertently served as shields for the PLO fighters). The agony that came with these IDF losses was added to the general feeling shared by many Israelis that the 1982 Lebanon War was Israel's first war ever that had not emerged from a "no alternative" sense of survival.

The young Israeli soldiers who fought in Lebanon in 1982 are the sons of the Israeli combatants who fought in the Six Day War. Many of them are also the grandsons of men who were members of the pre–1948 Palmach and Haganah organizations. To this day, these sons, like their fathers and grandfathers before them, are still fighting the wars in defense of Israel. The portrait of the Israeli soldier, then, is the reflection of Israel's history of wars. Together they continue to mold and shape one another.

Notes

1. The literal translation of Zvah Haganah LeIsrael is "Defence Army for Israel." The official translation, as insisted upon by Israel's first Prime Minister, Ben-Gurion, was "Israeli Defence Forces."

2. For the reader who is interested in a more complete review, there are several relevant resources (which also formed the basis of this chapter): Allon, Y. (1970). *The making of Israel's army*. New York: Bantam Books; Dupuy, T. (1984). *Elusive victory: The Arab-Israeli wars, 1947–1974*. Fairfax, VA: HERO Books; Herzog, C. (1983). *The Arab-Israeli wars*. Jerusalem: Edanim Publishers; Luttwak, E., & Horowitz, D. (1975). *The Israeli army*. London: Allen Lane; Rothenberg, G. E. (1979). *The anatomy of the Israeli army*. New York: Hippocrene Books, Inc.

3. Throughout the British Mandate period the Haganah remained an illegal organization whose many members maintained strict secrecy about their activities. This was one Russian revolutionary characteristic with which the Haganah was imbued and which in fact survives in the Israeli military to these days.

4. Allon, *The making of Israel's army*.

5. Ibid., pp. 11–12.

6. "Lehi" is the acronym for "Lohamei Herut Israel" meaning "Fighters for the Freedom of Israel."

7. Luttwak & Horowitz, *The Israeli army*, p. 18.

8. Allon, *The making of Israel's army*, p. 15.
9. Ibid., p. 19.
10. Ibid.
11. Ibid., p. 23.
12. Rothenberg, *The anatomy of the Israeli army*.
13. Even in prestate Israel, manpower statistics were surreptitiously kept. According to Ben-Gurion's personal diary (not made public until 1969 [see Ben-Gurion, D., 1969, *Medinat Israel Ha-Mithadeshet* (The reviving state of Israel). Tel-Aviv: Am Oved, p. 106]), by the end of the British Mandate (in May 1948), the Haganah forces consisted of the following numbers:

Palmach (three brigades)	6,000
Ground forces by brigades	
Golani	4,095
Carmeli	2,238
Alexandroni	3,588
Kiryati	2,504
Givati	3,229
Etzioni	3,166
Training	398
Air Force	675
Artillery	650
Engineers	150
Military Police	168
Transport units	1,097
New conscripts in training	1,719

Ben-Gurion's figures, however, did not include the relatively large (though static) home-guard forces, supply and support units or headquarters troops.

14. Herzog, *The Arab-Israeli wars*.
15. This would be comparable to the United States—in the mid-1980s—losing 2.3 million people to war, or Great Britain losing almost half a million of its present population. In contemporary Israeli numbers, this would translate to approximately 35,000, more than half the total number of Americans killed throughout the more than ten years of the Vietnam War.
16. A more detailed description of this reserve system is given in Chapter 2.
17. The commanders of the Air Force and Navy became members of this General Staff along with the heads of four administrative divisions (operation, quartermaster, manpower and intelligence).
18. Ben-Gurion, D. (1970). *Memoirs* (Compiled by Thomas R. Bransten). New York: The World Publishing Company, pp. 66–105.
19. The 101 unit was originally established by Dayan's predecessor, Mordechai Makleff, as a special commando unit. It was manned by a small group of hand-picked combatants. Though its appearance was quite unmilitary, the 101's combat performances were normatively impeccable. The first leader of this unit was a young unknown major by the name of Ariel Sharon.
20. Liddell Hart, the noted British military strategist and a known proponent

of the indirect approach, himself praised the 1956 campaign's plan as a "masterpiece" (quoted in Herzog, *The Arab-Israeli wars*, p. 113).

21. These figures are reported in Dupuy, *Elusive victory*, p. 337. The total Israeli strength in 1967, when all the reserves were fully mobilized, amounted to 275,000 troops, with an estimated 800 tanks—according to a press release by the International Institute for Strategic Studies, London, June 6, 1967.

22. See Luttwak & Horowitz, *The Israeli army*, p. 282. Figures concerning the Arabs' losses in the Six Day War are not definitive: the total number of killed in all three fronts varies from approximately 20,000 (Herzog, *The Arab-Israeli wars*), to 14,000 (Luttwak & Horowitz, *The Israeli army*), to 4,296 killed and 7,550 missing or captured (Dupuy, *Elusive victory*).

23. Rothenberg, *The anatomy of the Israeli army*, p. 150.

24. In Allon, *The making of Israel's army*.

25. Dupuy, *Elusive victory*, p. 335.

26. Ibid., p. 336.

27. The latter group was primarily composed of reserve combat officers who responded to these needs and volunteered for a predefined period (six months to a year) in the permanent service corps. Reentry into active duty, specifically to serve in the critical zones such as the Bar-Lev Line, earned these volunteers the nickname "Tigers."

28. Schiff, Z. (1970). *Knafaim Me'al LeSuez* [Wings over Suez]. Tel-Aviv: Ot-Paz, pp. 179–227.

29. Luttwak & Horowitz, *The Israeli army*, p. 302.

30. Sanua, V. D. (1974, May). Psychological effects of the Yom Kippur War. *The Source*, 2(3), 7–8.

31. According to Herzog's account (*The Arab-Israeli wars*), the entire Suez Canal front (some one hundred miles) was manned by only 436 reserve soldiers, with only three tanks positioned at the waterfront.

32. The battle on October 14 is considered by many experts to be one of the greatest Armor battles in recent war history. Approximately 2,000 tanks were fighting across the lines. By the end of the day, the Egyptian defeat was total, with more than 1,000 dead and 264 tanks destroyed by the Israelis. The Israeli forces lost only 6 tanks on that day. Herzog, C. (1975). *The war of atonement: October 1973*. Boston: Little, Brown and Company, p. 206.

33. Later that evening, in a telephone call to Golda Meir, Israel's Prime Minister, General Bar-Lev laconically reported: "It has been a good day. Our forces are themselves again...."(Herzog, *The war of atonement*, p. 206).

34. This pressure indeed led to the appointment of the Agranat Commission—a public commission of inquiry, manned by five Israeli legal and martial experts, who were charged with investigating both the military and civilian authorities' decisions which had led to the Yom Kippur "blunder." The findings and conclusions of the Agranat Commission led to the dismissal from service of several of the IDF's top generals (including the Chief of the Intelligence Branch and the Commander of the Southern Region) and the final resignation of Meir's cabinet.

35. These 1973 and 1982 figures were taken from *The Military Balance*, July 1973 and July 1983 reports, the International Institute for Strategic Studies, London.

36. Ibid.

37. Various assessments, made by both Israeli and non-Israeli military experts

provided the rationale for this IDF doctrine of increasing the number of combat units and at the same time decreasing their size. An example of one of these assessments is that of Dupuy who calculated that in the Yom Kippur War the average Israeli unit was about 2:1 superior to the average Egyptian unit and about 2.5:1 superior to the average Syrian unit (Dupuy, *Elusive victory*, Appendix B, pp. 628–633).

38. Reports by American military analysts, as quoted by Middleton, D. (1978, March 16). *New York Times*.

39. Herzog, *The Arab-Israeli wars*, p. 290.

2

MILITARY SERVICE IN ISRAEL

Two facts are central to understanding the nature of military service in Israel. The first is that the Israeli Defence Forces (IDF) was founded in the crucible of a war—the War of Independence. The IDF was born into the battlefield, and there it made its first steps. This has made it, from its first moment, a fighting army. The second major feature of the IDF is that since its foundation, it has been a national service: a full-scale draft system beginning with a conscript's compulsory service and continuing with a universal reserve service which practically involves almost every family in the state. In fact, military service in Israel is so deeply rooted in society that it is almost taken for granted. The importance of serving in the IDF is perhaps the only issue that has full consensus among the Israeli population.

The IDF is basically divided into three components: (1) compulsory service, into which virtually everyone is conscripted at age eighteen; (2) permanent service, which is basically the leadership and training structure of the military and is composed of career officers and NCOs; and (3) reserve service, which is the main body of the Israeli armed forces. Of these three components, the first two comprise the standing army and involve continuous active duty, while the reserves involve periodic active duty. All three include both Jewish men and women, and Druze men, who are citizens or permanent residents of the State of Israel.

"Sherut-Hova"—Compulsory Service

At the beginning of every month, large posters (an example is Figure 2.1) appear in public places throughout all cities and towns in Israel, ordering all men and women who are soon to reach the age of seventeen to report for military registration in one of the five recruiting centers.

Figure 2.1
Order to Report for Registration at District Recruiting Offices

MANPOWER BRANCH

Defence Service Law, 1959
(CONSOLIDATED VERSION)

Order to Report for Registration at District Recruiting Offices

Male and female citizens or permanent residents, who were born between April, 3, 1965 and September 26, 1965, both dates inclusive, must report for registration at their district recruiting office in accordance with the Order to Report for Registration which they have received.

The men and women born between these dates who do not receive through the post an order to report for registration will report at one of the recruiting offices listed in Table A, at 8.00 a.m. on the date given in Table B, in accordance with their date of birth.

TABLE A

Jerusalem	Recruiting Office, 103 Rehov Rashi (Mekor Baruch)
Tel Hashomer	Recruiting Office, Tel Hashomer, near Kiron
Haifa	Recruiting Office, 12-14 Rehov Omar Khayyam
Tiberias	Recruiting Office, Rehov Natzrat
Beersheba	Recruiting Office, 22 Rehov Yad Vashem

TABLE B

DATE OF BIRTH		DATE OF REGISTRATION	
BETWEEN	AND	MEN	WOMEN
1. Apr. 3, 1965	Apr. 17, 1965	Mar. 28, 1982	June 13, 1982
2. Apr. 18, 1965	May 2, 1965	Mar. 29, 1982	June 14, 1982
3. May 3, 1965	May 17, 1965	Mar. 30, 1982	June 15, 1982
4. May 18, 1965	June 1, 1965	Mar. 31, 1982	June 16, 1982
5. June 2, 1965	June 16, 1965	Apr. 7, 1982	June 17, 1982
6. June 17, 1965	July 1, 1965	Apr. 4, 1982	June 20, 1982
7. July 2, 1965	July 16, 1965	Apr. 5, 1982	June 21, 1982
8. July 17, 1965	July 31, 1965	Apr. 6, 1982	June 22, 1982
9. Aug. 1, 1965	Aug. 15, 1965	Apr. 11, 1982	June 23, 1982
10. Aug. 16, 1965	Aug. 30, 1965	Apr. 12, 1982	June 24, 1982
11. Aug. 31, 1965	Sept. 14, 1965	Apr. 15, 1982	June 27, 1982
12. Sept. 15, 1965	Sept. 28, 1965	Apr. 18, 1982	June 28, 1982
13. Those liable for National Service *(sadir)* or Reserve Service		June 7, 1982	

Male Israel citizens or permanent residents, who were born between January 1, 1930 and September 6, 1964, and who immigrated between October 1, 1951 and the date of publication of this Order in *Rishumot*, and who do not receive an order to report for registration for defence service by June 6, 1982, must report, as directed above, at their nearest recruiting office on June 7, 1982.

Those reporting are required to appear on the date and at the time indicated in the Order to Report sent to their home — or in accordance with the above table if they do not receive such an order.

UNDER NO CIRCUMSTANCES MAY A PERSON REPORT ON A DAY OTHER THAN THAT GIVEN UNDER THE ORDER WITHOUT THE PRIOR PERMISSION OF THE OFFICER IN CHARGE OF THE RECRUITING OFFICE.

Those reporting should bring their identity card or Ministry of the Interior registration certificate *(teudat rishum)* or birth certificate. Immigrants should also bring their *teudat oleh* and passport.

A married woman who is a mother, or is pregnant, and who does not have a certificate testifying that she is legally exempt from defence duty, is required to come to a recruiting office and to bring documents testifying to her personal and family status, in order that she may be issued a certificate exempting her from duty.

From the date of publication of this notice, everyone who is required to report and who wishes to go abroad, must obtain a permit to do so from the officer in charge of a recruiting office.

Note. The full text of the Order to Report for Registration will be published in *Kovetz Hatakanot*.

Aluf-Mishne Moshe Ya'ari
Chief Recruiting Officer   Manpower Branch

In addition, these notices are published in newspapers and serve to remind those individuals who may not have received their written notifications to report for registration. This order to report derives from the Defence Service Law and applies to every citizen or permanent resident of Israel. Those permanent residents who arrive after the age of eighteen will be called at some later point and will have a reduced length of service.

Of the non-Jewish minorities in Israel, only male Druze are formally required to register and serve. However, each year a few Arab Bedouin and a handful of Arab Christians are allowed to volunteer to serve as well. But, as a general rule, the approximately 550,000 Arabs living in Israel are exempted from military service. With the traditional enemies of Israel being the Arab states surrounding it, drafting Israeli Arabs into the military has traditionally been considered a security risk.

In practice, then, the draft system applies to virtually all Jewish men and about 60 percent of the women. While precise figures are not available, it is estimated that approximately 92 percent of the male manpower pool is called to active duty each year.[1] The 8 percent who are not called consist of those eighteen-year-old Israeli citizens who are not physically present in Israel at the time of drafting and those who are legally exempted from service because of religious constrictions. That leaves as exempted only the severely disabled who could not function in any capacity in the IDF. It is obvious, then, that Israel is stretching to its utmost limits its manpower resources in order to man its armed forces.[2] In this way, with a Jewish population of approximately 3.28 million people, Israel manages to have a standing defense force of 172,000 men and women of which over 120,000 are conscripts. Together with the reserve forces, the total IDF strength is close to 500,000.[3] Thus, hardly a family in Israel does not have a member serving in the military at any given time. To be an Israeli adult means in one way or another to be a soldier.

With regard to women in the IDF, while they too are subject to draft as part of national compulsory service, there are more exemption categories for them. Briefly, these are (1) marriage or formal engagement; (2) religious beliefs; and (3) less than eight years of formal education. In addition, the physical and mental criteria for women are more stringent than for men. As a result, considering all of these exemptions, only about 60 percent of all women are actually drafted.[4]

The duration of this compulsory service, generally, is three years for the men and two years for the women. However, there are many exceptions to these rules. First, in many of the special units in the IDF, there is a requirement for a longer period of service—sometimes four or five years or even more. Examples of this include some of the special commando units, submarine crews and naval officers, pilots, and some job specialties in the Intelligence corps. The rationale for this extended service stems from the length and expense of training involved and the need to fully utilize the services of these personnel when their training is completed.

Second, any male who becomes an officer during compulsory service incurs an additional obligation of one year. Any female who becomes an officer must have at least one year of active duty remaining in order to be commissioned.

Third, extended service also applies to those who choose to participate in the academic reserve program. This basically defers military service while the individual completes his or her academic studies. When they do begin active duty, they will serve within their specialty, for an extended period of two years, bringing their total obligation to five years.

The result of all of these extension categories is that a substantial proportion of the conscripts in compulsory service are in much longer than three years—sometimes four or five years or longer. There are fewer cases of those serving less than three years, either because of health problems, age (those who have immigrated to Israel after reaching the age of eighteen), or socio-economic reasons.

Whether a person serves two or three years, or even longer as in the case of specialized fields, military service can be a very long and critical period in the life of any young Israeli adult. In no other Western country is there such a long period of universal compulsory military service. Israeli youngsters spend their most important years after high school in full military activity, with minimal monetary compensation (comparable to about $25 per month) and with total commitment of time and energies to this activity. The military service precludes any outside activities at all. Furthermore, serving in the IDF, by its own nature, involves (in most cases) high likelihood of combat, severe stress and tension, and usually very high responsibility. Although no systematic studies have demonstrated the possible outcomes of such demands, it is easy to assume that these factors combine to condense the maturation process of young Israeli adults. Indeed, it is a common observation by many visitors to Israel that the Israeli youth embody maturity and seriousness to a degree not seen in most other Western cultures.

At the completion of their compulsory service, conscript soldiers are discharged from active duty. On the day of discharge they report back to the Induction Center where they had been initially processed into the military. At the center they turn in most of their military equipment except for one uniform and a pair of boots. They are then immediately processed into their reserve unit. They take with them their prior military rank, whether as officers (2nd or 1st lieutenants) or enlisted personnel (corporals or sergeants), and their specialized military occupation. Some of them, however, will choose not to be discharged but rather to continue with their military service. Hence they will sign a statement of obligation to extend their period of service and thus will join the small group of Keva—the permanent service corps.

"Sherut-Keva"—The Permanent Service Corps

Very little has been written to this date about the permanent service corps of the IDF, compared to the abundance of literature concerning the career service of the U.S. military and other Western militaries. Only a few comprehensive studies specifically focused on the IDF's Keva corps.[5] This small group of Israeli military professionals is normally referred to only when discussing the IDF in general. But the "Sherut-Keva" members of the IDF are quite different from the other two components (the compulsory service and reserve service) of the IDF. These are the individuals who have chosen the military profession as a way of life. In the citizens' army, which is the IDF, these permanent service personnel are the closest to what is usually referred to in the United States as military careerists.

The permanent service is the core of the IDF. As small as it is (various sources estimate its size, in the early 1980s, at around 50,000)[6], this is the backbone of the military organization, responsible for its training and war preparations, the development and implementation of new weapon systems and the maintenance of the military's resources. While during compulsory service an officer may achieve the rank of captain, all of the higher command positions, as well as the command of all training bases and other military installations, are designated for permanent service officers. As to the reserve units, while the rule is that reserve officers command reserve units, when it comes to the higher echelons, the key command positions are held by permanent service officers. Normally, at the division level, the division commander and most of his staff will be permanent officers, while at the brigade command level, there will be a mix of reserve and permanent service officers.

The permanent service corps obviously includes more than unit commanders and staff officers. A large portion of it includes professional officers and NCOs in various military specialties. As a military which depends so heavily on armories ready for activation at a moment's notice and on sophisticated equipment which is continuously used either for training or actual combat, there is a serious need for a strong infrastructure of maintenance, repair and supply specialists. Similarly, there is a need for research and development specialists as well as professional planners, inspectors and so forth. For most of these areas the compulsory service is not sufficient. Therefore, in the IDF these positions are filled by permanent service personnel with the auxiliary assistance of conscripts and occasionally with reserve reinforcements or military-employed civilians.

While not everyone might be qualified to join the permanent service (as will be discussed shortly), there are those who are automatically required to have periods of permanent service. Mentioned earlier were those conscripts who volunteer to special units as well as those who are commissioned as officers and pilots. As a prerequisite for volunteering, they commit themselves for a period of between one and four years beyond their compulsory service. For many of them, this additional obligation leads to a long military career, sometimes until their retirement. However, others in this category merely end up with their required years in the permanent service and subsequently return to civilian life and to reserve service.

This category of required extended service also includes the academic reserve. These are conscripts who chose to defer their recruitment in order to pursue their academic studies before beginning their compulsory service. Military authorities approve such deferments only for those interested in academic professions which are significant to the military. In addition, individuals applying to the program are carefully screened, including the officer selection procedure, because all academic professionals in the IDF occupy officers' positions. The academic reserve candidates spend their summer vacations in military training such as basic training, junior command course, etc., so that when they finally begin active duty, they are already trained soldiers. Shortly after induction they will complete the officers' course and be commissioned as specialist officers in their respective academic professions.

A few years ago the IDF conducted an experiment in which graduates of the academic reserve program were assigned to combat command positions, most frequently as platoon leaders, with no relationship to their academic specialties. Although these young lieutenants had already demonstrated a higher intellectual level than most of their counterparts, they failed in most cases to translate their intellectual superiority into effective leadership. The IDF conclusion from this experiment was that the ability to lead combat units effectively required something more than, or perhaps different from, academic prowess and hence demanded a selection and training process independent of civilian schooling.

The main bulk of the permanent service corps, however, does not come from the academic reserves or the extended compulsory service corps. The majority are officers and NCOs who made the decision at the completion of their compulsory service period, or sometimes a year or two after discharge, to continue with, or return to, military service. Sometimes this is a decision for a lifetime career; more frequently it is a decision to try it for two or three years before deciding about a longer career. However, many of those who start it on a trial basis end up with a long career in the military.

The permanent service corps is quite selective even though the IDF usually needs additional officers. In an attempt to keep the high quality of its permanent service corps, the IDF established, several years ago, special procedures a candidate must follow in order to join the permanent service corps. In addition to obtaining highly positive recommendations from the candidate's commanders, if the candidate has a lapse in service greater than three years, he is subjected to evaluations, including psychological batteries, similar to those required of officer candidates. While very few fail these additional evaluations, it is assumed that these requirements maintain the high quality of applicants to the permanent service corps. Whether it also guarantees that the "cream of the crop" of Israeli soldiers do indeed join the permanent service corps is still open to question.

> In an article published in 1975, Meir Pa'il, a retired colonel in the IDF, noted that the best and brightest officers of the IDF are not necessarily the ones who remain in the permanent service. Pa'il warned that as time passes the "quality gap" might grow between the young conscript officers and the corps of permanent officers who eventually constitute the high echelons of the IDF command structure.[7]

During the period of self-criticism and introspection that came after the Yom Kippur War, charges were made that the professional conduct of the IDF permanent service corps, especially the officers, had sharply deteriorated in the previous years. Thus, for example, the IDF officers' corps was accused of becoming more career oriented and less committed to maintaining the force.[8] This "laxity" was, no doubt, a result of the overconfidence among the Israeli military as a result of the extreme success of the Six Day War, after which there ensued a period of "resting at peace." As a result there was deterioration in the quality of critical thinking and creative planning. The failures of the IDF during the Yom Kippur War were blamed to a large extent on this deterioration. The Israeli military quickly learned its lesson, and after the Yom Kippur War, many of those negative characteristics observed before the war virtually disappeared. A greater attention to military professionalism and higher standards for personnel quality were required from the permanent service corps. Concerns such as these, along with the significant expansion of the size of the permanent service corps, resulted in the implementation of many changes (including the introduction of the screening procedure mentioned earlier).

Various attitude surveys conducted within the permanent corps of the IDF in recent years have indicated that the main attraction for this type of military service comes not from utilitarian factors such as promotions and economic benefits but rather from factors related to the military profession—its importance, the inherent authority, and the challenge. In reality, it is not that glorious. The mission of an IDF Keva member is excessively demanding. Being the nucleus of Israel's standing army, these individuals constantly carry the responsibility for the day-to-day security of Israel. This involves responding to frequent terrorist attacks and continually preparing for major combat involvements even during peacetime. Almost every month, along various borders, there will be periods of warm-up alerts in response to enemy activities across the border. Each one of these receives all-out consideration down the line, since none of these enemy activities can be underestimated. On many of these alerts, senior commanders must also decide whether or not to call up, or request the call-up of, reserve units. Since reserve call-up is a very costly decision, both monetarily and psychologically, it is usually kept as a last resort. Whatever decision they make, they still carry the heavy burden of securing Israel's borders.

It is not surprising then that the material compensations provided to the permanent service corps are rather generous. The IDF career officer's pay grade is one of the highest in Israel. Throughout the years there has always been a constant effort to maintain, if not to increase, that pay rate to adequately compensate these individuals. Despite high pay, however, service conditions for most permanent service members are most frequently Spartan: accommodations in the units are sparse; individuals sometimes do not see their families for extended periods; and the job frequently will require relocations or extensive commuting.

Along with the salary, the military provides its permanent service members with service-related benefits: every officer from the rank of lieutenant colonel and above has a military automobile for unlimited use both on and off the job. The lower ranks (majors, captains, and lieutenants) will share cars between two or three service members. Substantial housing subsistence is provided (either by providing quarters with minimal rent, or loans at below-market rates toward purchase of a house, or by paying the service member's rent). All higher education costs for the member are paid by the military. Free medical care is provided the service member and his or her family, along with exchange and commissary facilities offering significant price discounts. And finally, a generous retirement benefit program is available after the member has completed ten years of permanent service and also reached the age of forty. All of these benefits make life more bearable for the permanent service member and family as they cope with the hardships found in the Sherut-Keva way of life.

The work norms of the Keva members are, indeed, exceptional. In rear headquarters, but more so in field units, commanders and their immediate staff spend long hours in their offices, often into the early hours of the morning. A common saying is: "the lights were on throughout the night," which may contain the hidden message that turned-on lights do not always mean that crucial work is being done, but rather expected work norms are being followed. The issue of overwork has been discussed on occasion both by the General Staff and local headquarters, but normally without any significant impact on the problem. This phenomenon of overwork is sometimes related to the post-Yom Kippur impact, seen as a collective unconscious expression of the guilt feelings that many permanent service members still carry with them.

Service in the permanent corps of the IDF is still considered, in most cases, as national service at the highest level, which is somewhat idealistic, almost altruistic, and involves many difficulties and real danger. Thus in Israeli society, the military profession has been traditionally perceived as being one of the most prestigious professions available.[9] However, in the last decade, and particularly since the Lebanon War (1982), this perception has eroded significantly. One of the consequences of this erosion could be seen among young officers and NCOs in the mid-1980s who were contemplating joining or continuing service in the IDF's permanent corps. They have recently found themselves with problems of conscience which originate from the role of the IDF in the controversial War in Lebanon.

The Israeli professional soldiers—the Sherut-Keva members—are currently in a transition period. In the past they always refrained from being labeled, or perceived, as "career officers" or "career NCOs," preferring the perception that they were motivated by moral and national commitment rather than by occupational considerations. However, more recently, the Sherut-Keva has been gradually transformed into a guild of essentially professionals. Though still composed of very talented, highly devoted and extremely proficient servicemen, the IDF permanent service corps has not completely escaped the malaise of many other Western military organizations. The early feelings of priesthood, intimacy, and ultimate altruism which had characterized the founders of the IDF permanent service corps have been partially replaced by the more trendy entrepreneurial, competitive, and occasionally utilitarian aspects which characterize the more recent generations of IDF careerists.

"Miluimm"—Reserve Service

The reserve service of the IDF ("miluimm") is the largest component of the Israeli armed forces. For a small country, with a population of only a little over 3.5 million inhabitants, whose very survival and defense depend on a large and strong Army, a reserve corps is the only solution. Furthermore, since defense issues are daily concerns, and the military finds itself involved in a full-scale war on the average of every eight years, the reserve corps must maintain a high level of readiness and combat effectiveness. Such are, indeed, the main characteristics of the miluimm units of the IDF.[10]

The miluimm paradigm, which began concurrently with the establishment of the IDF in 1948 (and was partially patterned after the structure of the Swiss reserves), is very simple. Every able man who has completed compulsory service (where he received extensive training and military experiences) serves as a reserve soldier until he reaches the age of fifty-five. The same applies to women, except for them the maximum age is thirty-four, or earlier if they marry. By regulation, reserve members will be called to active duty at least once a year for a maximum of thirty-five days for enlisted and forty-two days for officers, up to the age of thirty-nine. After this age the period of annual reserve duty is decreased. As former Chief of Staff Yigael Yadin once remarked: "Every Israeli citizen is a soldier on eleven months annual leave." However, in actuality, most reserve members are called more than once and for longer periods, sometimes as much as a total of sixty days a year. In time of war those periods may even extend to several months, as was the case in the 1982 War in Lebanon. Basically, reservists are paid a very small amount as pocket money by the military. Reservists who are employees receive their full salary from their employer while they are on periodic active duty. Self-employed reservists receive compensation from the government treasury.

Age restrictions apply to men in combat reserve units. At approximately the age of forty (but sometimes even earlier in those units such as paratrooper, which require the highest physical conditioning), these men are shifted out of combat units and into behind-the-line support units. However, it is common among reservists to request permission to remain with the reserve unit they have served in for so many years and through several wars until "retirement" age.

In my reserve unit (an elite reconnaissance unit with great pride and a long tradition), we had a fellow nicknamed "Jake." He was long past forty but consistently refused to be reassigned, even though it was required, to a civil patrol unit. Jake, who had participated in the fighting in Jerusalem during the Independence War (1948) and later in the Sinai campaign (1956), found himself again involved in the battles to liberate Jerusalem in 1967, fighting shoulder to shoulder with men, many of whom were babies during his first combat experience. In order to prove that he still belonged in the unit, Jake was always the first one to carry the heaviest weapons or pursue the most arduous missions. As a matter of fact, all of us in the unit shared his own perception that he did indeed belong in the unit. Men such as Jake can be found in many of the elite reserve units.

The reserve units, even more than the regular units, gradually become like extended families. The Israeli "miluimnick" may sometimes spend two or more decades of his life in the same reserve unit, basically in the same company, and with the same core of peers and leaders. Only the wars change.

Indeed, these reserve units, especially the line units, resemble the regimental model of traditional militaries. These units preserve their history and tradition, even while they are creating their own. Many reserve units are organized by territory so that most people in the unit normally live relatively close to one another. While the primary reason is, of course, for rapid mobilization, there are side benefits as well. This closeness contributes to unit cohesion. Although the miluimnicks are as militarily efficient as the regular units, these reserve units differ uniquely in that they retain a certain civilian flavor. Rank and saluting are not highly emphasized. Officers, even high-ranking ones, are often called by their first names by their troops. Thus one finds a relaxed esprit de corps replacing the traditional military hierarchy. A great deal of role reversal often occurs in this transition from civilian to military life, in which superiors may find themselves under the command of their employees, professors under their students, and even lawyers under their clients.

Combat readiness, however, is the top priority of these reserve units. Each of these units has its own armory in which the equipment for the unit, team and individual members will be stored. Only the uniforms and personal belongings are kept with the reservist at home. The close relationship between the men and their equipment is so important that in the armor units, for example, each tank crew has its own specific tank. The same applies also to artillery units, mechanized infantry units, and other ground units. It is always the team for that particular weapon system that assumes the responsibility for its own equipment. Only in between reserve calls is the equipment maintained by small maintenance teams from the regular service, who insure that the equipment is always kept combat ready. A common story among these maintenance teams is that in almost any inspection the senior inspector (normally a high-ranking officer), in order to verify equipment readiness, will point at random to one of the vehicles and ask that it be started. It is a source of great pride for these maintenance teams to start up, on the first try, any equipment so selected.

For the front-line reserve units this is more than just a matter of pride. It is a matter of necessity. The Israeli-Arab wars, and especially the Yom Kippur War, have repeatedly demonstrated how crucial combat readiness and rapid mobilization can be to the nation's security. The Yom Kippur War, again, exposed many deficiencies within the armory system of the reserve units. Many fact-finding committees established following the war discovered incidents of negligence in equipment maintenance. Consequently, since 1973 the combat readiness of the reserve armory system has received high priority. A tremendous effort has been made to improve the depots to maximize equipment maintenance and to develop sophisticated techniques to guarantee immediate deployment at a moment's notice. Even the locations of these depots were carefully chosen: they are strategically placed, usually close to major roads, yet at some distance from densely populated areas.

The sight of military armories is a very common one to anyone traveling Israel's main roads. These huge gray structures, frequently constructed like aircraft hangars, contain rows of tanks, APCs, trucks and tank transports. The latter can frequently be seen, with their tank loaded, driving on the roads, especially during an alert. It is, indeed, one of the most striking impressions of any tourist first arriving in Israel—the numerous military vehicles which are a common sight in everyday traffic.

The IDF's policy regarding the employment of reserve units exemplifies the Israeli military way of thinking. For example, take the case of a reserve armor brigade which has just completed its forty-day period in, say, southern Lebanon. It will be replaced by another reserve armor brigade, which will be identical in size and equipment. While the most obvious, and certainly most economical, approach would be to use the same equipment for both brigades, this is not what will be done. Instead, at the end of its term, the first brigade will redeploy, with all of its equipment, to its armory, where the men will spend another two or three days performing maintenance to make the vehicles fully operational. At the same time, the new brigade will arrive at the same site, again with its own equipment and vehicles. While this is certainly not the most economical approach, it characterizes, nevertheless, the IDF doctrine that a combat unit is an inseparable combination of men, equipment and vehicles.

Furthermore, even within each small unit, personnel stability is carefully maintained. Tank crews, APC crews, and artillery teams are consistently made up of the same individuals. The same four tankers who are assigned to a specific tank in a reserve unit may have been together for several combat operations, not to mention the hundreds of training hours they have shared. They know each other intimately. At times, they will be able to "read" each other's minds to the point that words are not necessary. Above all, they have developed a high level of trust and confidence which not only enhances combat effectiveness but also enables them to better cope with the extreme stresses of combat, thereby minimizing their rate of psychiatric breakdown.

These close relationships are often maintained beyond duty periods. Since the reservists are located in the same geographical area, many of them socialize together in their civilian lives, and their families will be closely related as well.

> During the first days of the Yom Kippur War, when information from the front lines was scarce, the families in the rear experienced a great deal of stress and worry. A large group of women—the wives and girlfriends of a paratroop battalion fighting in the Sinai—gathered at the home of the mother of one of the battalion's officers. There, in that hospitable home in Jerusalem, these women spent their days and nights listening to the radio news being reported on the war. After a couple of days of uncertainty, the telephone rang. It was a member of that paratroop unit who had called to deliver "group greetings" to the waiting women. On the phone he read the men's names, knowing most of their wives or girlfriends would be there and would share the message with the rest of the families.

During peacetime years reservists spend about half of their active duty in various types and levels of training. This training is carried out either in special training centers near urban areas or in the field at the different fronts in Israel. The latter is done in order to familiarize them with the differing terrains they may have to defend. The other half of their active duty is normally spent on routine security matters such as patrol, guard duty, and observation along Israel's borders. These two types of activities normally will occupy the reservist for thirty to forty-five days each year. In addition to these planned activities, reserve units are occasionally called for short periods (usually two or three days) either to replace a regular unit or to be familiarized with a new weapon or system which has just arrived. Thus, total reserve time may in actuality exceed forty-five days per year.

Several times a year the Israeli miluimnick is awakened in the middle of the night by a phone call or knock on the door as part of a readiness exercise designed to examine the efficiency of the reserve's alert procedures. Immediately after this notification, the reservist reports to his or her predesignated assembly area, where the reservists sign in and check their address and phone number on the alert roster to insure that they are up-to-date. Another method of notification of a readiness exercise involves radio broadcasts where the two-word code names of reserve units are read on the air.

The burden for officers and senior NCOs in the reserves is considerably greater than that of the lower-ranking reservists. These commanders are continually involved in reserve activities throughout the year. Usually at least once a month they are called in for additional command training, updates through briefings, staff meetings or short trips. Reserve pilots, for example, are required to fly their particular type of aircraft at least once every month. Similar training requirements apply to various other specialties.

Reserve officers who are unit commanders (i.e., at the battalion or brigade level) spend many hours of their civilian time handling the daily problems of their units. This may include a quick visit to the unit depot, checking one of their subunits which is training in a nearby center, or participating in a staff meeting in their higher headquarters. But mostly it will involve handling the personal problems of their troops. Specifically this usually involves talking with individuals who feel they will be unable to attend the coming call-up period. The commander will have to determine whether the individual's reasons are indeed urgent enough to excuse him or her from portions of that training. This, however, is seldom the case, since the commander's primary concern is to insure the maximal readiness of the unit.

> The intrusion of reserve matters into the daily life of the Israeli reservist is tremendous. I recently spent an entire day in the office of a friend who is a senior manager in a large manufacturing plant near Haifa. He is also an Armor battalion commander in the reserves. During the course of our day together I counted no fewer than twenty-two phone calls he received or made, all of which pertained to his reserve unit, and most of which involved personal problems of his troops. This was, he told me, a normal working day for him.

The reserve corps forms the bulk of the combat forces of the IDF. According to the International Institute for Strategic Studies,[11] approximately 65 percent of the IDF's combat units are reserve forces. The security and ultimate survival of the State of Israel depend on the combat readiness and rapidity of deployment of the reserve units. Every Israeli reservist is fully aware of this and therefore takes reserve duties very seriously. The little sticker that every Israeli miluimnick carries with the two-word code name for his or her reserve unit is a constant reminder of the reservist's role in the defense of Israel.

The reserve corps naturally is an integral part of the overall Israeli society. In sharp contrast to the regular military, which is apolitical and geared toward implementing national policy, the civilian environment in Israel is political, controversial and vocal. As long as there is a national consensus regarding defense issues of the state, the reservist will make a military contribution without reservation. Active duty will be performed without regard to his or her political opinions or party affiliation. However, many reservists will find themselves fighting and risking their lives for goals whose legitimacy they may question whenever a conflict arises regarding the use of the IDF for certain political goals. Such was the case in the 1982 incursion into Lebanon. How does the miluimnick cope with such a situation?

Any active resistance or refusal generally occurs before the reservist reports to the unit. These actions can be in the form of refusing to be sent to a specific location or by covert attempts to elude being called at all. In the history of Israel there have been few periods in which such actions have occurred with any frequency. However, in the period following the Lebanon War, which was perhaps the most serious example of lack of national consensus, there were (by early 1985) 150 cases of reservists refusing to serve in Lebanon, including a few junior officers. All who refused to serve were convicted during courts-martial and were sentenced to one to three months in military prison. While this is a negligible number compared with the total number of reservists called to active duty during that time, it may be an indication of the greater numbers of individuals who covertly eluded their call to active duty. One thing is almost certain, though. Reservists, despite any personal convictions they may have, will virtually never refuse to carry out their military responsibility once they are in their unit. The influence of the military unit and commanders is almost always stronger than the most resistant individual. Although they may discuss their beliefs at great length and with great emotion, the moment they receive the order by their immediate commander, reservists will, almost without exception, join their peers to complete their assigned mission.

During the days of the Lebanon War, there were frequent scenes such as the following: A reserve unit has just returned home after two or three months of exemplary active duty in Lebanon. Several of its members go directly home, change from their uniforms into civilian clothing, and proceed to join the demonstrations taking place in front of the Ministry of Defence building in Tel-Aviv, protesting against the War in Lebanon. They are careful to avoid violating the law which prohibits soldiers from political acts. Thus they are dutiful soldiers one minute and concerned citizens virtually the next minute.

This is indeed one of the most telling characteristics of the IDF as a civilian militia. In a state where almost one out of every seven citizens is a soldier (either full-time or part-time), it is almost impossible to distinguish between society and the military. This is a double-edged sword; from these close bonds the military draws its strength, but this is also its vulnerability.

Notes

1. Feldman, O., & Milshtein, A. (1983, May 25). General Moshe Nativ: A farewell interview. *Bamahane, 37,* 12–14 (information from p. 14).
2. The German Army during World War II was also based on a full draft, but projected recruitment was planned at 75 percent of each age group. Though as the war went on this figure might have gone higher, the armed forces in Germany, at its peak strength in 1943, was approximately 10 percent of the total population. From van Creveld, M. (1982). *Fighting power: German and U.S. Army performance 1939–1945.* Westport, CT: Greenwood Press.
3. *The Military Balance, 1984–85.* London: The International Institute for Strategic Studies.
4. Nativ, M. (1984, Summer). IDF manpower and Israeli society. *The Jerusalem Quarterly, 32,* 140–144.
5. Among these are Peri, Y. (1977). The ideological portrait of the Israeli military elite. *The Jerusalem Quarterly, 3,* 28–41; Peri, Y. (n.d.). *The professional ethics of the military.* Unpublished manuscript.
6. *The Military Balance, 1984–1985.*
7. Pa'il, M. (1975, January). Israeli defense forces: A social aspect. *New Outlook,* 40–44.
8. Hasdai, Y. (1979). *Truth in the shadow of war* (Translated from Hebrew by M. Kohn). Tel-Aviv: Zmora, Bitan, Modan Publishers.
9. In a survey conducted in late 1974, on a representative sample of Israeli adults, military employment received relatively high scores on an overall career-prestige scale. Thus, for example, a colonel in the permanent service was ranked 96 (on a 1-to-100 scale) falling just below a university professor and somewhat higher than a rabbi or a psychologist. A Keva major was ranked 81 (equivalent to a pharmacologist), and a captain (ranked 76) received slightly higher prestige than a commercial pilot. See Kraus, V. (1981). The perception of occupational structure in Israel. *Megamot, 26*(3), 283–294.
10. Ben-Gurion, one of the founders of this system, described the IDF's reserve corps "as the Minute Men of the American Revolution who in seconds could exchange farming implements for rifles in the cause of their country's freedom." From Ben-Gurion, D. (1970). *Memoirs* (Compiled by Thomas R. Bransten). New York: The World Publishing Company, p. 98.
11. *The Military Balance, 1981–82.* London: The International Institute for Strategic Studies.

3

WOMEN IN THE IDF

The stereotype of Israeli women, equal with men and sharing in the national defense burden, has its roots in the Zionist socialist ideology. This ideology, which was a secular-sectarian reaction movement against the traditional religious Judaism of the Diaspora, stressed sexual equality, especially with regard to work roles. Prior to the establishment of the State of Israel, women were quite involved in the activities of the pre-IDF military organizations (the Hashomer, Haganah, Palmach, Irgun and Lehi). During World War II, women served as volunteers with the British women's Auxiliary Territorial Service (ATC). However, in none of these organizations have women directly participated in combat fighting, but rather they served in various support occupations such as signalers, nurses, secretaries and drivers. Women in the kibbutzim were incorporated into guard duties, and in the Palmach several women were assigned as commanders of mixed units but usually not in units engaged in fighting.[1]

During the War of Independence (1947-48), however, there were occasions when women were directly involved in incidents of guerrilla warfare or participated in combat operations. One hundred and fourteen women were killed in this war while under active military service, eighteen of whom were members of the Palmach.[2] Though these figures represent a small portion (2.8 percent) of the total Jewish combatant fatalities of that longest and deadliest war, they have nevertheless generated a vast and long-lasting mythical lore about Israeli combat women, obliged to fight in the front line, shoulder to shoulder with their male comrades. This legend has no basis in modern Israel. The IDF policy regarding women's military service has always been (since 1943) that women are to be prohibited from going into battle with their units.

> The office of the IDF Spokesman published in 1980 a special pamphlet describing the Israeli women's corps.[3] The pamphlet begins: "Sorry to disappoint you if you have been influenced by the Hollywood image of Israeli girl soldiers being amazon-type warriors accoutred in ill-fitting male combat fatigues and toting sub-machine guns. Today's Israeli female soldiers are trim girls, clothed in uniforms which bring out their youthful femininity. They play a wide variety of non-combatant, though thoroughly essential, roles within the IDF framework and within certain sectors of the civilian community."

Whether by design or not, the Hebrew acronym for the IDF Women's Corps is "Chen" which as a word means "charm." Indeed, the Chen brings charm and gentleness into an otherwise tough and mission-oriented milieu.

Originally modeled after the British ATC as an independent corps, the Chen today is not a corps in the true sense of the term, but rather an administrative cadre, responsible for the training, initial assignment and the well-being of IDF females. The female soldiers themselves belong to the various units, branches or corps to which they have been assigned. However, in each unit the size of a battalion or above, there is at least one Chen officer (obviously, a woman) who sees to it that the female soldiers are well integrated into that unit and are given suitable accommodations and working conditions. The Chen officer, sometimes assisted by female NCOs, also helps women soldiers in solving personal and professional problems and, at the same time, provides orientation and counseling to the commanders in matters regarding women's duties. In regard to daily matters of discipline, female soldiers are treated the same as their male peers in the unit by their immediate commanders, who are most frequently men. Should it become a court-martial case, however, a female soldier can only be judged by a female (Chen) officer. This is done in order to prevent incidents of sexual harassment.

Although not an independent corps, the Chen is directly responsible for a number of units, whether for training or other special missions (discussed below). The Chief Commander of the women's corps, a colonel, ordinarily reports to the Chief of Personnel but may occasionally report directly to the Chief of Staff on matters pertaining to the conscription and utilization of female soldiers in the IDF.

Women's Conscription

The Israeli Defence Service Law, originally adopted in 1949, makes all Jewish women who have reached the age of eighteen liable for conscription for a two-year period of military service within the IDF, in peacetime as well as in wartime. Female conscripts, like males, are also required to serve in the reserves following their initial service tour. Reserve service for women commonly applies until they become mothers, or reach the age of twenty-four, although some (those trained in very special areas of importance to the military) may continue in the reserve service until the age of thirty-four. The latter, however, will also terminate their reserve service with their first pregnancy. In addition, some women also continue to serve in the permanent service corps, where they constitute about 10 percent of its total strength.[4] Women's military service, then, is a common phenomenon in Israel. However, because of a series of modifications in the conscription law, resulting mainly from political and religious pressures, the women's draft today is far from total.

Women in a number of categories are exempt from compulsory military service. Married women and mothers of children are exempt. This exemption category also applies to women already doing their compulsory service. If these conscripts get married or become pregnant (and intend to carry to full-term), the IDF requires that they be separated from the service. In addition, female conscripts who have been accepted to pursue a college education receive deferments. Women in this category, however, are required to perform their full period of military service upon graduation, regardless of their future marital status.

The largest category of women's exemption from military service, however, has traditionally been for religious reasons.[5] Such has been the case since 1948, when it was established in law that women from Orthodox families would not be drafted. In July 1978 the ruling coalition in the Israeli Knesset passed a modification to the religious exemption law, making it even easier for women to be exempt from military service. All that a woman now needs to do is to attest before a judge that her religious convictions preclude her military service and to sign an affidavit stating that she observes Jewish dietary laws and does not travel on the Sabbath.

This modification in the law, in fact, made exemption from military service so easy that some military authorities feared a sharp decline in women's rate of enlistment. This has not happened, however, partly because the exemption law has been circumspectly enforced, but mainly because the norm for women's military service is still prevailing among most Israeli youth. Thus, in an attitudinal survey conducted in April 1980[6] on a small random sample of prospective female conscripts ages seventeen to seventeen and a half, about 90 percent of the surveyed females expressed a highly positive attitude toward their future conscription. Furthermore, more than half of them admitted they would have volunteered to serve in the IDF even if there were no draft. Notwithstanding religious and political demands, it seems that serving in the IDF is still a predominant norm among young Israeli women.

> In a recent interview, Colonel Dalia Raz, former commander of the IDF's women's corps, said: "First of all, I should like to speak about the importance of women in the IDF.... What I view as important is not only serving the IDF but contributing to one's country. There is an obligation to the country in which one lives: both women and men are compelled to cooperate in insuring their nation's security—and this is not just a matter of equal rights. This cooperation does not mean that men and women are compelled to fulfill the same roles, but rather it means taking part in bearing the burden—this is a responsibility of the highest order."[7] (P.44)

In addition to the various exemption and deferment categories, it has been observed[8] that the IDF still does not take all eligible eighteen-year-old women, but rather selects each year the number of women it needs to meet its annual manpower requirements. Consequently, a somewhat higher-quality index entry score will apply for women than for men. (The cutoff point for that score may vary slightly from time to time.) As a result, the second largest category of women's exemption from service is that of low level of education or intelligence. Around 10 percent of Israeli female youngsters are exempted from military service because of low quality.

Because of the different exemption categories for women's conscription to the IDF, only approximately 60 percent of all Israeli females join the military service, compared to about 90 percent of all males.[9] Furthermore, their average quality is consequently higher than that of the males. Thus, for example, 20 percent of the female recruits fall within the top 55–56 quality category (Kaba, see Chapter 5), while only 10 percent of the males do so.[10]

In spite of the females' restricted representation, their presence within the IDF is, nevertheless, very apparent. There is not a single unit in the military which will not have several female soldiers. They are assigned to all sorts of units, including first-line combat units, albeit in non-combatant roles only. In 1977 eighteen new non-traditional specialties were opened to women. Among these were arms instructor (in the infantry, artillery and armor schools), weapon repairman and communication technician. At present 516 out of 775 existing military occupations are open to women in the IDF.[11] However, between 50 and 60 percent of all women conscripted serve in secretarial and clerical jobs.

> One assignment to which Chen women have been recently posted is that of platoon sergeant in an all-male basic training program, where

these women perform exactly the same duties as their male counterparts. Despite initial disbelief by male colleagues and the recruits themselves, the women have succeeded outstandingly. New recruits do not dare complain of muscle aches and pains or drop out of a long-distance run when it is being led by a female sergeant.[12]

A certain proportion of Chen soldiers serve within their own corps. These are the instructors and commanders of the Chen training bases. In these schools (the Chen's Basic Training Base, Chen's NCO School and Officers' School) the entire cadre is female. Starting in mid–1984 female officers were required upon their commission to extend their compulsory service period by six months (thus making it a total of thirty months). No significant declines in number of women candidates have been reported as a result of that change.

Within branches of the military in which high technology is predominant, women's representation in non-traditional specialties has been expanded in recent years. For example, about 45 percent of the Air Force jobs have recently been opened to women.[13] These trends emerged as a result of the growing shortages of manpower in the IDF and the policy of "freeing all able men for combat." In part, however, it also reflects a growing acceptance within the predominantly masculine-oriented IDF of women's participation in non-traditional occupations.[14]

The frequent discrepancy between the women's quality and their assigned tasks is reflected in some of the surveys recently conducted with Chen soldiers. In one of these surveys[15] female soldiers reported at their day of separation from service (most frequently at the end of two years of service) their retrospective view of their military experience. About three-quarters of the sampled females expressed a high level of satisfaction from their service. However, a lower percentage (62 percent) felt that their military job had enabled them to use their personal capability to the fullest.

In another survey,[16] sampling 1,000 female soldiers from all branches of the IDF, a majority of women soldiers reported seeing themselves as being highly (48 percent) or somewhat (30 percent) overqualified for their jobs (in terms of their overall competency), and only half of them (53 percent) expressed high levels of satisfaction from their jobs. Thus, for the majority of the Israeli young women, the military does not create a highly gratifying work place.[17] This is not out of line with their expectations, however, for the military service is perceived by most young Israeli females as being an exciting opportunity to exercise their independence from home and family, to be exposed to new social relationships and a different style of life, and for some perhaps a place to chance upon their future husbands.[18] While the sense of duty and the willing-

Table 3.1
Sample of IDF Specialties and Frequency of Preference by Chen Conscripts

Specialties	"Highly preferable" or "Preferable" responses
Radar operator	53%
Company clerk*	38%
Electronic technician	34%
Personnel clerk	31%
School teacher**	28%
Medical corpsman	24%
Electric-power tech.	14%
Truck driver	13%
Vehicle mechanic	8%
Telephone operator	6%

*Refers mainly to combat units.
**Female soldier-teachers are assigned to public elementary schools in remote development towns.

ness to participate in national service also play a role in women's motivation to serve in the IDF, it is less apparent with them than it is with the men.[19]

When asked about the kind of military occupation which they would choose (the actual placement procedure for women's assignments is normally done at the end of their basic training), the women's preferences reflect a compromise between their hope for a challenging job and their realization of the scarcity of such jobs for them. This compromise is clearly demonstrated in the Table 3.1 in which occupational specialties are ranked in diminishing order of preference, as reported by samples of Chen soldiers.[20]

Though this list is not all inclusive, it shows, on the one hand, a high preference for front-line, operative types of specialties (i.e., radar operator, company clerk) while, on the other hand, it reflects a concession to the reality that administrative clerk and medical corpsman are among the most frequent jobs available for women serving in the IDF. Regardless of their actual military job, when asked at the end of their two-year service about their feelings, the majority of the Chen soldiers expressed remarkably favorable sentiments toward their military service. Of the surveyed women 92 percent claimed that they had indeed fulfilled their initial expectations of making a personal contribution to the state defense while serving in the IDF (only 82 percent of the men responded the same).[21] Job satisfaction, apparently, is not the only significant component in women's analysis of their military service.

The female soldiers in the IDF also have an additional, non-assigned though culturally encouraged function. With their visible femininity, in sharp contrast to the rugged army milieu, these women soldiers serve as a nurturing factor, especially in the combat units. They soften the atmosphere in the unit, bringing to the barracks a touch of warmth and affect, reminiscent of home and family. While wearing their uniforms, (even occasionally the fatigue outfit), many will consciously conserve their feminine appearance in their discreet use of make-up and nail polish and sometimes wearing modest jewelry.

> In the infantry unit where I served in my early military career as a platoon commander, we had a company clerk, Corporal Lea. This pleasant girl used to receive the company mail every day and distribute it herself to each individual soldier, sharing one's cheer when a letter from home or from a girlfriend was received, and occasionally reassuring another when his letters failed to arrive. She was liked by all soldiers in the company and was a close confidant with all the company's officers. It was clear to everyone, however, that her role in the unit could not allow her an intimate relationship with any particular man in the company. Her role was as a sister-figure, even somewhat of a mother-figure, for all of the members of the unit.

Women in Combat Units

Assignment to a combat unit is highly sought after by many women soldiers in the IDF. Indeed, they have to volunteer to serve in line units stationed along the borders and normally will serve there for one year. For their second year in service they may either stay in the same unit or request transfer to a rear unit. However, the rules in these line units regarding the females' roles are sharp and clear: as soon as the unit is deployed for actual combat, the women are immediately evacuated. Although under a surprise attack, this might sometimes be of no avail (in the Yom Kippur War of 1973, at least three women soldiers were killed and many others injured, under the surprise assault of the Arabs), the policy of detaching the women from combat engagement is an unequivocal dictum in the contemporary IDF.

The recent example of the Lebanon War is self-evident: as the Armor and Infantry troops started their advance from the northern borders of Israel toward Lebanon, the women escorted them along the road, then returned to the rear posts. It was not until two months later that female soldiers were allowed to visit their respective units in Lebanon but were still required to return to the Israeli side of the border before dusk.

What are the reasons for this rigid policy of excluding women from combat? The prevailing rationale offered by Chen personnel is the fear of Israeli women being taken prisoners of war by Arab soldiers. While the periodic occurrence of IDF (male) soldiers being taken as POWs makes such a fear undeniable, it is only one explanation. The other possible explanation is rooted in Israeli society's contemporary view of women's equality. Unlike in some other Western cultures (notably the United States) this issue is not enthusiastically pursued in Israeli culture, or among Israeli women in general nor among women in the military in particular. Addressing the current problems Israeli women face in defining their own identity in the military, Colonel Amira Dotan, Chief of the Chen Corps recently stated: "One thing that I said all the time is that equality doesn't mean identity.... One of my tasks is to make females in the army understand that we fight for equal rights and opportunity, but we fight also to remain women and not to become a man."[22]

Thus combat roles in Israel's war-experienced society are still predominantly perceived as men's roles. It is this particular portion of military service that Col. Dotan is reluctant to share with Israeli men. Though many of the Israeli female soldiers grievously complain throughout their two years of military service that they are not utilizing their full intellectual potential, they nonetheless do not wish to better their situation by insisting on combat roles. Instead, other avenues for self-fulfillment and satisfaction are continually sought.

Special Chen Units

Like the IDF in general, the objectives of the Chen corps in particular are not strictly military but include some oriented toward Israeli society at large. Such an orientation is carried out by three special units under the Chen command: the Teachers Unit, the "Chiba" Auxiliary Police Unit, and the "Yachas" Auxiliary Nursing Unit.[23]

The Teachers Unit

In cooperation with the Israeli Ministry of Education, this unit provides school teachers and youth leaders to remote regions in which civilian manpower for youth education is deficient.

The women soldiers who serve in the Teachers Unit are either graduates of civilian teachers' seminars or carefully selected volunteers who start their military service with a special training course which commissions them as school teachers. These teachers-in-uniform are assigned to developing towns and remote settlements where they teach in kindergarten and elementary schools, work in youth community centers, teach Hebrew to immigrants and illiterate adults, and eventually become involved with the daily life of the community. Like other conscripts in the IDF, both males and females, these women soldiers in the Teachers Unit earn only a little spending money (their accommodations are provided by the local community). Their real compensation is the unique personal and professional experience which they acquire in the course of their military service.

The Chiba Auxiliary Police Unit

This unit is also a result of the unique conditions and demands of the Israeli environment. Due to increasing terrorist activities in Israeli civilian centers, the security authorities have developed an intricate network of security guards, placed at crowded streets and in marketplaces, at shopping centers, at theatre entrances, on trains and in buses, and in air terminals. While the assigned responsibility for this security is that of the Israeli Police Department, the serious shortage of manpower for this enormous task has required some innovative solutions—the main one was the establishment of the Chiba unit. Women in this unit are assigned by the Army to the state Police Department, where they undergo special basic training under the instruction of both military and police personnel. Upon completion of this training, they are assigned to towns and cities across the country where they perform around-the-clock shifts of security tasks. Their activities include making security checks in entrances to major public sites, and patrolling in crowded streets, on buses and trains, thus providing vigilant surveillance against possible terrorist activities. While the Chiba soldiers are subordinate to the police, they retain the rights, privileges and responsibilities of soldiers. They are noticeable, in their Chen uniforms (but without any weapons), on every main street and public place in Israel.

The Yachas Auxiliary Nursing Unit

This unit was first established, on an experimental basis, in 1976–77, with an initial group of 300 women who normally would not have been inducted into the IDF because they were below the IDF's minimum standards for women. The Chen command took this special program under its responsibility and named it Yachas (Hebrew acronym for "nursing unit," but as a word it means "rapport"). The idea was to try to rehabilitate girls who were frequently themselves victims of an underprivileged social environment by employing them in useful social welfare–nurse's aid duty in civilian hospitals.

The women in this program go through a six-week basic training course, which is specifically designed and conducted to grant gradual adaptation to military demands. This is followed by another six-week, on-the-job training course in hospital duties, medical hygiene, interpersonal relationships and other related subjects. The Yachas soldiers are then assigned to hospitals[24] where they are employed as general nursing assistants, social-worker aids and various auxiliary nursing roles. While serving in the hospitals, the women study general academic subjects, hence expanding their professional knowledge and enhancing their own personal growth. Indeed, some of them stay on to work in "their" hospitals as civilians, after they complete their two-year military service.

The Yachas project emerged, after its experimental phase, as a successful framework for the rehabilitation and resocialization of many of the underpriviledged young Israeli women. Part of its success is because of the tremendous care and attention given to the project by the Chen headquarters. As with the other two special programs—the Teachers Unit and the Chiba soldiers—the Yachas program successfully combined military service with civil duties, and individual growth with community needs.

Conclusion

The Israeli women's corps exemplifies the IDF's dual functions: as a professional army, its primary function is guarding the security of the State of Israel; its other function, an ideological one, is that of socializing the Israeli youth in the basic values of the society. Anne Bloom, a dedicated student of the Israeli female soldier, has noted that "as Zahal [the Hebrew name of the IDF] has played out this dual character, males dominate in the sphere of the professional meritocracy, and the women recruits are funneled into the sphere of social maintenance and the ideological side of military functions. As experience shows, with the professionalization of an occupation, women are expected to be the idealists."[25]

If this insightful observation places the IDF, or rather Israeli society, in a somewhat paternalistic state in contemporary Western terms, it is certainly not so perceived by Israeli women themselves. In fact, for most young Israeli females, the two years' service in the military is appreciated as a personally, though not always professionally, self-fulfilling and gratifying experience.

Notes

1. Allon, Y. (1970). *The making of Israel's army*. New York: Bantam Books.
2. Source: Ministry of Defence, Tel-Aviv. Cited in Bloom, A. (1982). The women in Israel's military forces. In N. Goldman (Ed.), *Female soldiers: Combatants or non-combatants*. Westport, CT: Greenwood Press.
3. *CHEN translates charm: CHEN—the Israel Defence Forces' Women's Corps*. (1980, February 27). The Israeli Defence Forces Spokesman.
4. *Report on the status of women*. (1978, August). Jerusalem: Prime Minister's Office.
5. Goldman, I. (1982, April). An interview with Colonel Dalia Raz, Commander of the IDF Women's Corps. *IDF Journal: Israel Defense Forces Spokesman*, 1(1), 43–46. Col. Raz noted that approximately 20 percent of all women exempted from military service are exempted for religious reasons. Major General (Res.) Moshe Nativ, the former IDF Chief of Manpower, reports that in 1984 24.7 percent of all eighteen-year-old Jewish women are exempted for religious reasons. In 1977, however, this figure reached 32 percent. See Nativ, M. (1984, Summer). IDF manpower and Israeli society. *The Jerusalem Quarterly*, 32, 140–144, figures from p. 140.
6. Amiad, P. (1981, January). *Attitude survey among conscripts regarding service in the IDF* (Research Report). Department of Behavioral Sciences, IDF. The major results of this survey were reported by the author; see Gal, R. (1982, February). *Modes of adjustment and coping with military service in the IDF*. Paper presented at the 18th Conference of the Israeli Psychological Association, Haifa, Israel.
7. Goldman, An interview with Colonel Dalia Raz.
8. For example, see Dickerson, V. (1974, May). *The role of women in the defence force of Israel*. Alexandria, VA: Defense Documentation Center; and Bloom, The women in Israel's military forces.
9. Nativ's updated figures are 62.1 percent and 88.0 percent. See Nativ, IDF manpower and Israeli society.
10. *Report on the status of women*.
11. Goldman, An interview with Colonel Dalia Raz.
12. *CHEN translates charm*, p. 7.
13. Goldman, N. L., with Wiegand, K. L. (1984). The Israeli woman in combat. In M. E. Martin & E. S. McCrate (Eds.), *The military, militarism and the polity* (pp. 201–230). New York: The Free Press.
14. The former Commander of IDF Women's Corps, Col. Dalia Raz, denies any women's pressure for more significant utilization in the service. In her

interview (with I. Goldman) she claimed: "New specialties—formerly occupied only by men—are now being opened to women, not in response to feminist demands but due purely to IDF requirements for electronics and radar technicians, tank instructors, etc. The end result of this development may be greater equality for women, yet this was not the original consideration" (p. 44).

15. Segal, R. (1980, January). *Attitude survey conducted on the August 1979 cohort of conscripts on their day of discharge.* Unpublished manuscript, Unit of Military Psychology, IDF, Israel. Note: Parts of this report were presented at the 18th Conference of the Israeli Psychological Association, Haifa, Israel.

16. Israelashvilli, M. (1982, April). *The CHEN survey: attitudes toward conscription, adjustment and satisfaction from service among conscript female soldiers.* Unpublished manuscript, Department of Behavioral Sciences, IDF, Israel. Note: Parts of this report were presented at the 18th Conference of the Israeli Psychological Association, Haifa, Israel.

17. In an academic conference on psychological aspects of adolescents, the IDF's chief mental health officer noted that "roughly eighty percent of the female conscripts spend their military service period in a state of 'frozen' intellectual development.... For many of them this results in a sense of unworthiness, apathy and depression." See Talshir, R. (1984, November 30). Eve's services. *Ha'aretz,* p. 6.

18. This insightful and frank comment was made by the current Chief of Women's Corps, Col. Amira Dotan, on her visit to the U.S. National Defense University, Washington, DC, December, 1983.

19. Israelashvilli, *The CHEN survey.*

20. Combined from the following two studies: (1) Israelashvilli, *The CHEN survey*; and Kalay, E. (1982, April). *Professional preferences among CHEN basic trainees.* Unpublished manuscript, Department of Behavioral Sciences, IDF, Israel.

21. Segal, *Attitude survey.*

22. Doctoroff, M. (1984, January 26). Col. Dotan and woman's place: At home, in the military. *Washington Jewish Week,* p. 5.

23. The following description is based mainly on the IDF Spokesman pamphlet *CHEN translates charm.*

24. In Israel there are no military hospitals. All main civilian hospitals are available for military personnel during peacetime and are specially equipped for emergency operations in wartime.

25. Bloom, The women in Israel's military forces, p. 158.

4

Motivation for Military Service

Israelis are generally known for being uncooperative with the law. They do not obey traffic rules; they hate to comply with any directions or sign-posts; they defer bill payment as long as they can; and they will simply ignore civilian duties such as cleaning your front yard or reporting your new address.

All this changes when it comes to military duties. Here, the rules are different; so is the entire orientation. When an Israeli youngster receives his first call for conscription (this usually happens at the age of seventeen), he is well prepared for it. He will not wait for a second notice. In many cases he will report to the local recruiting center in response to a public announcement in the newspaper, even before receiving his first written notice. In the full-draft system which has been operating in Israel for thirty-five years, it is still the case that more than 99 percent[1] of all eligible conscripts report for recruitment on their specified date willingly, without any need of threat or warning. Cases of conscientious objectors are very rare (and they, too, will eventually enlist without force, frequently to non-combat units), and a phenomenon such as draft-dodgers is unheard of.[2]

The Israeli soldier is called for a substantial period of compulsory service—three years for men and two years for women. For some highly specialized jobs, this will turn into an even longer commitment. The conscripts are placed in jobs which they did not necessarily ask for, receive the most arduous training amid inconvenient conditions, and are paid a small amount (equal to about $25 a month) which is hardly even pocket money. During this period of active duty, many of them have a good chance of engaging in real combat, perhaps even in an all-out war[3] and, consequently, may even be wounded or killed. Notwithstanding this, the motivation among youth in Israel to serve in the Israeli

Defence Forces is very high. It has remained high during wartime and peacetime equally. How can one explain this?

Obviously there is the sense of duty to do a national service as required by the law. Most conscripts would not even think of *not* appearing at the induction center on their due date. The Israeli youth is not required to reach a decision about whether or not he should enlist. That decision was made long ago for him and has been upheld by thousands before him. In a paradoxical way, the full-draft system (as contrasted with a selective-draft system or an all-voluntary system) spares the Israeli youth the effort of exploring exemption routes, the fear of being forced into service, and feelings of relative exploitation. The legal requirement of *all* Israelis to participate in military service makes it, in short, a fact of life, not an option. However, this legal requirement for military service does not explain the high level of motivation among young Israeli conscripts to serve in the IDF. A broader and deeper explanation is needed. This can be found in the normative system of Israeli society.

Military service in Israel is not perceived as compulsory, even though it is. It is not perceived as a penalty, even though it constitutes a major interruption in the life course of Israeli men and women. It is not considered a calamity, even though it is extremely stressful, sometimes even fatal. It is a normative part of the Israeli ethos—an integral phase in the life of any Israeli youth. Furthermore, being basically a positive norm, service in the IDF usually receives unequivocal support from society. Parents in Israel discuss with their adolescents their prospective military service in the same way American or European parents discuss college studies with their teenagers. When teenagers are sixteen or seventeen, military service is already the predominant subject of their conversations. Seventy-seven percent of Israeli youngsters at these ages sampled in 1980[4] indicated that they were already "very interested" or "interested" in subjects related to the military. Furthermore, 80 percent of them claimed it was "very important" or "important" for them to "succeed in their military service," not just to "get away" with it.

A frequent scene among Israeli seventeen-year-old boys is to see them preoccupied with physical training, in preparation for their coming recruitment and the pending basic training period. Some will persistently indulge in long-distance jogging, occasionally with some extra load on their shoulders; others will practice map reading or be engaged in assembling model airplanes or combat vessels—depending on their respective dreams about their military service. Their perseverance is quite remarkable, if not excessive. Indeed, several years ago a tragic event happened, when a seventeen-and-a-half-year-old teenager drowned in a public swimming pool, in his relentless efforts to stay two minutes under water—as part of his self-dictated training toward his anticipated recruitment into the naval commando unit. The ethos regarding the extremely demanding training in the IDF combat units is effective long before the young Israeli conscripts are actually drafted.

Serving in the IDF, then, is a well-established norm in Israeli society, anchored in a basically positive attitude toward that service and supported by the individual's family and his social network. Within the Western industrialized democratic states of Europe and North America, in the decade following Vietnam, which has also seen the emergence of a nuclear-disarmament movement, this basic attitude toward military service is unique. What are some of the indicators of this exceptional phenomenon, and what are the sources of this high motivational level? The answers to these questions are the focus of this chapter.

Motivation Indicators

Obviously, the ultimate measure of an individual's motivation for military service can be obtained only on the battlefield. The soldier's readiness to risk, perhaps sacrifice, his life in the face of battle is the highest indication of military motivation in its purest sense. The Israeli soldier's combat motivation, as demonstrated on the battlefield, will be discussed in the following chapters. At present, the initial motivation to join the military and to duly serve in it should be examined. In addition to the factual evidence mentioned earlier, that there is almost, as a rule, a 100 percent report rate of conscripts on their due date, several other measurements have been traditionally used to assess motivation to serve in the IDF.

Attitudinal Surveys

The Department of Behavioral Sciences (previously called the Unit of Military Psychology) in the Manpower Division of the IDF conducts periodic attitude surveys among various populations within the military. One of these surveys is administered to potential conscripts as they attend to their preenlistment medical and psychological examinations, which normally occur six to twelve months prior to actual induction. The items in this survey are aimed to assess the perception, knowledge and attitudes of the prospective draftees toward their anticipated service. The fact that this type of survey, using the same questionnaire, is conducted every few years enables the researchers—as well as the IDF—to trace any possible changes or trends in new recruits' level of motivation toward the service.

In the 1980 preinduction survey[5] one particular question was phrased as follows: "If service in the IDF were to become completely voluntary, how would you react?" Ninety percent of the close to 1,000 subjects participating in that survey responded positively to this item, using the following optional alternatives: 57 percent of the subjects responded, "I would volunteer for the same full service." Another 33 percent said they would volunteer too, but for a somewhat shorter period of time. Only 10 percent declared that they would not serve in an all-voluntary army. Similar responses to an equivalent item had been obtained in previous surveys.[6]

A more recent survey of the same sort, conducted in Spring of 1984, again yielded comparable results,[7] in spite of the strong controversy which the 1982 War in Lebanon had evoked in Israel. In response to the 1984 survey, 25 percent of the prospective recruits reported that the Lebanon War only increased their motivation to serve in the IDF. About the same percentage reported a decrease in their motivation, while half of the survey subjects said the Lebanon War did not affect their military motivation at all. The results of this recent survey came as comforting news to many Israelis who had feared a possible decline in military motivation of Israeli youth resulting from the Lebanon War.

Even if such a decline did occur during a period of debate and confusion about the use of the military for questionable political goals, there is enough accumulated data to ascertain that motivation for military service in Israel may undergo, at times, a temporal impairment, only to again be replaced by a renewed increase in motivation to serve. Such vacillations have occurred before in Israel, as, for example, those noted after the Yom Kippur War. But the average figures in these attitude surveys remain quite stable over the years.

The attitude surveys among prospective conscripts include additional items pertaining to the conscripts' feelings and expectations toward their anticipated service. Table 4.1 summarizes some of the findings from the 1980 survey.[8]

Since the surveyed sample was representative of the seventeen- to seventeen-and-a-half-year-old male population in Israel, it demonstrates that the Israeli teenagers show high interest in military issues about a year before they are drafted; most of them feel pride in being entitled to serve in the IDF; and the majority of them will prefer a combat to a non-combat unit to serve in.

Rates of Volunteering

Another indication of military motivation is rates of volunteering to special units. While military service is mandatory in Israel and placement is determined primarily by manpower needs of the military, there are several elite units in the IDF which are composed entirely of volunteers.

Table 4.1
Responses on the 1980 Preinduction Survey

The item	Response alternatives	Distribution (percentage)
To what extent are you interested in military subjects?	very interested	26.8
	interested	49.8
	not so interested	18.6
	uninterested	4.8
Are you proud of the fact that you are going to serve in the IDF?	definitely yes	45.2
	yes	41.6
	no	10.0
	definitely no	3.2
If you are assigned to a combat unit, will you make an attempt to change it to a non-combat assignment	definitely yes	16.3
	yes	19.9
	no	33.3
	definitely no	30.5

These include pilots in the Air Force, paratrooper units, several Navy units (i.e., submarines and naval commandos) and several of the Army reconnaissance units. Conscripts in good physical condition and qualified on the psychological tests (to be described in Chapter 5) may volunteer for each of these units, either during the preenlistment examination period or at the first day of induction. The proportion of these volunteers from the total number of conscripts is one of the primary indicators of motivation to serve in the IDF.

The actual numbers (or proportions) of these volunteers are highly classified. However, for our purposes, suffice it to say that these numbers have not changed a great deal over the last two decades. If anything, they have gradually increased.[9] On various occasions during the last few years, corps commanders of the Army, Air Force and the Navy have declared that at no time were the volunteer units short of candidates. Instructors from these units who show up at the Induction Center to recruit volunteers are frequently overwhelmed by numerous applicants who vie to join those elite units. A frequent scene during induction day is that of a conscript who had graduated from a vocational school (hence will most probably be assigned to a technical support unit) fighting desperately for his right to volunteer to one of the special combat units.

Indeed, because of the large overflow of candidates, the volunteer units have developed, in addition to the formal selection routine, their own selection procedures, which are sometimes extremely demanding and quite deterring. These "procedures" (see more about them in Chapter 5) are also the first confrontation of the fresh draftee with the "real army" and may either totally frighten or further encourage the initially enthusiastic volunteers. The ones who are finally accepted to these volunteer units immediately gain high status, while most of the rejected ones receive the news with a great deal of disappointment.

Conscripts may express their willingness to join not only the actual volunteer units, but also other non-volunteer combat units such as Infantry units, the Armor tank units, missile boat units in the Navy, etc. Although stating their preferences does not necessarily guarantee their placement in those units, it will certainly be considered by the recruiting personnel during the placement procedure.

Consequently, it may be indicative to examine the Israeli conscripts' preferences regarding both volunteer and non-volunteer units because the choices are made while the conscripts are still in their preenlistment examination period. Questions regarding the conscripts' preferences are included in the surveys administered periodically in the recruiting centers. In the 1980 survey, a general question was included: "If you have the required qualifications, would you select one of the volunteer units in the IDF?" Of the 870 randomly sampled male conscripts, 73.7 percent responded "definitely yes" and "yes" to that question.

Table 4.2 presents the response distribution of two such surveys, conducted in 1974 and in 1980, to several items pertaining to conscripts' attitudes toward various volunteer and non-volunteer combat units in the IDF.[10]

The overall readiness of prospective conscripts to volunteer to frontline, combat roles as can be seen from this table is quite high. Generally, this level of readiness seems to have been increasing from 1974 to 1980.

Unquestionably, the most desirable, and admirable, role in the IDF is that of a pilot. Indeed, it has the highest priority in the IDF. The Air Force is the first to select its pilot candidates from each pull of new draftees. Only after the Air Force achieves its needed share will the

Table 4.2
Percentage of Conscripts Expressing their Willingness to Serve in Volunteer (V) or Non-Volunteer (NV) Units/Corps in the IDF

Unit/Corps	1974 (n=1150)	1980 (n=900)
Air Force pilots (V)	49.0	53.0
Paratroopers (V)	41.4	42.7
Golani (Infantry Brigade, NV)	13.6	27.0
Naval units (NV)	28.0	38.5
Armor (tank units, NV)	18.9	15.5

conscripts be available for other combat units. Being a pilot is strictly voluntary. It also requires a commitment for seven years of service—four additional years beyond the three already required. Yet, more than 50 percent of the conscripts were "strongly willing" or "willing" to become pilots in 1980—a slightly higher percentage than in 1974. The famous slogan of the Israeli Air Force—"Hatovimm Latyees" ("the best to pilots") is not just an empty slogan: The Air Force pilots are the *crème de la crème* of Israeli youth, and they possess the highest status of all military professions.

Not too far behind come the paratroopers. More than 40 percent of all conscripts expressed their desire to join the paratroopers, to wear the red beret and red shoes. While only a few of them will eventually be fortunate enough to wear the paratroopers' uniforms (both because of the units' small size and because of the rigorous entry standards required), the percentages presented in the table reflect the superior image that the paratrooper corps has. This high level of volunteering has been the case since the late 1950s, when paratroopers became the spearhead of all ground combat forces of the IDF. Though small in number, their history includes most of the heroic operations performed by the Israeli armed forces throughout the years. The rate of conscripts' volunteering to the paratrooper corps has always served as a sensitive barometer of the Israeli youths' combat motivation. This rate has always shown a sharp increase immediately after a war period or a daring military operation. Though the paratroopers' toll in dead and wounded has always been high on such occasions, this seemed, somehow, only to further increase the attractiveness of the red berets.

An excellent example of this trend is also demonstrated in the conscripts' attitudes toward the "Golani" infantry brigade. For years, this brigade was in the shadow of its counterpart, the paratroopers' brigade. Being a non-volunteer unit, it utilized the next best manpower quality level after all-volunteer units recruited their own candidates. In the 1973 Yom Kippur War, the Golani brigade performed a gallant assault (although with very high casualties) on Mount Hermon in the northern part of the Golan Heights in order to recapture from the Syrians an important stronghold located on the top of that hill. This heroic operation and the unit which performed it were widely publicized in the Israeli media and boosted significantly the Golani's image as a determined and highly devoted unit. A series of across-the-border operations completed successfully by units from this brigade (during the period between 1973 and 1980) further elevated its status. And so, in 1980, 27 percent of the prospective conscripts wished to join this non-volunteer unit. Indeed, the Golani brigade commander announced, on several occasions, that his brigade was now manned only by soldiers who had directly requested to serve in it. Recalling the high-quality standards required in all Israeli combat units, this story of the Golani brigade may well reflect the trends of motivation for military service among Israeli youth.

The story of Israeli Navy units is the same. From a rate of 28 percent of conscripts who had expressed strong motivation to serve in those units (mainly missile boats) in 1974, the percentage increased to 38.5 percent in 1980. This development reflects, again, the changing image of these units from a non-aggressive coast-guard type of service into a high-performance, front-line combat corps in recent years. The more that was publicized about the naval units' participation in combat operations, the greater its desirability to young draftees. Once again, it is the combatant, high-risk, no-nonsense image of those units that attracts the Israeli youth.

Finally, this is also the case with the Armor corps. The tank units, which are the backbone of the Israeli ground forces, also suffered, in absolute numbers, the highest casualty toll in the Yom Kippur War. Here again, joining the Armor corps is not a voluntary act, yet many of the conscripts express a clear desire to become a "shiryonair," a tank crew member. More than 15 percent in 1980 and about 19 percent in 1974 (this somewhat higher percentage is probably due to the post–Yom Kippur War effects) of all young Israeli males who reported to the recruiting centers declared the tank units in the Armor corps to be their first preference for service.

These figures regarding the expressed willingness of prospective conscripts to volunteer to various combat units were further analyzed with regard to the respondents' background information. Hence, the level of motivation appears to be strongly associated with the conscripts' level of education, socioeconomic background and locale. The most positive attitudes toward volunteering for combat units, in both the 1974 and 1980 surveys, were found among conscripts with higher education, those raised in well-to-do families and those predominantly from kibbutz and "moshav" settlements. (A moshav, quite similar to the kibbutz, is a cooperative village, incorporating features of both private and collective farming.)

> One target of volunteering for many highly educated conscripts is the "Nahal" brigade. Nahal, an acronym for "Noar Halutzi Lohem" (Fighting Pioneer Youth) is basically a combat-ready infantry brigade, which combines military with agricultural training. Nahal units are based on youth groups which have been consolidated for several years within youth movements and have formed "Garinim" or "nuclei," part of which are designed to become the kernel of new agricultural settlements. Prior to basic training, the youths are sent to agricultural training in one of the established kibbutzim, where they become acquainted with various aspects of farming and with the kibbutz way of life. Basic training is conducted at the Nahal Training Base, and the entire "Garin" participates together (the females, however, in separate companies) and graduates together. During the course of their service, the group will spend time engaged in both security and agricultural work in a "target settlement"—usually a newly formed outpost in a strategic area—while continuing to be military units in all other aspects. In the second year of their service, the male members of the Garin complete an additional few months of advanced military training within the paratrooper corps, hence becoming some of the best-trained and most highly motivated line units of the IDF. The continual flow of volunteers to the Nahal framework over the years is just another indicator of Israeli youths' motivation for meaningful military service.[11]

Young Israelis, then, especially those with high education and "good" backgrounds give combat units and combat roles their highest preference. This is further enhanced (as well as induced) by the fact that these units are also given (by the military authorities) the highest priorities, in terms of quality allocations, during the actual enlistment and placement procedures. Placing the highest priority and status on those units inevitably dictates the general standards for military motivation among the Israeli youth.

However, among certain social groups, although limited in size, one can also identify strong norms of resentment and objection to military service. Typically, this may be found among teenagers with very low socioeconomic status, those with adjustment problems, high school dropouts, and juvenile delinquents. Although these youngsters seldom try seriously to dodge the draft (which is almost impossible in a small and isolated country like Israel), they will nonetheless try to avoid any combat roles and definitely would not join a volunteer unit. Ironically, these conscripts are the ones who might benefit the most from their military service, in terms of their future assimilation into society.

Desire to Be an Officer

In the 1980 attitude survey among conscripts regarding their readiness for service in the IDF,[12] 59 percent of the subjects answered "definitely yes" or "yes" to the question: "If you are qualified, would you volunteer to become an officer?" Serving in elite combat units, albeit voluntarily, is still within the framework of the three-year compulsory service period for men, but volunteering to become an officer in the IDF is something else.

In committing themselves to be officers, men are required to sign for one additional year of service (while the women's requirement is for six months). Hence, when a soldier agrees to attend officers' school (this will normally happen sometime during his second year of service), he knows that his term will be four, rather than three, years of fully committed military service. For these young men, most of whom intend to begin their higher education work after they complete their national service, this fourth year is yet another postponement to their career preparation. Yet, it is particularly among these youngsters that being an officer is especially desired. In all the preenlistment surveys, favorable attitudes toward being an officer were positively correlated with level of education. Thus, for example, in one of these recent surveys the percentage of those who wished to become officers was 84 percent among high school graduates, while among those who had completed only ten years or less, this dropped to 59 percent.

Officers' roles are extremely demanding, whether in combat or noncombat units. This high level of demand implies not only more time, energy and responsibility than the average non-officer soldier, it also has its high toll in terms of casualties on the battlefield. The Israeli officers, in all the recent wars, were three to four times more likely to be battle casualties than were enlisted men.[13] Furthermore, throughout all his reserve service, which will last until the age of fifty-five, the Israeli officer will be required to serve more tours, and more days each tour, of active duty than his enlisted counterpart. Serving as an officer, then, in the IDF is an all-consuming mission. Yet, it is highly desirable. Trends and fluctuations of this desirability may serve as subtle measurements of military motivation among the quality groups in the IDF.

With all the extra demands associated with the officer's role, and in spite of the difficult selection procedures involved, the IDF has never been short of officer candidates. In addition to the high status resulting from being an officer, it is also considered among most of the young soldiers to be a great personal achievement. Being commissioned as an officer, for the majority of Israelis, means to exert one's abilities and skills—as well as one's capability to contribute to one's society—to their utmost.

As the Chief Psychologist of the IDF, a position I held between 1977 and 1982, it was my responsibility to make the final decisions on soldiers' appeals regarding their officers' selection tests. Obviously, all the appeals came from individuals who had failed those tests but could not accept the fact that the route to becoming an officer was blocked for them. There were hundreds of them each year, and many, who were given a second chance and failed again, kept appealing again and again, desperately insisting upon their wish to become officers. Those endless appeals may be seen as indicators of high desirability attached in the IDF to an officer's position.

The desire to become an officer is, furthermore, a delicate sensor, responsive to any changes in mood and attitudes regarding military service among the civilian population of Israel. Thus, for example, when during the 1982 War in Lebanon a critical response toward the Israeli military involvement in Lebanon had developed among broad parts of the Israeli population, it had its immediate reflection also in attitudes pertaining to volunteering to become an officer. In the winter of 1983 (while the Israeli armed forces were still deployed in Lebanon, including Beirut) the media in Israel were suddenly preoccupied with scattered reports regarding "serious" decline in kibbutzniks' motivation toward the military service. It became clear, eventually, that indeed there had been a significant change in kibbutz members' readiness to volunteer to become officers. (There were no changes, apparently, in any other volunteer behaviors of those socially elite youth during that period.)

An IDF official confirmed that the rate of commissioned officers among all kibbutzniks dropped from a normal rate of 40 percent to about 20 percent, but attributed that change to the fourth year of service required from those becoming officers. The young kibbutzniks, said the official, are reluctant to stay another year in the service. However, since the fourth-year requirement was announced in 1977, it is questionable whether it was, indeed, the reason for the kibbutzniks' more recent behavior. More likely, it was a reflection of the lack of consensus among many Israelis regarding the IDF's involvement in the War in Lebanon that deterred many kibbutzniks (generally known for being politically attuned), and perhaps others as well, from seeking leadership roles during their military service.

During several private conversations with young kibbutznicks, I received similar responses: We have no doubts about our duty to serve in the IDF, and we will continue our traditional way of volunteering to elite combat units. But three years are enough. And under the current circumstances we have no enthusiasm to serve beyond duty requirements, certainly not as leaders.[14]

While these reactions may be temporary, they demonstrate how labile this motivation is and how sensitive are these motivational indicators to political changes. In a society where military service is mandatory and results from the need to defend one's home, the motivation for this service does not fluctuate according to changes in unemployment level or economic conditions. Rather, the motivation to serve springs from deeply rooted sources in Israeli history and society.

Sources of Motivation

Before turning to the historical and social forces which are specific to Israel, one should mention a factor which is universal—that of age. From a psychological-developmental perspective the age period of eighteen to twenty is when the physically mature young adult begins to explore mental challenges. The same forces that drive youngsters of this age of other countries to launch backpack journeys around the world, to join exotic religious sects or to vigorously demonstrate against the world's evils are the very forces which channel Israeli youth into military service. Here he undertakes adventurous journeys, becomes part of a cohesive group and also feels part of an ideological mission.

The specific origins of Israeli society's attitudes toward, and motivation for, military service can be viewed from four perspectives: historical, national, social and normative.

Historical

From the early days of the Jewish settlement in Palestine, involvement with defense, security and military (or paramilitary) activities was always associated with high status and respect. The early members of the Hashomer movement were aristocrats who had abandoned both their wealth and patrician life in Europe in the late 1890s to become professional armed guards, fully engaged in self-defense activities. Similarly, the Palmach members were elitist, the cream of the crop of Israeli youth. As an army that was born during its nation's War of Independence, the IDF's early core of senior commanders was composed mainly of highly intelligent and creative young men. Many of them were the sons of parents who themselves belonged to the social elite of the Jewish community or were the founders of many of the prestate institutions. In short, the military service in Israel, since its early days, has been regarded with great respect and has attracted the best and the most capable of Israeli youth. Furthermore, because of its constant occupation with genuine operations and war-related activities, which were so essential to the very survival of the newly born state, the "cutting edge" components within the IDF always gained the highest respect of all.

To this, one has to add the collective memory among the Israeli population of the Holocaust. Every Israeli soldier, be he a Sabra, a Sepharadi, or an Ashkenazi, carries within him the remembrance of the 6 million Jews extinguished by the Nazis. The notion that the security of the State of Israel is the only guarantee that "this wouldn't happen again" is deeply rooted in every Israeli citizen. Thus the IDF is perceived as being the only force guaranteeing that security.

National

Defense is, unequivocally, the highest priority among Israel's national goals. The physical threat to its existence is perceived by the Israeli population not as a mere possibility but as a definite certainty. The recurring wars since 1948 have served only to strengthen this perception, while the 1973 Yom Kippur War almost made it happen. Hence, the high priority given to, and great prestige associated with, the Israeli Defence Forces are apparent in Israel, in both practical and perceptual senses.

In monetary terms, Israel has spent an unusually high proportion of its national budget on defense from the earliest days of the state. Although the most recent figures are not available (the defense budget in Israel is considered a state secret), previous reports[15] indicate a pre–Yom Kippur War defense expenditure amounting to 32 percent of Israel's

Table 4.3
Israeli Ministers of Defence since the Establishment of the State of Israel

David Ben-Gurion (also Prime Minister)		May 1948-Jan 1954
Pinchas Lavon		Jan 1954-Feb 1955
David Ben-Gurion		Feb 1955-Nov 1955
David Ben-Gurion (also Prime Minister)		Nov 1955-Jun 1963
Levi Eshkol (also Prime Minister)		Jun 1963-Jun 1967
Moshe Dayan		Jun 1967-Jun 1974
Shimon Peres		Jun 1974-Jun 1977
Ezer Weizmann		Jun 1977-Jul 1980
Menachem Begin (also Prime Minister)		Jul 1980-Aug 1981
Ariel Sharon		Aug 1981-Feb 1983
Moshe Arens		Feb 1983-Jan 1985
Yitzhak Rabin		Jan 1985-present

total government expenditure (20 percent of Israel's GNP). However, in less than three weeks, the Yom Kippur War cost the nation a whole year's GNP.[16] A more recent evaluation[17] estimates Israel's defense expenditure for 1982-83 at $8.2 billion dollars, or 37.9 percent of GNP. These figures do not include various sources of foreign aid that Israel traditionally receives, primarily from the United States.

The Israeli defense budget, probably one of the highest per capita in the world, is just one indicator of the IDF's high national priority. Other indicators show it too. The Ministry of Defence (in Hebrew "Misrad Habitachon," literally meaning "Ministry of Security") has been traditionally the most critical office in Israel's government. The position of Minister of Defence was always considered the most important one next to that of the Prime Minister, with the Prime Minister frequently occupying both positions, as illustrated in Table 4.3.

The high priority clearly given to the military in Israel stems not only from its main function as the shield for Israel's survival, but also from the central role the IDF plays as being directly involved in building the nation in areas such as education, settlement, absorption of immigrants and rehabilitation of juvenile delinquents. The IDF is perceived in Israel not just as a military force, but as a national resource, capable of carrying out almost any national goal. In a rather mythical way it has become a common belief that there is nothing that the IDF cannot accomplish, in addition to its combat missions, if and when called upon. This image of the IDF may be attributed not only to its efficiency in performance, but also to its perceived superior moral standards and its remaining apart from any local or political interests. Whatever the sources of this image are, the IDF's top priority in Israel's hierarchy of national priorities is perhaps the only issue which receives a complete consensus among the Israeli population.

Social

Average Israeli youths find themselves, as early as their teenage years, under severe social pressure to serve compliantly, if not ardently, in the IDF. In a nation where military service is conceived, literally, as home-protecting, there is no measure of tolerance toward any signs of evasiveness. In fact, attempts to dodge the draft, though not completely unheard of, are typically considered to be deviant behavior. Any youngster between the ages of eighteen and twenty-one who is not in uniform is looked upon with suspicion. The fact that serving in the IDF means high risk and a possible loss of life only makes universal service in the IDF more imperative. The societal consensus is that the share should be everyone's and the toll should be evenly divided.

Service in the military has become an entrance ticket to Israeli society in general and to the job market in particular. The first thing required for any young person who looks for a job is his "teudatt shichrur" (certificate of discharge from the military). Not only does it verify that the candidate has fulfilled the requirement for military service, but it will indicate the rank achieved, and it will include a brief evaluation regarding conduct. In most cases this will be considered far more evidential than any other form of recommendation. Hence, an Israeli young person who for some reason (health problems, adjustment difficulties or others) did not serve in the Army or did not complete the required service will face serious problems in making his or her way in Israeli society. On the other hand, successful service in the IDF may serve as a springboard for upward social mobility. This is especially true for youngsters coming from lower socioeconomic groups and for whom the military service provides a great opportunity to advance rapidly in social and economic roles and to finally free themselves from their prior social origins. The IDF, with its adherence to criteria for promotion based on fairness, competence and actual achievements, has been successful in enhancing the upward mobility of certain segments of the Israeli population. In any case, having served in the IDF continues to be an important biographical reference throughout the life of most Israeli citizens.

> The importance of military service in the Israeli's career does not diminish with one's age and progression. Sometimes the opposite is true. Even among Knesset (the Israeli parliament) members, an occasional charge leveled toward an opposing member will be: "Where did you serve in Zahal?" And even when the response will confirm that the distinguished representative has indeed done his share in the military, the baleful question will still return: "Yes, but as a non-combatant, wasn't it?"

Normative

Indications of the normative roots toward military service can be found in every aspect of Israeli life. From folk songs to classic poems, in colloquial speech as well as in the educated language, the favorable influence of the IDF is undisguised. Even radical changes in the political and attitudinal atmosphere in Israel have not changed the basic norms regarding the IDF in Israeli folklore. A colloquial word such as "jobnik" (which refers to a soldier serving in a non-combat job) still has a strong negative connotation for the average Israeli youth. In contrast, it is typical for teenagers to wear brown high-topped boots (used traditionally by the elite paratrooper units) or commando rubber shoes (the type used by the naval commando fighters) or to be dressed in the popular IDF combat parka called a "dubon."

A content analysis of Israeli contemporary folk songs would yield a high proportion of songs pertaining to military issues. Furthermore, most of these songs will include themes idealizing the warrior image of the Israeli soldier.

Similar phenomena can be seen in the literature. In addition to the "industry" of valorous books and stories generated after each war (this was especially the case after the Six Day War, though much less so after the Yom Kippur and Lebanon wars), there are also the endless memorial books and monographs published by the families, fellow soldiers or community members of many of those killed in action. This literature serves not only to commemorate the beloved lost ones, but also to idealize and to sculpt the heroic images of devoted combatants in the mind of the Israeli youth. This is the normative background for most Israeli teenagers as they approach their period of compulsory military service.

A typical "confession" made by Illan, an Israeli reserve combat soldier, is reported in a study conducted recently with war veterans. Illan's words demonstrate how deeply the norms regarding combat military service are rooted.

"In those of us who are sabras [Israeli born], who went through primary and secondary schools, with a strong involvement in the youth movements especially, the image of the hero was clearly implanted. ... Moreover, if you accept this ideal, you volunteer for a certain kind of army service, as I did. ... This was what we felt was socially demanded of us. We wanted to conform with the image. ... I didn't feel any internal conflict."[18] (P. 245)

Conclusion

The various forces that drive the Israeli soldier on the battlefields—that is, his fighting spirit—will be further discussed in Chapter 8. In the present chapter the motivation to serve, the Israeli soldier's military motivation, was delineated. The indicators of such motivation are reflected in both the expressed attitudes and the actual behavior of the Israeli conscripts (i.e., reporting to duty, volunteering to special assignments, etc.). These indicators, though they may undergo serious fluctuations, are nonetheless surprisingly stable across the years.

The roots of this motivation to serve obviously cannot be explained simply as compliance with the legal requirement for mandatory service. They can be accounted for by looking at universal developmental factors such as age, adventure seeking and youth searching for meaning. Moreover, though, this motivation becomes clear in light of the historical, societal and national perspectives of Israel's population. These become the ingredients of the extremely powerful normative system which makes serving in the IDF so highly appreciated, so socially desirable and—for most Israelis—so taken for granted.

Notes

1. Quoted in (1982, April 21) *Bamahane* (the IDF magazine) (29–30), 44.

2. An increasing number of refusals to report for active duty in Lebanon were noted among reservists in the period following the Lebanon War of 1982. This phenomenon will be further discussed, especially in Chapter 13.

3. In its thirty-seven years of independence (1948–85), the State of Israel has gone through five such wars: the War of Independence (1948–49); the Sinai campaign (1956); the Six Day War (1967); the Yom Kippur War (1973); and the Lebanon War (1982). This makes an average sequence of one all-out war every eight years.

4. Amiad, P. (1981, January). *Attitude survey among conscripts regarding service in the IDF* (Research Report). Department of Behavioral Sciences, IDF. The main

findings of this survey were reported by the author at the 18th Conference of the Israeli Psychological Association, Haifa, February 1982, and were partially published on April 21, 1982, in *Bamahane* (29–30), 44–46. The survey was conducted on a random and representative sample of potential conscripts reporting for early examinations to the recruiting centers. Age range was between sixteen and a half and seventeen. Of the sample, 95 percent were males, and only 5 percent were females.

5. Amiad, *Attitude survey*.

6. Ibid.

7. Eshet, M. (1985, April). "Peace for Galilee" did not change motivation for service. *Bamahane* (Special issue for reservists abroad), 5.

8. Amiad, *Attitude survey*.

9. *Bamahane*, 1982, April. Also *Yediott Ahronott* of October 24, 1984, reported (quoting the IDF's Induction Base Commander) that in the latest induction cohort there were five times more volunteers for paratroopers and Air Force pilots than slots available. The report also said that patterns and trends of volunteering to elite units in the IDF have not changed in the last few years.

10. This table is adopted from Amiad's report (*Attitude survey*). It was also presented at the 18th Conference of the Israeli Psychological Association, Haifa, Israel, February 1982. Each figure in the table represents the percentage of subjects who answered either "strongly willing" or "willing" to the question: "To what extent are you willing to serve in the following unit/corps?" Responses to each unit/corps were given independently.

11. This description was based on the IDF Spokesman Report, *The unique character of the Israel Defence Forces*, 1982. A detailed description of Nahal structure, training and phases of service is found in Bowden, T. (1976). *Army in the service of the state*. Tel-Aviv: University Publishing Projects.

12. Amiad, *Attitude survey*.

13. In the Yom Kippur War, 28.5 percent of total Israeli casualties on the battlefields were suffered by officers. In the Lebanon War this percentage was 24. For details, see Chapter 7.

14. In *Ha'aretz* of June 26, 1984, an article entitled I am not willing to die for nothing: Kibbutznicks, on the eve of their induction, confronting army generals, described some of these reactions.

15. Keegan, J. (Ed.). (1979). *World armies*. New York: Facts on File, Inc., p. 361.

16. *Facts about Israel*. (1979). Jerusalem: Ministry of Foreign Affairs.

17. *The Military Balance, 1982–83*. London: The International Institute for Strategic Studies, p. 56.

18. Lieblich, A. (1978). *Tin soldiers on Jerusalem Beach*. New York: Pantheon.

5

THE SELECTION, CLASSIFICATION AND PLACEMENT PROCESS

The manpower needs of the Israeli Defence Forces can best be characterized as requiring both maximum quantity and maximum quality. Given the small population of Israel and the immense defense requirements, the optimal utilization of available manpower is an absolute necessity. This is achieved, indeed, by means of the IDF's rigorous screening system (involving selection, classification and placement) for new recruits.

The screening process of the IDF is based on several premises: (1) the entire population is available for drafting; (2) screening for military service has to take into account both physical and mental capabilities (i.e., it is both a medical and a psychological screening procedure); (3) rejection rates must be minimal, yet effective, in order to utilize as much of the available manpower as possible; (4) placements have to be based primarily on the military's needs (the individual's preference is secondary and will be granted only if it also fits military demands); and (5) for some specialties, the best screening is achieved throughout the initial service course rather than prior to recruitment.

Based on all of these premises, the screening procedures in the IDF are composed of preentry, entry, and postentry stages:

Preentry screening occurs during the two visits each prospective conscript makes to his or her recruitment center. The first visit takes place when the recruit is about seventeen years old, and the second one at roughly the age of seventeen and a half. In these preenlistment processing phases, the candidate will go through medical, mental and supplementary screenings.

Entry screening occurs at the Induction Center on the conscripts' first day of active duty, normally at the age of eighteen. This screening phase is based primarily on the information gathered during preentry screening and consists of placement in a military specialty with specific screening for special units.

Postentry screening involves continuous monitoring throughout the initial period of service for advanced courses, junior command and officer training.

Preentry Screening

Medical Screening

Medical screening is one of the first phases in the preenlistment screening procedures. The IDF uses a medical profile that has a numerical scale, ranging from 21 to 97. (For some historical reasons no scores are used below 21 or above 97.) A score of 21 designates an individual totally unacceptable for military service. A score of 24 indicates an individual with a temporary deferment for medical reasons. Conscripts with scores above 24 are drafted. The highest score—97—means superb physical condition. The scores falling between 25 and 97 are used to determine assignment possibilities. Thus, for example, conscripts with scores below 65 can be assigned only to units that are stationed to the rear. An individual with a score of 65 and above may be assigned to front-line units. Those with scores above 65 are further classified into assignment categories, such as infantry and paratroopers, who are required to have a score of 72 and above, and pilots, who are required to have a score of 89 and above, and so on.

The medical screening procedure is rigorous and thorough: conscripts are given a thorough medical checkup by a physician, fill out an extensive medical history questionnaire, take laboratory tests, and occasionally are referred to other medical specialists. The end result of this screening procedure is a precise indication in the form of a medical profile, aimed primarily to assess the conscript's combat fitness. By this thoroughness the medical screening system allows the drafting of even moderately disabled individuals and uses them in appropriate assignments.

A special area in medical screening is that of psychiatric screening. Because of the extreme demands and the stressful situations which characterize the military service in general, and combat service in particular, psychiatric stability of the individual is very important. The potential adjustment of the conscript is tested thoroughly by means of psychiatric interviews and occasionally psychological testing. Those conscripts who are found to have severe adjustment problems are not exempt from service but are enlisted in a special enlistment category.

Until 1974, conscripts with psychiatric articles referring to potentially severe adjustment problems were exempted from drafting. These individuals (as well as another small group of conscripts who had extremely low intelligence or educational level) were considered as unfit for military service. This exemption was dropped after the Yom Kippur War with its high rate of casualties and the public pressure for everyone to share equally in defense. In addition it was also a chance given to these individuals to overcome their adjustment problems by functioning in the structured setting of the military. A special program was established (called "Makam" which is an acronym for the Center for the Advancement of Special Populations) to handle the special needs of these draftees. That included modified basic training, which was longer and more slowly paced, special occupational courses to provide them with vocationally transferable skills, carefully selected placement assignments, constant follow-up to assess their functioning, and more tolerant standards in regard to their discipline. The Makam project initially evoked a great deal of reluctance and objections from commanders, who worried about the effect of these conscripts on the overall combat readiness of the IDF. However, over the years the Makam soldiers have become an integral part of many of the IDF's units, and the relatively high success of that project guarantees its continuation.[1]

Mental Screening

The name given to the psychological testing procedures that take place at the various recruitment centers is not psychological testing or mental screening; rather, and for many good reasons, it is termed "quality screening." Its final product is the "Quality Group Score" (in Hebrew "Kaba"—an acronym for "quality category") which is determined for each individual through a series of tests and interviews taken at the recruitment centers during the preentry period. The conscript's assigned Kaba combined with his medical profile will consequently affect his fate throughout most of his military career.

The Kaba system. The nature of the IDF's Kaba has been frequently described in professional literature.[2] It has been regularly used by the IDF for psychological screening since the late 1950s. Throughout the years it has shown relatively high stability and predictive validity and was perceived by the IDF manpower authorities as an extremely useful tool. Recently, however, the IDF's psychologists have been working on an improved and modified version of this measurement.

The Kaba is made up of four components which are combined by an actuarial procedure into a single score varying from 41 to 56. The four components are:

1. An intelligence evaluation score. For test reliability it is called the Primary Psychotechnical Rating (the acronym in Hebrew is "Dapar"—a term which has become, in Israeli slang, a synonym for IQ or intelligence). The Dapar is derived from a version of the Raven's Progressive Matrices and an Otis-type verbal test.[3] The Dapar score ranges from 10 to 90, with 90 being roughly equal to an IQ of 135 and above.
2. Level of formal education. Simply the total number of years of schooling that the conscript attended before recruitment.
3. Command of the Hebrew language. The estimated level of the conscript's fluency in reading, writing and speaking Hebrew. While obviously depending, at least partially, on whether the conscript had been raised in Israel or not, this component becomes crucial in assessing a soldier's quality in a military where orders, instructions, manuals and forms are all in Hebrew.
4. A motivation-to-serve index (called "Tsadach," an acronym from its Hebrew wording). This is an overall estimation of the conscript's initial motivation to serve in the military, particularly in combat units. In addition, this index reflects the conscript's prospects for successfully adjusting to a combat unit. The index is derived from a semi-structured interview, roughly twenty minutes in length, administered by trained enlisted specialists (most of them female soldiers), who have received a three-month course in conducting such interviews. Six traits are assessed in this interview: activeness, motivation to serve in a combat unit, sociability, responsibility, independence and promptness.[4] From the responses given by the interviewee in these six areas, the interviewer then generates an overall prediction score which reflects the conscript's projected probability of success in a field unit.[5] The motivation-to-serve index is finally compiled by summarizing some of the interview scores and the weighted prediction score into a total score, ranging from 8 to 40.

Thus, the Kaba reflects the individual's intelligence level, education level, mastery of the official language, and projected adjustment to combat service—four factors that in the Israeli's eyes comprise those measurable attributes relevant to potential fighters.

Women's Kaba. The Kaba screening system, with all of its four components, applies for male conscripts only. Female conscripts have Kaba scores based on only three components—intelligence, education level and language. The motivation index, designed specifically to predict adjustment to a combat environment, is not included in the women's Kaba.

Validity of the Kaba for men. The four components of the Kaba score are not simply added up. Rather, they are empirically weighted, based on results obtained from continuous validation studies which are conducted periodically by the research psychologists in the Psychological Testing Branch. As such, the Kaba index provides a highly stable, reliable, and considerably validated predictive index. Some examples of this validity can be seen in Table 5.1.[6]

Table 5.1
Range of Validity Coefficients (Pearson correlation) and Multiple Correlation Coefficient (MCC) of the Kaba and Its Components

Intelligence Evaluation ("Dapar")	Level of Education	Command of Hebrew	Motivation Index ("Tsadach")	KABA (total score)	MCC
.41--.44	.46--.48	.34--.37	.39--.42	.52	51--.54

The criterion against which the Kaba scores were validated, and which is traditionally used by the testing experts as a measure of successful service, was the soldier's rank upon his discharge from the compulsory service period.[7] This criterion may vary from early discharge through enlisted ranks up to officer's rank (the Israeli officers, as will be described in Chapter 8, are trained and commissioned during the compulsory service period). As one may conclude from the table, the prediction power of the Kaba, as represented by the multiple correlations, is fairly high. The two highest single scores among the Kaba components are the intelligence evaluation and the level of education. Considering the non-specific nature of the predictors and the criterion, on the one hand, and the many additional variables that obviously intervene in between, on the other hand, the coefficients presented in the table indicate a decently validated screening system.

Kaba categorization. The Kaba scores are normally assigned by the manpower personnel to three major categories: from 41 to 46 are termed low quality; 47 to 50 are moderate quality; and 51 to 56 are high quality. This categorization indicates, approximately, the prospective assignments of the conscripts. The vast majority of those within the high Kaba category are assigned to combat roles, and many of them will eventually be channeled to become officers or NCOs in command positions. It is from this category, also, that pilot, naval officer and other special units will receive their volunteers. A small portion of conscripts with Kaba scores of 51 to 56 will be assigned to high-tech or highly sophisticated specialties. However, as a general rule this category is reserved for the front-line units of the IDF. The moderate quality category mainly includes individuals who will consequently be assigned to support and service specialties, but still within field or combat units. The lowest category, conscripts with Kaba scores of 41 to 46, are normally assigned to non-combat auxiliary units, for non-combat service specialties.[8]

A more detailed illustration may clarify what the various Kaba scores mean: a conscript with a high Kaba score of 56, for example, will have an IQ above 135, have completed at least twelve years of school, is completely fluent in Hebrew and shows high adjustment capability along with strong desire and motivation to serve in a combat unit. At the other end of the scale, a conscript identified as a Kaba 43, for example, will most probably fall at the 70 to 80 IQ level, have no more than four or five regular years of consistent attendance at school, show poor verbal performance and will be a poor prospect for adjustment to the military environment. Most typically such a conscript will also express reluctance, if not overt objection, to being drafted.

Viewed as such, it is no surprise, then, that the highest Kaba categories include mostly well-educated (i.e., high school graduates) youths who come from financially "comfortable" families, who have traditionally shared positive attitudes toward the military service. Most of the kibbutzim youth, the kibbutzniks, and the moshavim members have high scores. By contrast, the lower Kaba scores are characterized mainly by youth from underprivileged families, many of whom had immigrated to Israel during the 1950s, mostly from Islamic states (called Eastern Jews or Sepharadim as opposed to Ashkenazim who are Western Jews). While the former (high Kaba) will eventually serve mainly in line units, in combat roles, and most typically end up as officers or NCOs, the latter (lower Kaba) will mostly serve in support and service roles and normally remain at lower ranks throughout their military service.

Kaba and military performance. Figure 5.1 graphically displays the relationship between Kaba scores and consequent achievements during military service (compulsory period only), as reflected by ranks upon discharge and early discharges.[9]

The picture is clear: the higher the conscript's quality, the greater the probability that he will end up serving in a command position, either as an officer or an NCO. In the IDF that also means a high probability for a line-unit assignment.

Thus, for example, of all conscripts who belonged to the highest quality group (i.e., a Kaba of 56), 50 percent have eventually become officers, and another 38 percent have completed their service as NCOs. Only 10 percent of this quality group remained at lower ranks, while 2 percent received early discharges. One should recall that the IDF is a full-draft system and has full control over a conscript's assignments. The above figures, then, reflect, from the military point of view, a maximal utilization of the highest human quality resources.

The figure also demonstrates that the entire officers' corps (with the exception of 1 percent) comes from the high-quality category (Kaba scores of 51 to 56), with the larger proportion at the higher scores. Similarly, the main bulk of the NCO corps, even though scattered along the entire

Figure 5.1
Distribution of Ranks by Kaba (Quality Group) Scores

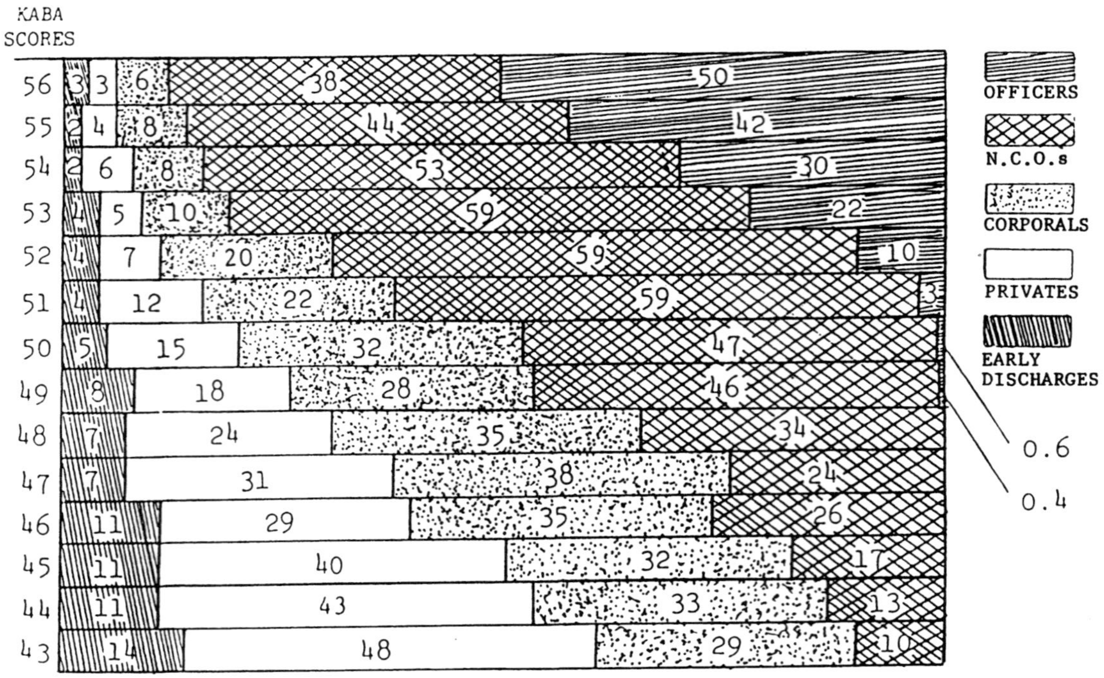

range, stems from the high- and middle-quality categories. The lower ranks (privates and corporals) are most frequently found as one goes down the Kaba scales, while early discharge cases are more frequent at the lower qualities, although they can also be found at the higher levels. (The data in the figure do not include conscripts from the 41 to 42 Kaba scores. Their rate of early discharge, however, is significantly higher than shown here for even the 43 quality group.)

Kaba and the demographic distribution. The IDF preserves a linear, positive correlation between the quality level of its manpower and their ranks and positions within the service. The Kaba score of the Israeli conscript becomes, accordingly, a key factor in determining his military career. Viewed from the individual's perspective, this might become either a positive opportunity for upward mobility or a label that hampers forward progress. From a broader point of view, however, the predominancy of the Kaba system and the way it is used in the IDF create one of Israel's paradoxical phenomena: While the IDF is indeed typically viewed as a full representative of Israeli society, it also generates demographic "distortions." For example, a tiny group of kibbutznik conscripts (roughly 3 percent of the national population) are extremely overrepresented among command positions, elite units, and special occupations (i.e., fighter pilots). Education level, rather than being proportionally distributed, is strongly skewed toward field units and combat assignments. The better-educated and stronger-motivated soldiers are overly condensed within the IDF in units most likely to see combat, where failure is least tolerable.

Kaba as a manpower planning tool. The quality groups screening system is essential to the manpower distribution of the IDF's strength. Since the Kaba score, like the medical profile, is firmly established before induction day, it enables the IDF's personnel authorities to plan their annual manpower charts ahead of time. Since various branches, units and military occupations receive their respective distributions of percentages of different Kaba "slices," these percentages can already be translated into real numbers and, consequently, into individual assignments right at the Induction Center. Furthermore, in order to guarantee that each corps will eventually generate its own officers, the high-quality category (Kaba 51 to 56, the prerequisite for officer's candidacy) has to be proportionally distributed among the various corps. Finally, a small portion of the top Kaba scores (54 to 56) is identified, and conscripts are further encouraged to volunteer for advanced screening procedures and special assignments (to be described shortly).

Hence, the Kaba system is not only a validated screening procedure, it is also a useful planning device which enables optimal utilization of Israel's limited human resources. By first establishing a valid estimation of each conscript's soldierlike potential, then updating the Army's quantitative and qualitative requirements, and, finally, matching these two measures, the Israeli military is able to achieve one of the nation's primary goals—making the best use of its qualitative resources.

The new Kaba. During the late 1970s, the IDF's manpower authorities (with the noticeable personal involvement of then Deputy Chief of Staff for Personnel, General Moshe Nativ) concluded that the nearly twenty-year-old Kaba system had been losing its sharp discriminatory capability (i.e., the capability of classifying draftees into accurate quality categories pertaining to their military performance potential). Each of the Kaba's four components seemed to have become outdated: the Dapar intelligence score, with its two archaic tests, could not respond to the increasing variety of sophisticated specialties entering the various branches of the military; the education-level index lost, to an extent, its high validity, since over the years Israeli law had enforced schooling up to the minimum of the eighth grade (thus squeezing the possible range for education-level variance); and, most important, the enlistment of growing numbers of lower quality conscripts and their difficulties in adjusting to any form of military environment made it necessary to develop a motivation-adjustment measure which would not be exclusive for combat units only but would also predict success in any military framework.

The new Kaba system, which emerged after four years of research and development, is basically similar in its underlying conceptualization to its ancestor. Only the Hebrew-mastery test was deleted from the system while some of the inner components of the other tests were replaced or expanded. The Israeli draftee will still be evaluated in the future for the same major attributes—his intelligence, level of education, and motivation for and prospective adjustment to combat assignments. However, each of these areas is now assessed in a much more sophisticated and elaborated way. The net outcome, it is hoped, will be a more refined and accurate selection and classification system—hence, a better utilization of the scarce human resources available for the IDF.[10]

From the perspective of an outsider, the enormous research and development activities which were involved in developing the new Kaba system may tell a great deal about the high priority given to this screening system by IDF authorities. At various stages of the process, thousands of conscripts were administered the experimental version of the new tests (in addition to the ongoing screening tools), which required each individual to spend an extra two or three days at the recruiting centers. The whole project, the largest of its kind ever undertaken in Israel, involved the expenditure of a great amount of resources. However, all of the resources required were given, with no strings attached, to the behavioral scientists who directed the project. Since 1985 the new and improved Kaba has been gradually replacing the old Kaba, which for all of these years effectively fulfilled its mission.

In search of quality. The concept of quality, for the IDF, is not just a screening category or a manpower planning parameter. Rather, it is the only exclusive advantage that Israel, a country with a little over 3 million inhabitants, has over its enemies—the Arab states of the Middle East, with over 200 million inhabitants. With its total draft and reserve systems and with its nearly static population, Israel can find no new sources to increase its military quantity. Neither can it beat the Soviet-backed Arab nations in the size of its arsenal. Israel's only superiority is its quality superiority.

It is no surprise, then, that the IDF is constantly scrutinizing, with great concern, any fluctuations in the overall annual distribution of the Kaba scores of its new conscripts. After all, this is, by definition, the distribution of its own quality! While the concerns pertain to each of the Kaba components, very little can be done by the IDF to preserve or enhance any of them: the intelligence level (Dapar) is, by and large, innate; education and language are already fixed prior to draft; and motivation is apparently determined by education and the larger societal norms. Yet, all these quality indicators are anxiously kept under surveillance by IDF authorities.

Assuming the intelligence level of Israeli soldiers follows the normal distribution curve for the entire population, the entire Israeli population is fully represented in the compulsory service. Within the IDF, however, the intelligence scores curve is clearly biased toward the combat roles and combat units. Thus, for example, the mean intelligence (Dapar) score of 150 combatants, randomly sampled from various combat units (mostly armor and infantry) which participated in battles in the Yom Kippur War, was 69.2. (Note: the Dapar scores range from 10 to 90, with a structured mean of 50.) The intelligence level of fifty-one medalists, members of various front-line units, was even slightly higher; their average Dapar score was 71.8, reflecting the eighty-sixth percentile of the total population.[11] Apparently, the Air Force and the Navy, because of their high technological skill requirements, get conscripts with even higher intelligence scores than those of the Army conscripts.[12] However, because of the rigorous selection standards for officer candidates, the intelligence level of the IDF officers in all three branches is, on the average, higher than the average Dapar score of the total conscripts' population.[13]

Unlike the intelligence capability, the education level of an individual depends basically on his or her own achievement and exploitation of available resources. In general, the average educational level, which apparently (see Table 5.1) is the strongest predictor among the four Kaba components, is constantly increasing among IDF recruits. In 1981, 60 percent of all conscripts had at least twelve years of school, while only 13 percent had fewer than eight years. Projections for the coming years estimate the percentage of high school graduates among conscripts to increase to around 80 percent in the year 1990, while the percentage of poorly educated will practically diminish to none.[14] (It is the IDF policy to see to it that every conscript who has fewer than eight years of schooling will attend a special school, prior to his discharge, which will bring him at least to the level of junior high school.)

The mastery of the Hebrew language is closely related to, and also highly correlated with, the education level. The exceptions are new immigrants, who may possess a higher education but do not speak the Hebrew language. For this reason young immigrants are deferred from immediate enlistment until they can improve their level of mastery. In addition, if necessary, these conscripts will begin their military service with a three-month intensive course of Hebrew. This will enable them, at the very least, to understand orders, to read written instructions and to fill out forms—all necessary requisites of any good soldier.

Last, but not at all the least, the constant search for maintaining high quality focuses on the motivation factor. The motivation for service, as shown in Chapter 4, is quite sensitive to changes in current political situations and to the extent of societal consensus regarding military activities. This is true, however, mainly with regard to the reserve soldiers and only partially so to the permanent service corps. As for the young conscripts, their motivation level remains basically stable over the years. This can be seen objectively in the motivation index of the Kaba. This index, across annual flows of conscripts, has not changed much throughout the years.

Since the motivation index is viewed as a predictor for field or combat adjustment, it is no wonder that combat units are characterized by especially high levels on that index. For example, the mean score (on the motivation index) for forty recipients of medals for bravery during the Yom Kippur War was 29.1, reflecting the ninety-fifth percentile of the entire IDF population. Even more striking is the fact that even for the non-medalists from the same combat units, the motivation index mean did not differ significantly from the medalists' and fell, too, in the high percentiles.[15]

Supplementary Screening

Once the conscript's Kaba and medical profile have been determined, he is prepared for his draft and for his prospective military assignment and will not be burdened with additional visits to the recruitment center until induction day. However, a small proportion of the conscripts are invited for supplemental screening. Based on their exceptionally high

Kaba scores and medical profiles, these individuals (mostly men, but also some women) become candidates for special assignments, such as fighter pilots, several elite combat units, and some specific high-tech specialties.

While information regarding the special tests applied to these highly selective candidates is classified, it is known that most of these tests had been specially designed and developed by IDF psychologists and were tailored to the IDF's specific requirements. Thus, for example, psychological screening for pilots at this stage includes tests for complex mechanical coordination and for spatial perception. The medical examinations for these pilot candidates concentrate on vision and vestibular fitness.

The assessment procedures, both medical and psychological, performed at the recruitment centers during the year prior to induction have one main goal: to collect all the necessary data regarding a conscript's capabilities so that on the conscript's first day of active duty minimal time will be spent on placement procedures. With two (for women) or three (for men) years of compulsory service, the IDF authorities regard every service day as too dear to spend on preliminaries. Whatever can be achieved before the date of draft is done.

Entry Screening

Placement in a Military Specialty

The famous Induction Center of the IDF ("Bakum"—an acronym for the Hebrew words "Induction and Placement Base") is located in Tel-Hashomer, a suburb close to Tel-Aviv, in the center of Israel. The Bakum base is quartered in a pre–World War II British-made camp, and most of its buildings are old-looking wooden shacks which certainly do not represent for the new draftees the modern military machine that they are going to operate in a few weeks.

At the Induction Center, the new draftees receive, on their first or second day of induction, but based on their preentry screening results, their actual unit placement and thereby assignment to a specific basic training course within the respective corps. For a relatively small group of draftees who have been initially placed as candidates to some special units, the Bakum will also be their host for a few more days, during which their final acceptance for these special assignments will be assessed. These two functions of the Bakum center apply, however, only to the men. The women draftees are all sent, immediately after processing, to the Central Women's Basic Training Base. Their placement procedures will only occur at the end of their basic training period.

The actual placement of the male conscripts is executed by special placement officers (most frequently reserve specialists with no formal training in placement techniques but a great deal of experience in this job) and is based on the evaluation information already known about the draftee from his preinduction assessment procedures. Although the guiding line is the Army's demands and requirements, the draftee's preference is also incorporated into the decision-making process regarding his future placement. Before entering the placement officer's office (this will normally occur during the second day in the Induction Center), each conscript is given a form which lists all the possible specialties which are available, along with a brief description of each. The conscript is then asked to rank his three preferences as first, second and third. During his interview with the placement officer, the details of his preferences are discussed, and further information about the optional alternatives is provided, when required. The final decision is made by the placement officer in an attempt to match, if possible, one of the conscript's preferences, even if not the first one, to the available slots.

In fact, the placement procedure does not have too many degrees of freedom: a given distribution of Kaba scores and medical profiles is dictated beforehand by the manpower placing authorities. Further limitations of certain medical articles and exact combinations of the Kaba are sometimes attached to certain MOSs (military occupational specialties). Occasionally, some personal or family problems will also affect the individual's placement. Finally, the draftee's preference is strongly regarded. All of these factors are finally condensed to determine the conscript's actual placement.

A relatively small percentage of draftees who have severe family problems, health restrictions or predicted adjustment problems—are assigned to serve "near their home." This translates in Hebrew into the acronym "Kallab"; hence, Kallab has become a synonym for a "troubled soldier" who cannot serve in remote units. Similarly, conscripts who are only sons can not be assigned to combat units without a special agreement signed by their parents. Even more strictly, sons of bereaved families (most typically with an older brother or a father who had been killed in action during his military service) are formally restricted from combat units. Most of them, however, will persist in it, and with their parent's (mother's) approval will be stationed according to their wish.

The entire process of placement, albeit very brief, is highly emotional for the conscript. Indeed, it determines the conscript's fate for many years, particularly considering the long years of reserve service facing him in the future, and may be quite critical to his life. At the end of this placement process in Bakum, which takes several hours, one can see bursts of excitement from the conscripts—some cheerful, others agonized. With their placement assignment completed, however, they are transferred to their next phase.

Specific Screening for Special Units

The special screening procedures are used with the special volunteer units which require more rigorous screening. These units are air crews in the Air Force (these candidates have already completed a portion of their special screening in the recruiting centers); naval officers, submarines crews, and frogmen in the Navy; and paratroopers and special reconnaissance units in the Army. All of these units can, in fact, afford more rigorous selection since the number of applicants usually far exceeds the number of spaces available. The special screening procedures are designed to identify those personality predispositions required for each of these specific units.

The IDF retains remnants of traditional screening procedures which were used by the American OSS (Office of Special Services) and the British model for the Officer Selection Board. These procedures are situational tests which incorporate simulation attempts of their prospective tasks and continual observations of a candidate's performance of various tasks under very stressful conditions. Most typically, these situational tests will consist of a series of unexpected tasks (such as having to push uphill a "stuck" command car, crossing a natural obstacle, etc.) performed during several days in the field under strenuous conditions.

> These situational screening procedures are called "Gibush" which translates to "getting cohesive." This term was used in order to disguise the real purpose of these activities. Terminology, however, was not the only problem of these inventive procedures. First, each unit developed its own methods, frequently without appropriate professional control, which resulted in unusual, albeit innovative, testing situations. In addition, because of the applicants' high level of motivation (for many of whom, especially the kibbutzniks among them, there could not be a greater disgrace than failing these tests), they would often overexert themselves to the point of exhaustion. Quite frequently these candidates would begin their basic training not only tired but also injured. Because of this, there were constant debates about the exact validity of these procedures. In the early 1980s the IDF established formal guidelines to reassert control over these screening procedures.

The Air Force screening procedures for their air crews are somewhat different during this entry stage. Before introducing their applicants to the situational testing in the field, they are first given a battery of personality tests, plus specific tests to measure selective attention and speed and errors in dealing with competitive information.[16] A junior psychometrician reviews the results of these various tests and forwards his report to a senior psychologist who reads it, then interviews the applicant. Applicants who meet the screening standards are then sent on for the field situational testing. The air crews' situational testing (Gibush) occurs at the flight school and lasts several days. During this period heavy use of sociometric (peer evaluation) techniques is made, in addition to scrupulous observations of the candidates' behavior by their future instructors and trained behavioral scientists. Candidates who have successfully met the requirements during all the phases of aviation screening will be sent to take the applicable aviation coursework. The conscripts who failed are returned to the Induction Center, still in time to be tested for the other available volunteer units.

Postentry Screening

While the use of preentry and entry screening is common to all militaries, the use of formal postentry screening is unique to the IDF. Postentry screening is used with both female and male conscripts. It is especially applied to the latter for selection to junior command courses and officers' school.

Screening Procedures for Women

As mentioned earlier, most of the women draftees (with the exception of a few whose military occupation had already been determined at the recruitment center) arrive at the Central Women's Basic Training Base without any placement assignment. In addition to being trained throughout their one-month basic training phase, these women are evaluated by their immediate training staff regarding their general capabilities and their specific skills. Toward the end of their basic training, their actual placement occurs, based in part on these evaluations and in part on their stated preferences. However, their final placements are determined by the ongoing manpower needs of the military.

The women's basic training is also used to identify potential candidates for junior command positions and especially for officer candidate selection. For this purpose women trainees are evaluated not only by their supervisors but also by each other by means of peer-rating techniques. Such techniques, using sociometric questionnaires, are among the most widely used methods in the IDF's continuous postentry screening procedures. Further examples will be discussed in the following paragraphs.

Selection of Men for Junior Command and Officer Training

All Israeli field officers come from the ranks. They begin their respective basic training like everyone else. They serve for a while as regular soldiers, then are selected for junior command courses and, consequently, serve as NCOs in positions such as squad leaders or tank commanders. Only then are they selected for officers' training. This entire screening and selection process occurs roughly during the conscript's first year of service. A brief description of these procedures has been provided by various authors.[17]

Toward the end of their specific basic training, a sociometric questionnaire for peer evaluation is administered at the platoon level. In these questionnaires, each conscript is asked to rank his "best friends" in the platoon, followed by a requirement to rank the "best potential squad leaders" in the platoon. While the real purpose of this peer evaluation is the selection of junior leaders, including the "best friend" item allows for partialing out the impact of popularity on selection. However, empirical studies have repeatedly shown that the two lists are strongly correlated. It is the case, apparently, that those who are perceived as having leadership potential also tend to be relatively popular.

Based on their initial quality scores (Kaba), immediate commanders' evaluations, and their sociometric scores, candidates from each specific basic training course are selected for their respective junior command courses. These courses include infantry squad leaders, armored tank commanders, artillery crew leaders and various other similar NCO courses.

During these junior command courses, a similar screening occurs in which candidates for officers' training are selected. Just completing the junior command course is, in itself, a part of the selection process since these courses are the most difficult in the IDF, and not everyone completes them. Again, toward the end of this course, the sociometric questionnaires are administered; only this time the leadership item pertains to the "best potential officer."

The sociometric score of each soldier becomes part of his personnel file. An interim evaluation by his immediate commanders is also placed in his file. These two indices, together with his original Kaba score, will determine whether or not he is considered, sometime during his junior command course, for additional screening at the Officers' Testing Center. This additional screening currently consists of a battery of psychological tests and a clinical interview (a further detailed description of which can be found in Chapter 8). In the past, the Officers' Testing Center was patterned after the British model using a board of senior regular officers who evaluated a series of Gibush-like situational test results. In the early 1970s the board system was replaced by the current, much shorter evaluation process which emphasizes the clinical-psychological aspects. The final determination of whether an individual is selected for officers' school will be based on a composite score derived from the Kaba score, the sociometric score, and the psychological test scores obtained at the Officers' Testing Center. Of these, only the Kaba is a preentry score; the sociometric score reflects his achievement as a soldier during the initial training phases, and the psychological tests delineate his personality as a soldier at that time.

Classification for Specialties and Teams

The ongoing screening processes throughout service apply not only to junior command and officer selection. In a limited way it also contributes to the specific classification of various specialties within each corps. One of the best examples for this can be seen in the Armor corps. The particular classification into the three tank specialties—the driver, loader and gunner—occurs only toward the end of Armor basic and advanced training phases. It is based, to an extent, on the conscript's specific abilities as demonstrated during those training periods. Thus, for example, gunners are selected mainly on the basis of their actual performance in gunnery. Another consideration is manpower planning needs (i.e., distributing high Kaba conscripts equally throughout all three specialties so that unit disruption is minimized when selected soldiers are sent to the junior command course).

The initial phases of training (combined basic and advanced) are used in the Armor corps not only for individual selection but also for team building. A unique use of the sociometric technique was applied in the late 1970s in an attempt to assemble tank crews in a systematic way. The immediate reason for using the sociometric device was to improve performance levels of tank crews. However, the initial stimulus came from psychiatric considerations: the combat experience of the Armor corps in the Yom Kippur War demonstrated the importance of tank crew cohesion as a significant means of enduring sustained combat stresses and even coping with psychiatric breakdowns.[18]

The sociometric questionnaire was administered at the end of the combined basic and advanced Armor course. Each soldier was instructed to rank six individuals from his company with whom he would prefer to be teamed in his tank. The crews were then assembled according to these stated preferences. While the experiment successfully demonstrated a significant improvement in performance,[19] it became evident that this "teaming" technique resulted in the emergence of "good" teams in which good crew members selected other good crew members, and conversely "poor" teams were composed of the less desired (thereby also less competent) group members. Furthermore, in a subsequent study[20] it was demonstrated that an optimal use of the Kaba scores in assembling tank crews can provide an even better predictor for tank crew performance than a sociometric assemblage. Not only did crews with high Kabas perform significantly better than crews with low scores, but the performance level exhibited by a uniformly high-scoring crew far exceeded the performance levels expected on the basis of individual crew members' quality scores. Teaming high Kaba combatants, then, not only ensures superior performance of each member of the team, but also enhances remarkably the effectiveness of the team as a whole.

Another example of the combining of initial test scores with ongoing performance evaluation is that of the screening procedures of the Israeli Air Force. Candidates who achieved the necessary scores on the preentry and entry tests are sent to the situational testing phase (Gibush). Here, as in the other Gibushim, candidates are placed in both real and simulated stressful situations and are constantly observed and evaluated. In addition, toward the completion of the Gibush phase, they are administered a sociometric questionnaire which asks them to rate their peers in terms of "how good a pilot they will be." All of the available information for each candidate is incorporated into a statistical equation (multiple regression) which is reported[21] to produce a relatively high prediction score (R of 0.51) for successful performance in the aviation course. The aviator's screening, however, does not end even at this phase: every phase in the aviator's course serves as a predictor of success in future phases. His performance score, along with a new sociometric score from each phase, will be combined with his prior prediction score to produce an updated one which will determine whether or not he will proceed to the next phase of aviation training. As it is reported the sociometric test alone has achieved "an accuracy level of over 90 percent during the two decades since it was introduced."[22]

The repeated use of peer evaluation constitutes, as shown above, an important part of the overall screening process for aviators. Consequently, the Israeli aviator, the end product of this process, is not only technically proficient but is also characterized as a "sociometric star."

Reassignment

A somewhat different example of the ongoing screening that occurs during service is that used for reassignment. Although the IDF's selection and placement procedures for regular units are designed to successfully place each conscript in a definite specialty for the three-year period of compulsory service, a certain amount of attrition, though minimal, nonetheless occurs. These dropouts result from inability to adjust to some particular demands of their military service or from inadequate performance in their assigned specialties. Many of these individuals come from the lower Kaba categories and are especially characterized by low potential adjustment indices, as shown by either psychiatric articles in their medical profile or in their motivational-adjustment Tsadach index.

These dropouts are sent back to the Induction Center to a special office which reevaluates their files and reviews the history of their military performance. Sometimes these individuals will be given additional tests. Sometimes additional medical evaluations will be made with the option of changing the medical profile. As a result, these soldiers are reassigned to a new unit, and sometimes even to a new specialty. A few of these soldiers return, sometimes even again and again, during their service. Each time, an attempt is made to better place them, instead of discharging them, unless it cannot be avoided. Whether these latter cases reflect a failure of the screening procedures, or the individual's determination to fail, remains open.

Conclusion

Israeli manpower screening concepts stem from a combination of inherent factors: a limited, insufficient manpower supply versus a wide range of military needs, all within the context of compulsory service. Under these conditions, the various screening methods usually manage to effectively integrate the individual's mental and physical qualifications with his or her motivation to place them in the optimal assignment. The fact that this attempt is not successful 100 percent of the time does not detract from the effectiveness of this system, especially if one considers the tremendous difficulties associated with enlistment and placement totally dictated by the military system.

In the United States Army and in the Canadian armed forces, which are both all-volunteer forces whose members receive adequate monetary compensation, an attrition rate of 30 to 40 percent[23] during the first year of service has been reported. By comparison, in the IDF, which is compulsory service with minimal monetary compensation, the attrition rate during the three-year service period averages less than 10 percent. Obviously this can be partially attributed to the fact that military service in Israel is mandatory, essential and normative. But it can also be seen as a result of the meticulous though lenient structure of the selection, classification and placement system of the IDF.

Notes

1. The IDF Spokesman (1982, March). *The IDF contribution to the rehabilitation of disadvantaged youth.* Tel-Aviv: IDF Spokesman's Office.

2. Reeb, M. (1968). Construction of a questionnaire to replace a valid structured interview in the Israeli Defence Forces. *Megamot*, Behavioral Sciences Quarterly, 16, 69–74; Amir, Y., Kovarski, U., & Sharan, S. (1970). Peer nominations as a predictor of multistage promotions in a ramified organization. *J. of Applied Psychology*, 54, 462–469; Reeb, M. (1976). Differential test validity for

ethnic groups in the Israeli army and the effect of educational level. *J. of Applied Psychology, 61*(3), 257–261; Gal, R. (1983). Courage under stress. In S. Breznitz (Ed.), *Stress in Israel*. New York: Van Nostrand Reinholt; Tziner, A., & Vardi, Y. (1983). Ability as a moderator between cohesiveness and tank crew performance. *J. of Occupational Behavior, 4*, 137–143.

3. This verbal intelligence test is a modified—and translated into Hebrew—form of the old Army Alpha Instructions Test, which was developed for the U.S. Army during World War I.

4. Reeb, Differential test validity. See also Tubiana, J. H., & Ben-Shakhar, G. (1980). *An objective group questionnaire as a substitute for a personal interview in the prediction of success in military training in Israel.* Unpublished manuscript, Hebrew University of Jerusalem, Jerusalem, Israel.

5. The six Tsadach scores are similar to combat-effectiveness-related characteristics identified by Egbert and his colleagues: Egbert, R. L., Meeland, T., Cline, V. B., Forgy, E. W., Spickter, M. W., & Brown, C. (1957, December). *Fighter 1: An analysis of combat fighters and non-fighters* (HumRRO Technical Report # 44). Monterey, CA: U.S. Army Leadership Human Research Unit.

6. Source: Selection Branch, Induction Center, Tel-Hashomer, IDF. The figures in the table represent a range of correlation coefficients for each component, obtained throughout the recent years.

7. The expected contamination between the predictors and the criterion (that is, the fact that selection for higher ranks is, at least partially, based on the Kaba scores) is statistically controlled in this table of validity coefficients.

8. Until 1974, many of the conscripts with Kaba scores of 42 (who also had psychiatric articles) and all of those with scores of 41 were not drafted at all—in view of their poor prospects for adjustment to military service. In recent years they have been drafted as a special group (called Makam, as discussed earlier in this chapter).

9. Source: Selection Branch, Induction Center, Tel-Hashomer, IDF. The information regarding the exact years and sample size to which this figure refers was not released for publication. It is known, however, that the data on which the figure is based had been accumulated over several years.

10. A detailed description of the new Kaba system was given November 21, 1984, in *Bamahane, 9,* 34–35.

11. Gal. Courage under stress.

12. Pa'il, M. (1975, January). The Israeli defence forces: A social aspect. *New Outlook: Middle East Monthly,* 40–44.

13. While this is true regarding the young generation of conscript officers (2nd and 1st lieutenants), the intelligence average declines among the main bulk of the permanent officer (Keva) corps, since only a small portion of the conscript officers, and not necessarily the brightest among them, stay in the Keva corps for a military career. This trend will be further discussed in Chapters 7, 9 and 13.

14. *Bamahane* (1984, February 22) *26,* 5.

15. Gal. Courage under stress.

16. Lester, J. T. (1973, June 26). *Israeli military psychology* (ONR Report R–13–73). London: Office of Naval Research, U.S. Navy, Branch Office.

17. Ibid.; Gabriel, R., & Gal, R. (1984, January). The IDF officer: Linchpin in unit cohesion. *Army*, *34*(1), 42–50.

18. Steiner, M., & Neumann, M. (1978). Traumatic neurosis and social support in the Yom Kippur War returnees. *Military Medicine*, *143*(12), 866–868; Levav, I., Greenfeld, H., & Baruch, E. (1979). Psychiatric combat reactions during the Yom Kippur War. *Am. J. Psychiatry*, *136*(5), 637–641.

19. Tziner & Vardi. Ability as a moderator between cohesiveness and tank crew's performance, pp. 137–143.

20. Tziner, A., & Eden, D. (1985). Effects of tank crew composition on tank crew performance: Does the whole equal the sum of its parts? *J. of Applied Psychology*, *70*(1), 85–93.

21. Lester, J. *Israeli military psychology*.

22. Ravid, Y. (1984, May). Sociometric pilot testing saves time, lives, and money. *Defense Systems Review*, 44–45.

23. Doering, Z. D., & Grissmer, D. W. (1984, May). What we know and how we know it. A selected review of research and methods for studying active and reserve attrition/retention in the U.S. Armed Forces. *Proceedings of the Second Symposium on Motivation and Morale in the NATO Forces* (pp. 251–299). Brussels: NATO.

6

THE FIRST STEPS: INDUCTION AND BASIC TRAINING

Eighteen is perhaps the most significant age for Israeli youth. "When you are 18..." is something Israeli children hear a lot. For many of the younger Jewish generation who have grown up in Israel, it is even more significant than being bar-mitzvahed. It is their "coming of age," a time when they leave behind their teenage joys and enter into the rigorous framework of military life. For some it will happen virtually overnight after their graduation from high school, while for others recruitment may be delayed for a month or two. This period of time will usually be spent pursuing pleasures and "charging the batteries" prior to their entry into this exciting though extremely demanding phase of their life.

Preparing Israeli Youth for Induction

Are Israeli youth at the age of eighteen mentally prepared for their military service? Apparently so. All of the atmosphere, education and folklore in which Israeli children grow up prepare them for their entry into this phase. As teenagers they have developed a multitude of expectations regarding their future military service. These expectations, while based on hearsay, are nonetheless surprisingly realistic. For example, a survey conducted among future conscripts asked them to rank those factors which they expected to play the most important role in their pending military service. The responses of the sixteen- to seventeen-year-olds reflected realistic perceptions held by these youngsters. The highest expectation was associated with having commanders who would take good care of them: 91 percent selected this factor as being the most important. Similar expectations regarded serving with "good guys" (90 percent). Only in third position did they rank "contribution to the state" (79 percent), followed by "acquiring a useful job skill" (60 percent). The lowest expectation pertained to a convenient service location (37 percent).[1]

Despite these well-enunciated expectations, entering the military is usually accompanied by worries and anxieties, and even real fear among those who know they will be assigned to fighting units. In another survey[2] of Israeli youth conducted some months prior to induction, they were asked about their anticipated difficulties during their early military training. The predominant concern was "being hassled" by their military instructors: 44 percent felt they would have difficulties coping with this source of stress. Another 38 percent felt that they would have difficulty coping with the restrictions on personal freedom imposed by the military. Less than 10 percent indicated difficulty in transitioning to the new social environment and missing home and family. The apparent overriding source of concern—the fear of physical injury—was obviously not included in this questionnaire.

In an attempt to ameliorate some of these fears, the IDF has instituted preparation programs to be given in preinduction situations, and especially in high schools. Such programs are conducted, as part of the regular curriculum, by school teachers with the guidance of military authorities. But more frequent are those special meetings with IDF representatives in which various facts about military service are provided, various difficulties are discussed, and the students are encouraged to inquire about whatever concerns them about their forthcoming military service. The IDF utilizes servicemen (predominantly officers) from all branches and ranks, including senior officers, for this program.[3] However, it seems that the greatest success among high school teenagers is accomplished by those servicemen who are closest in age to their audiences—that is, soldiers who have served just one or two years in the Army, very junior officers, or officer cadets. (They are even more effective if they are also graduates of the same high school.)[4]

Another approach the IDF uses to prepare soon-to-be draftees is a special publication[5] entitled *To You, the Draftee*, which was prepared by a team of psychologists and educators. In this booklet, which is given to the conscripts shortly before induction, there are brief chapters referring to the various sources of stress in the military, especially in the early phases, with some practical suggestions on how to cope with these stresses.

The table of contents of the booklet *To You, the Draftee* includes the following topics:

—away from home
—the basic training structure
—how can the group help?

Induction and Basic Training

  —how can the group be horrible?
  —what do you do about sex?
  —why do we need discipline?
  —the commanders
  —being hassled
  —how to get through

Written with wit and humor, this brief "how-to" manual indeed encourages the fresh draftee to use humor and to "take it easy" as primary coping mechanisms during the basic training phase. Overall it seems that it succeeded in "hitting the mark."[6]

Several reasons were behind this IDF effort to develop these preparation programs. First, it reflected the IDF's desire to maximize the motivation of new recruits. The school meetings, booklets, and information provided were all designed to enhance the conscripts' level of preparedness and readiness as they embark on their military service. Second, only recently have IDF authorities also responded to the realization that the induction process is accompanied by a high level of anxiety which may sometimes jeopardize the soldiers' coping abilities which are so essential, especially during the first month of training. Such a realization was strengthened after the 1973 Yom Kippur War, with its high death toll, and again during the IDF's involvement in Lebanon, when macabre attitudes became common among the potential conscripts. All sorts of cynical marching cadences evolved during these periods, involving fatal wounds on the battlefield and deforming or crippling injuries. These expressions, which were initially generated as a part of soldiers' lore, were ultimately conveyed to future conscripts and obviously had an adverse impact. The direct contact between soldiers in uniform and soon-to-be soldiers is so unavoidable in Israel that it exposes the future conscripts, long before their actual conscription, to the gory reality of combat.

In one of the preinduction conscript surveys, conducted after the Yom Kippur War,[7] subjects were asked to individually evaluate various sources of information about the military in terms of the primacy of these sources. The results generated the following order of information sources:

friends who serve in the military	49%
friends not currently serving in the military	36%
parents	35%
relatives	32%
various media sources	8–14%
school teachers	12%

A common scene on Friday evenings is that of new soldiers talking to their civilian friends, entertaining them with stories of military life. While the information gathered from these friends in the military may be the most enthralling, it is not always the most accurate or reliable and, in fact, may be counterproductive. That was an additional concern of the military authorities who opted to use the structure of the preparation programs to provide more balanced information.

The IDF, then, puts forth a substantial effort into the prospective conscripts long before their drafting in order to maximally prepare them for their pending military service. The level of initial motivation, the kind of expectations, the levels of fear and anxiety, and the adjustment ability of the fresh conscript may be critical during the first month of military life. The basic training phase, especially in the combat units, as will soon be described, is considered to be one of the most difficult times in the life of a young Israeli. Despite the constant exposure of Israeli youth to aspects of military life, it is obvious, then, that additional preparation is essential.

Day of Induction

Four times a year, during the months of February, May, August and November, the IDF inducts all qualified eighteen-year-olds into service. Dividing the process into four intervals helps to spread the annual recruitment throughout the entire year. It also fits into the scheduling of the various military courses in the IDF. Although there is an attempt to equally disseminate the quality of recruits throughout the four intervals, there have developed, nevertheless, specific characteristics for the different draft cohorts. Thus, for example, the August and November cohorts are considered to be the more successful, since they have high frequencies of recent high school graduates. On the other hand, the February and May cohorts are viewed as more problematic and consist more of conscripts who were not in attendance at a regular school and thus could be drafted in the middle of the school year.

No matter what the draft season, during those induction months, in various reporting centers across the country are typical scenes of farewell from family and friends, when the fresh draftees are loaded onto buses to head for the Induction Center, located in the center of Israel. Each morning during the draft months, these excited youth can be seen gathering in the reporting areas, sometimes accompanied by boyfriends or girlfriends and almost always escorted by their parents who show a mix of pride and anxiety. Although it is very clear that within a short while their children will be under the total control of the military, these parents try, nevertheless, to give them one more piece of advice, a little more encouragement, and, in the tradition of the classic "Jewish mother," an apple or sandwich for their journey. An Israeli writer once described this scene as "Isaac's Sacrifice," referring to the fact that some of these youngsters will not return from their service and also to the hidden pride of the parents, especially the fathers, when they escort their sons into this national service. This author saw it as reminiscent of the dramatic scene in which Abraham, in compliance with God's will, is going to sacrifice his son Isaac. Though some may not like this analogy, there is no doubt that this farewell scene has the characteristics of a *rite de passage*.

This is, however, still the easy part of the induction process for the conscripts. From these reporting areas they are bused to the Induction Center, commonly called the Bakum, where they will get their first real taste of military life. Here they will usually spend a day or two involved in in-processing activities, including receiving their personal issue and going through their final evaluations and placement assignments (this process was detailed in Chapter 5). Here, too, on their first day of military life, the new recruits will take their oath of allegiance in a formal and impressive ceremony that will take place that night.

> "I hereby swear, and fully commit myself, to be faithful to the State of Israel, to its constitution and its authorities, to take upon myself, without reservations or hesitancy, the rules of discipline of the Israeli Defence Forces, to obey all commands and orders given by authorized commanders, and to devote all my strength, and even sacrifice my life, to the defence of my country and the freedom of Israel."

At this time the young conscripts are ready to begin the rigors of military life, starting with the specific basic training course to which they were assigned.

Types of Basic Training

The IDF has a number of basic training bases, which can be categorized into three types: general, corps, and brigade.

Generalized Basic Training

These bases train soldiers for non-combat assignments for all the different branches and corps of the IDF. Such is the Central Women's Basic Training Base, which, practically speaking, trains all women recruited to the IDF. (Unlike several other Western militaries, the IDF does not have mixed-sex basic training.) The men too have a similar base, the Central IDF Basic Training Base, which trains men assigned to non-combat roles. These men all have physical limitations to a varying degree or other approved reasons which account for their assignments to this non-combat basic training in the first place. In this category, basic training lasts for a month for both the men and women and imbues them with basic military habits, trains them in the use of basic military weapons and orients them to the basic values of the IDF. The rest of the training will be accomplished in the specialized courses to which most of these graduates will consequently be assigned.

Corps Basic Training

All units of the combat corps, with the exception of the infantry, maintain their own specialized basic training bases. Recruits assigned to combat roles will attend one of these bases, determined by the combat specialty assigned to them in the Induction Center. These combat basic training courses last from three to four months, are extremely arduous, and although they encompass infantry-type training, they also include indoctrination into the recruits' assigned corps. In fact, from the first moments of their corps basic training, they become armor soldiers, artillery soldiers, etc. They are trained by personnel from their specific corps who instill in them esprit de corps. These instructors, mostly conscripts themselves who have already spent some time in the corps units, are specially selected to be training instructors. In many cases they will bring with them actual combat experience. Consequently, their instructions will draw from their real combat experiences rather than textbook examples. They normally will train several cycles of recruits before returning to their parent units or completing their compulsory service. At the end of this corps basic training, this cycle of trainees will begin the next phase of their corps training, the advanced training, after which they will be assigned, by groups, to the various corps units.

Brigade Basic Training

This category is exclusive to infantry recruits. The IDF's infantry and airborne brigades maintain different basic training bases for their units (i.e., the Golani brigade, paratroopers, etc.). These units, in part because of their compact size and uniqueness, foster their own identity, somewhat like that found in regimental systems, from the recruit's first day in the brigade's basic training. The training is somewhat different from the corps courses: the company which is created at the beginning of basic training will remain together as a company (recruits, NCOs and officers) to be integrated back into the parent unit after the basic training is completed. Indeed, among veteran paratroopers, for example, one will hear references to the specific training company they were members of, like "I belong to the November '80 company."

These brigade basic training courses are considered the most strenuous and difficult in all of the IDF. The courses last from four to five months, and at their completion the trainees in each company already constitute a cohesive, effective and committed group of combatants.

An interesting and exceptional combination of all three categories of basic training is found in the elite Nahal corps, (see Chapter 4) whose brigade-size basic training base includes both combat and non-combat recruits and both men and women. (The females, however, are trained in separate companies, and males with limited physical capacities participate in a modified program followed by military specialty training.)

General Characteristics of Basic Training

Generally, basic training in the IDF is demanding and realistic. This applies less to the generalized basic training because of the physical limitations of the recruits receiving it and more to brigade and corps basic training. The main emphasis for the latter two categories is on weapons usage, field training, individual training and team training. Very little, relatively, is devoted to pomp and circumstance (i.e., marching drills, parades, etc.). A significant part of the trainee's time is spent bivouacked in the field, with particular emphasis on night training to develop the trainee's confidence under night conditions. The main training components are the squads, headed by squad leaders who are conscripts themselves normally with the rank of corporal. Some activities are also performed at the platoon level but fewer at the company level. Hence, the platoon commander (usually a 2nd lieutenant), whom the basic trainees see only occasionally, is perceived by them to be a supreme authority while the company commander is almost next to God!

Discipline, too, is focused more on operational and performance accuracy than on ceremonial details. The requirement is more for a clean rifle than for spit-shined boots. Trainees are constantly disciplined to perform their duties within very tight time constraints; while a sharp uniform is not always essential, a sharp and timely performance is always demanded.

Starting on the first day of basic training, the recruits are issued their personal rifle (typically the Israeli-made Galil 5.56 mm rifle for combat unit recruits, and the M–16 or the Uzi submachine gun to non-combat recruits). This rifle is "attached" to them and literally never leaves their side until they complete their basic training. They carry it with them every minute of the day and sleep with it at night.

The continual holding of their rifles is quite typical of IDF soldiers in general, not just basic trainees, and is one of the most striking images tourists have when first visiting Israel: male soldiers, and sometimes females as well, are always seen on the roads to and from their bases, armed with their rifles or Uzi. This is not only because most of these soldiers serve in border areas (where carrying a weapon is mandatory) but also reflects the continual alert posture of the IDF. This physical attachment to one's rifle has evolved into a soldier's lore in which they often refer to being married to their rifles. But there is also a formal aspect to this attachment: losing one's rifle is a court-martial offense with severe penalty. This could be a year in the military prison or even more, depending on the specific circumstances.[8]

Basic training is centered around the group. Everything is accomplished within the squad or platoon framework. For example, the group always is together whether in classes, exercises, or meals, marching to the barber or to the pay officer, and even when discharged for short leaves. Everything is done with the same ten or twelve members of the squad. The training itself, though designed to get each individual to his "max," is always performed on the group level. For example, whenever they go on a forced march, the rule is that the group starts together, stays together, and finishes together, which sometimes means the stronger ones will literally carry the weaker ones, but never leave anyone behind. Similarly, every field exercise culminates in "carrying the wounded" (so designated by the squad or platoon leader) back to the base.

Another characteristic of basic training focuses on developing soldiers who are stout-hearted, decisive and willing to endure the extreme stresses of the battlefield. From the first day of basic training, the demands are gradually intensified in terms of the physical efforts required, the distances covered during forced marches, and length of sustained training periods without sleep. Tasks that were initially viewed as impossible by the trainees are accomplished in a short period of time, forming the baseline for the next "impossible" task. An almost daily exercise is completion of the obstacle course. However, the requirements in terms of load carried and completion time are gradually increased.

A primary emphasis is given during basic training to the issue of credibility and independence. From their first days of training, the fresh trainees are given a certain latitude in their daily conduct. In return they are expected to be absolutely reliable, trustworthy and "marble constant." The stiffest penalty is given to a fabricated report coming from a trainee. Though not quite an "honor system" in the full sense, the basic training (especially with combat troops, pilots, special units, etc.)

INDUCTION AND BASIC TRAINING   105

is the first step of their socialization into highly reliable, relatively independent combatants.

Finally, there is also an emphasis on learning the country's borders, particularly areas of importance to the combat history of the unit. The best method for achieving this is "with the feet" (i.e., forced marches, journeys and training exercises in those areas). There is nothing like these activities along the borders of Israel to make apparent to the fresh soldier that he or she has truly become a part of the nation's defense forces.

> The book, *Self-Portrait of a Hero*, which is a collection of letters written by Col. Jonathan (Yoni) Netanyahu, the hero of the raid on the airport at Entebbe, includes a description of some of his experiences during paratrooper basic training:
>
> "Everything went on as usual until the evening of that same Tuesday. That night we set out on a twenty-two mile march with full battle gear and weapons which ended at 3 A.M.. [sic] The final six miles were turned into a stretcher-march—you lay the heaviest guys on stretchers and carry them. That's the hardest work you can imagine, especially when the march goes on for miles on end.
>
> "The next day, Wednesday, we got up and continued with regular training . . . they kept us awake till 1:30 A.M. . . .
>
> "On the following day, Thursday, we got up as usual. Again the exercises. And at three o'clock we went on another march, the second in three days. That was unheard of (at least among us). We had all come back from the first march, which was conducted at high speed, with sores, strained muscles, injuries and great fatigue. But it became clear that this was only intended as preparation for the second march. Well, on Thursday we set out on a march aimed at getting us 'acquainted with the borders,' with full packs (very heavy!). That day we marched until nightfall. We slept outdoors and continued in the morning until two in the afternoon. Morale was high."[9] (P. 40)

Basic training is not based solely on physical training, even though it is the predominant theme. The trainees also receive instruction on subjects such as the structure and history of the IDF, hygiene and health matters, and basic first aid. (Based on the experience of the Yom Kippur War, it was decided in the IDF that every combat soldier, not just medics, would receive sixty hours of field first-aid training. This approach proved itself during the 1982 War in Lebanon.[10]

During the tenure of General Rafael Eytan, an exceptional experiment was conducted. Eytan, as a Chief of Staff who strongly espoused patriotic values and ideology in the military, ordered that all basic training begin with an intensive indoctrination period. This was accomplished by the rescheduling of the week-long "educational workshop" from its usual occurrence at a later stage in military training to the very first week of basic training. Skeptically, the Education corps of the IDF developed a program which was centered around the "individual within the military system" and included subjects such as rules of discipline and behavior, the importance of teamwork, individual needs versus system demands, and expectations of military service.

The experiment was an unqualified success! In spite of all the skepticism of how to run a program such as this with soldiers who have not learned the basics of discipline and order, it became apparent that such an introduction to the military has many advantages in reducing fears and increasing motivation. But, above all, this method achieved an unexpected side benefit of establishing healthy relationships between the trainees and their instructors. This area, which was always problematic in basic training, was greatly improved because the workshop sessions were conducted by the actual training leaders. The discussions these instructors conducted with their fresh trainees provided them with an opportunity to come to know their prospective soldiers in a more personal light. At the same time, the trainees were also able to discover the non-threatening side of their soon-to-be drill sergeants.

Basic Training Instructors

The IDF is perhaps one of the few militaries in the world lacking the typical drill sergeant, as personified by a careerist who is mature (both in age and experience) and who is also a professional in training and indoctrinating new recruits. This reflects the fact that the IDF's non-commissioned officers in general do not have the typical characteristics of NCOs in Western militaries. (This will be discussed further in the next chapter.) The instructors for the IDF's basic training courses are young conscripts themselves, either corporals or sergeants, who completed a junior command course shortly after they had finished their own basic training. Thus, there is often little age difference between instructors and trainees, and it is even not unheard of for an instructor to be younger than his or her trainees. In other words, the junior command in all the basic training bases (for both men and women) is staffed by conscripts rather than careerists. This includes squad leaders, platoon sergeants, platoon commanders and sometimes even the company commanders as well. Only the sergeant major, the command sergeant major, and the senior officers will not be conscripts, but rather are career professionals.

Each platoon of basic trainees has four squad leaders, normally corporals; a platoon sergeant, usually ranked as a sergeant; and the platoon commander, generally a 2nd lieutenant. As mentioned before, most of the training activities are conducted in the framework of these squads. The squad leaders, especially in the combat bases, lead by means of personal example: they normally carry the same gear, live under the same conditions, head the forced marches, and participate in their trainees' activities as, for example, in "carrying the wounded" from the field exercises (this is also done by the officers). In some unique way these squad leaders manage to develop close relationships with their trainees while at the same time maintain the necessary distance to effectively lead. Because they are almost as young as their trainees, lack extensive experience, and are sometimes unsure of themselves certainly does not make it easy for them. Indeed, one of the unavoidable results of this situation, coupled with the IDF's tough training tradition, was the frequent occurrence of severe harassment of trainees by these instructors. While these phenomena have been significantly reduced in recent years, they are still noteworthy.

Doctrinal Approaches to Basic Training

In its three and a half decades, the IDF has gone through a number of policy transformations regarding basic training and, to an extent, the treatment of soldiers in general. During the early years the predominant approach was "break down the civilian in order to build up the soldier," utilizing harassment to accomplish this. To an extent, that approach came from the fact that the IDF, at that time, was a military consisting of new immigrants from varying cultures and diverse customs, none of which came close to a traditional military view of life. Historically, it should be noted that Jewish peoples in their home countries were remote from, and reluctant to be involved in, any military participation. The urgent need to develop a standing military to meet the existing threat from Israel's enemies laid the way for this "break them down" approach which dominated the IDF, especially in basic training, in an unofficial way for more than two decades. Two additional principles also contributed to the partial legitimacy given to the harassment approach (which was called "Tirturimm"—literally translated as "rattling"). The first was "tough in training, easy in combat"—a principle which was reinforced by the fact that combat experience was common in the IDF. The other was the belief that extreme harassment, albeit humiliating, when undergone as a group only strengthens the group and increases the cohesion.

The Tirturimm used by junior commanders incorporated severe physical demands with arbitrariness and dehumanization. Squad leaders used group penalties, which were disproportionate to their causes. For example, a squad leader could have decided that two of his squad members were three seconds late for morning formation. His response was to wake up the entire squad in the middle of the following night and require them to carry their made-up beds into the middle of the parade ground, carrying full military gear but wearing only their underwear. The beds will be set up in precise military rows, then the trainees will begin simulated timed daily training and will continue until their performance meets his standards of timeliness and absolute perfection.

While these principles as elaborated, with their resulting harassment of trainees, are not uncommon in most militaries, the extent to which harassment was a tool in the early days of the IDF was exceptional. Since such methods were used, in addition to the continuous tough training six days a week (and sometimes even on the Sabbath evening) for the four to five months of basic training, it is no wonder that many of the trainees ultimately broke down, physically or mentally, including an unexpected number (given the age group involved) of suicides.

Various attempts by senior commanders to alter this doctrine were generally futile because it was not official policy, rather it was mainly based on the traditional theme adopted by the young instructors that whatever they, the instructors, had suffered through, the trainees could also sustain. That theme was stronger than any guidance they received from higher commands.

The first serious attempt to correct this problem was made by General Rabin in the mid–1960s when he was Chief of Staff. In a training manual[11] that he initiated, two alternative principles were presented to counter the harassment doctrine: the importance of the soldier's pride in himself, and the building up of the soldier's full confidence in his immediate commander. The utilization of Tirturimm, claimed Rabin, destroyed both the soldier's pride in himself and prevented him from developing confidence in his commander—two attributes critically essential on the battlefield. The characteristics that were required from the junior commander were that he have respect in himself and others, show self-discipline and appropriate behavior, personally maintain and instill proper values, be the best soldier in his group, and exhibit training skills.

In spite of the efforts of IDF authorities, it cannot be said that the Tirturimm phenomenon has completely disappeared. In fact, the introspection that came after the Yom Kippur War resulted in a new emphasis on discipline in the IDF and, in an indirect way, perhaps by a misinterpretation of what military discipline really means—a rebirth of the mistreatment of trainees in basic training bases. After the Yom Kippur War, the Agranat Commission[12] included in its report a full chapter concerning the subject of military discipline. Among the wave of reforms

Induction and Basic Training

the IDF underwent after the 1973 war, there was a strong shift back to strict discipline, emphasizing especially the little details. Combat units, in particular, took upon themselves extraordinary restrictions, which extended to the first days of basic training. While most of these reforms took place behind the closed gates of the military camps, the public occasionally was alarmed by revelations concerning mistreatment of basic trainees. One such case happened in armor basic training and ended in a trainee's suicide. Several commanders at various levels were consequently court-martialled.[13] Another event which illuminated the problem was a film, "Masa Alunkot" (translated roughly to "Stretchers Forced March") released in 1980, describing paratroopers' basic training. In this movie, the central event is the death of a trainee, and whether the death is a suicide or accident is not clear, it is apparent, however, that mistreatment was involved.

The following is an excerpt from a discussion between twelfth-grade students and a senior IDF officer during a preinduction preparation program.[14]

Question: The subject of difficulties in serving in the IDF has recently been discussed in the media. Following the televising of the film "Stretchers Forced March," I would like to ask why do things like that happen, and is it at all necessary to have such a tough approach in the IDF?

Answer: The Army has an ultimate goal, which is to win wars, and in order to achieve that, we have to train people. Part of this training is [geared to produce] extreme physical fitness and high endurance. We need a certain level of toughness. The question is whether this toughness can be achieved by using harassment. . . .

The Army's policy clearly prohibits any sort of harassments. What the Army can do in order to enforce this policy is to provide means to prevent it. . . . There are clear orders. Then there is the commander, and above him the whole chain of command and every soldier's complaint is investigated. You can go as high as the Chief of Staff and the IDF Ombudsman. I, as a commander, find myself responding to soldiers' complaints at least two to three times a week. However, you have to remember that when you finish high school, you are leaving behind the world of the teenager, and are entering into an adult's world. This transition alone is tough enough, but you must also add to it the extra toughness required from us as soldiers.

In recent years there has been, again, an improvement in this area. The former Chief of Staff, General Rafael Eytan ("Raful"), himself the personification of the tough soldier, put his full weight behind changing the doctrine regarding treatment in basic training. Besides reemphasizing the regulations prohibiting harsh treatment, he also ordered that of the six-day training week, one day would be exclusively devoted to the trainees' "maintenance," in terms of taking care of their various personal needs. (This too, however, is accomplished within the framework of the group.)

Raful's message was clear: A trainee must be built up and taken care of rather than broken down in order to be built up. The current doctrine, thus, is one that legitimizes tough training but prohibits harassments. While maintaining a clear distinction between these two may still be a difficult task, especially for the inexperienced squad leader, the established doctrine, however, has been radically implemented.

One of the examples of this new policy is demonstrated in the contacts maintained with a trainee's family. In most of the basic training bases, it has become the custom for the base commander to send a letter to each new trainee's parents in which he explains to them what their child will experience, encourages them not to worry, and compliments them for bringing up their child to become a loyal soldier in the IDF. At least once during the basic training period, the parents are invited to visit the base. The scene on a day like this[15] is in sharp contrast to the normal all-military character of the bases. On such a Parent's Day the base is transformed from "all green" into a big family picnic, with scattered groups of soldiers and their parents fussing over them. The poor trainee, who is in the midst of the transformation from childhood to being a soldier, totally succumbs to the warmth and love of his mom and dad. The strong bond between the people and the military is demonstrated here in its most primary unit—the family.

Basic Training as a Socialization Process

The basic training period in the IDF not only is professional training but also involves socialization into military life. It includes all familiar components of the socialization process: identification figures, transition phases, occasional psychological crises, internalization of norms and values, modeling, and the creation of a new identity.

Because of the training intensity, the instructors frequently become typical identification figures for the trainee, provide a role model, and may remain as such throughout the trainee's entire military service.[16] The transitional and crises phases are typical throughout the basic training period, which begins with confused and bewildered teenagers and concludes with assured, competent and highly motivated soldiers. This transition, amazing both in terms of the degree of change and the short time span, involves also substantial changes in attitudes and motivation. As may be recalled, the initial assignments to the various corps and their respective basic training bases are determined by the needs of the IDF. Many of those who are assigned to non-volunteer combat units are not necessarily pleased with their assignments. Some may even attempt to change their assignment, but the basic training period, with all of its aspects, succeeds in changing such an initially reluctant attitude by replacing it with a more positive, indeed enthusiastic attitude toward the unit. An example of this can be seen in the Armor corps. While prior to induction, fewer than 20 percent[17] of potential conscripts express their willingness to serve in the Armor corps, during the armor basic training period, the number interested increases to 50 percent, and toward the end of advanced armor training, the percentage of those pleased with their assignment reaches 80 percent.[18] Similar figures are found in other Army corps as well as in non-voluntary Naval and Air Force units.

Basic training is not only adjusting to the military, the corps, and the unit, but also involves the strengthening of the recruits' identification and familiarization with the nation, its history, and peoples. In addition to the abundant marches criss-crossing Israel, the basic trainees are also taken for visits to the various types of communities such as the kibbutz, the moshav, developing towns, etc. Perhaps the most impressive visit they will make is to Jerusalem to see the Yad-Vashem, the museum memorializing the victims of the Holocaust. Here the young recruits will be reminded of the millions of helpless and unarmed Jews who were brutally exterminated by the Nazis. While the IDF training programs do not include indoctrination coursework per se, it seems, nonetheless, that all of these visits serve the same purpose of strengthening and deepening the soldier's understanding of the meaning of his or her military service.

One of the highlights of this process is the basic training graduation ceremony, which is held for the different corps in places which have a special symbolic meaning. Several of the basic training bases, particularly the Armor corps, conduct their graduation ceremony on the Masada—the rock fortress near the Dead Sea where nearly 1,000 Jewish defenders held out for three years against their Roman adversaries. Other units conduct their ceremony in the Yad-Vashem Holocaust Monument. The paratrooper trainee graduates receive their unit crest and insignia in a ceremony which takes place in Jerusalem near the Wailing Wall—another symbol of the continuity of Jewish history from the time of the Second Temple (2,000 years ago) to now and is a reminder of the paratroopers' victorious battles in Jerusalem during the Six Day War. Similarly, the Golani brigade celebrates its graduate trainees on top of Mount Hermon, one of the brigade's most bitter victories in the Yom Kippur War. All of these ceremonies serve to strengthen, even more than any formal indoctrination, the bonding among the Israeli soldier, his country and peoples.

Another important aspect of the socialization processes taking place during basic training is the "melting pot function," which brings together the different Jewish ethnic groups, especially the Ashkenazi (Western) with the Sepharadi (Oriental) Jews, the newly immigrated with the Sabras (native Israelis), and individuals from varying socioeconomic backgrounds. The melting pot process, while occurring throughout the entire military service, is intensified during basic training. This is especially so in the generalized basic training courses where the trainees, being non-selected (except for physical impairment), come from many diverse groups. In basic training they will share an intensive, albeit short, group experience, involving a great deal of stress and emotional arousal. While such a period may be too short to obliterate preconceived attitudes and patterns of affiliation, it is still intensive enough to enable them to establish personal relationships across different groups and to weaken, to an extent, their stereotypical ethnic conceptions.

Conclusion

The first steps of the Israeli soldiers in their military service are not merely training and skill acquisition. Starting in their preenlistment phase, these conscripts-to-be are prepared not only for the glory of soldier's life but also for the gory aspects of their possible future combat experience. Quite uniquely, the IDF as a military institution had taken upon itself not only the physical deployment of the Israeli youth but also its psychological preparation toward that deployment. These preparations, taking place at high schools and within other premilitary frameworks and involving the cooperation of military and educational personnel, may seem to the outside observer as examples of a militant attitude. The truth, however, is to the contrary: the purpose of most of the preinduction programs is to reduce existing fears and anxieties pertaining to military service and, occasionally, to defuse some anti-military attitudes.

Similarly, the IDF's basic training phase is not designed only to develop the soldier's physical condition and military competence. Rather, especially in its combat version, this training period facilitates group cohesion and unit identification from the very first day of basic training. Indeed, in many cases the same men who shared a tent in boot camp will continue to serve together, as a team, throughout their entire service, including, sometimes, all of their reserve years as well.

Furthermore, the basic training period also facilitates the Israeli soldier's bonds to his or her country, its past history, and its future prospects. Through operational or ceremonial activities conducted during basic training at various sites in the country, the full meaning of "defence forces" is transmitted to the young IDF soldier. The lack of a long military tradition of the kind most Western militaries preserve is compensated for in the relatively young Israeli military by drawing on an even longer history, albeit not necessarily military, which joins together the 2,000-year-old Jewish history in this land and Diaspora, with the current State of Israel, defending itself against its adversaries. This "connection-through-history" is the theme of the Israeli soldier in his first steps within the IDF.

Notes

1. Zinger, Y., & Shorek, U. (1975). *Attitude survey among future conscripts regarding service in the IDF* (Research Report). Unit of Military Psychology, IDF. The main findings of this survey were reported by the author at the 18th Conference of the Israeli Psychological Association, Haifa, Israel, February 1982.

2. Amiad, P. (1981, January). *Attitude survey among future conscripts regarding service in the IDF* (Research Report). Department of Behavioral Sciences, IDF. The main findings of this survey were reported by the author at the 18th Conference of the Israeli Psychological Association, Haifa, Israel, February 1982.

3. *Bamahane* (1979, May 9), 32.

4. A partial assessment of the effectiveness of these meetings with officer cadets can be seen in a recent evaluation study which found that 80 percent of the twelfth graders who participated in these meetings reported that the meetings contributed a great deal to their mental preparation for military service. See *Effectiveness of preparation program for induction* (1982, February). (Research Report). Department of Behavioral Sciences, IDF.

5. *To You, the Draftee.* (1981, June). Division of Manpower, Department of Behavioral Sciences and Chief Education Corps. Tel-Aviv: IDF.

6. The effectiveness of this booklet was also evaluated in a sample of soldiers during their basic training, and it was found that 90 percent felt that the booklet would be very helpful to a fresh recruit to better anticipate what he will experience during basic training. All basic trainees reported having in one way or another these same experiences as described in this booklet, and many added that after reading the booklet, they perceived the fears and feelings they had during basic training as being normal. See *Effectiveness of preparation program for induction.*

7. Zinger & Shorek, *Attitude survey.*

8. In *Bamahane* (1978, November), 9, it was reported that a soldier who lost his Uzi was sentenced to one year in prison.

9. Netanyahu, J. (1980). *Self-Portrait of a hero: The letters of Jonathan Netanyahu.* New York: Ballantine Books.

10. Personal communication from Brig. Gen. Eran Dolev, former Chief Surgeon of the IDF, as reported in Belenky, G., & Kaufman, L. (1984). Staying alive: Knowing what to do until the medic arrives. *Military Review,* 64(1), 28–33.

11. *Leadership of the junior leader in the IDF: Principles, methods, and means.* IDF General Staff publication, Chief, Educational Corps.

12. The Agranat Commission was established after the Yom Kippur War to investigate what was generally perceived as the "blunder" which led up to the war. A central concern of the commission's report focused on cracks in the discipline structure and reemphasized the need for continual, undivided discipline.

13. As reported in a story entitled The Chief of Staff is acting to terminate extreme harassment, published in the May 22, 1978, issue of *Davar*.

14. Goldstein, A. (Ed.). (1981). *Toward induction*. Jerusalem: Department of Education, Israel.

15. A vivid description of such a Parent's Day was reported by J. Marcus in *Ha'aretz*, June 15, 1984.

16. An interesting observation of a similar impact, this time involving U.S. Marine Corps drill instructors and their trainees, up to thirty months later, has been noted by Sarason, I. G. (1984, May). *Longitudinal study of Marine Corps drill instructors*. Paper presented at the Second Symposium on Motivation and Morale in NATO Forces, Brussels, Belgium.

17. Amiad, *Attitude survey*.

18. This was reported by Maj. Gen. Moshe Peled, Chief of the Armor Corps, in *Bamahane* (1978, October), 4. In his interview General Peled also indicated that after a year and a half in the service, when his soldiers are already in operational units, this becomes virtually 100 percent who are satisfied with their assignment.

THE LEADERSHIP CORPS

7

Military leadership is a major component in the dynamics of every military. It is through the military leadership that the army is not only led but also establishes standards, patterns of behavior, and ingrained values. Leadership is one of the two forces driving the military machine, the second one being the soldier's combat motivation. But the soldier's combat motivation is greatly influenced by the leadership example. The present chapter will address the leadership corps of the IDF at its junior levels—that is, from non-commissioned officers (NCOs) through lieutenant colonels—while the following chapter (Chapter 8) will address the Israeli soldier's combat motivation. (Chapter 9 will address separately the higher command of the IDF.)

Basic Premises and Historical Roots

The IDF leadership has been traditionally characterized by adventurous officers instead of cautious NCOs, leading from the front instead of issuing orders from the rear, demonstrating improvisation, initiative and flexibility rather than going by the book, and showing a sense of duty and commitment rather than career considerations. While these characteristics are found in many other fighting armies, they are particularly nurtured in the IDF.

Several premises are at the heart of the Israeli model of military leadership:

1. No military position (enlisted, NCO or officer) is permanent: every soldier enters as a private and proceeds to the position he or she is best suited for, based on abilities and motivation.

2. Being a leader is a privilege rather than a chore; an achievement rather than an inheritance.
3. The leader, whether on the squad, platoon, or company level, is the best soldier in his squad, platoon, or company.
4. The ultimate test of leadership is in combat, where the only effective way to lead is by personal example.

In addition to being a unified force (i.e., Army, Navy and Air Force all commanded under one Chief of Staff), the IDF is exceptional among Western militaries in two more respects. First, it does not have NCOs in the traditional sense. And second, all of its officers come up through the ranks. In contrast to the British Army (to which the IDF was greatly exposed) and other Western militaries, whose traditions are passed along by a stable corps of NCOs, the emerging Israeli military had neither such a corps nor the traditions to pass on. Furthermore, the fact that in the Israeli army all NCOs are potential officers, and most of them do become officers within a year of their service, is yet another reason for the lack of a traditional NCO corps in the IDF. Following the example of the Palmach and the Haganah (the closest the IDF comes to having a tradition), the best soldier on the team will become the team leader, and the best among the team leaders will become an officer. Hence, the typical Israeli NCO is young in age, stays in an NCO rank for a relatively short period and in most cases belongs to the upper range of the Kaba (quality) categories. Only a small percentage of NCOs will become careerist NCOs, and those will be primarily in the technical specialties or administrative positions.

With regard to officers, the IDF does not have officer academies or academic prerequisites for its officers and certainly not the requirement that they come from the "right" social class. Rather, all conscripts enter on an equal footing and proceed with regular training and duties, until the time that they may be selected for officer training. Instead of an officers' model which is predominated by lateral entry (common among Western militaries) the Israeli model is characterized by vertical progression from the bottom up.

Furthermore, since any combat officer has already served as both a soldier and an NCO, he is spared the tutorship of his NCOs on his first assignments. If anything, the opposite is the case. Hence, this latent function of the typical Western NCO is completely absent in the Israeli system.

The Soldier-to-Leader Progression

The IDF process of selecting its junior leaders—including officers—begins with conscription. All IDF officers-to-be—with the only exception of pilots and naval ship officers[1]—start their military service as conscripts. As described in Chapter 6, they will undergo three to five months of vigorous basic training if they have been assigned to a combat unit, or at least one month for those assigned to non-combat units. The latter, upon completion of basic training will, most frequently, be sent individually to their respective preassigned specialized courses, after which they will be posted to their designated units. On the other hand, combat-assigned conscripts, after completing their basic training, are posted as a group directly to their field units. Here they will continue their advanced unit training and will participate in various guard duties (in Hebrew "Batash" which translates to "routine security") along the Israeli borders. At this phase, the combat soldier—whether an Army ground soldier or a Naval sailor—will experience firsthand the realities of preparing for, and perhaps even engaging in, combat.

The first step in the selection of potential IDF leaders begins after serving five months in this phase. All soldiers are evaluated at this point for junior command courses based on their initial Kaba (quality) score, on the one hand, and on their immediate commanders' evaluations, on the other hand. Approximately 50 percent of the soldiers[2] at this time will qualify for further leadership training as squad or team leaders, tank commanders, and other types of NCOs. The junior command courses for the combat corps are regarded as the toughest courses in the IDF. They last approximately three to four months and stress technical skill acquisition along with basic leadership. Training is characterized by spending most of the time in the field, practicing navigations, performing live-fire exercises under both daytime and nightime conditions. Sleep is minimal and eating is hurried. Throughout the course, the trainees receive rotating command roles which they have to execute under realistic conditions while being carefully observed and evaluated by their instructors. The instructor personnel, like those in basic training, are mostly conscripts themselves who are carefully selected to become tutors in those schools.

In the tank commanders course, these instructors are referred to as "kindergarten teachers" ("Gananimm"), and like good kindergarten teachers they receive one group after another of young tankers and train them to become NCO tank commanders. During tank training, they sit in a special "chair," which is actually an inverted tank turret, positioned behind the tank commander trainee. From this vantage point the instructor will observe the trainee as he performs the role of tank commander. From here the instructor can also tutor and guide him in the basics of effective leadership.

"This is an enormous task, a day to day neverending effort to produce for the armor corps all of its tank commanders. This involves enormous numbers of individuals, each single one of them a whole world by itself. For each one of them you have to find the right approach, to discover the particular recipe in order to get the maximum out of him"—this is how one of these "kindergarten teachers" described his job in a recent interview.[3] (P. 18)

An important part of the junior command course is the leadership seminar. These seminars are conducted in the IDF Commander Training Institute and normally last for a week. The main goals of this seminar are: acquainting the future commander with his role in all its facets and characteristics, instilling the awareness of the human factors and military values in the effective function of his command, alerting the trainee to the command situations frequently encountered and providing him with the adequate tools to cope with these situations, and reducing anxiety of the future commander in his initiation into his role as a leader.[4] These goals are achieved in small groups of approximately fifteen participants guided by a coordinator, who is usually a behavioral scientist, using such methods as simulations, case analysis, group discussions, and role playing. The main focus in this seminar is on the personal and group aspects of leadership and on preparing the junior commander to cope with potential problems in these areas.

Once the junior command course is completed, these new junior NCOs (now squad or team leaders, or tank commanders) will return to their original units, thus reinforcing their bond to each other and their parent unit. They remain in their units for an additional operational phase ("Batash") which may vary from six to ten months, only this time they serve in junior command positions or as training instructors. During this period many of them may experience combatlike leadership while they operate with their troops in real operational activities.

In fact, this period is considered the phase for practicing military leadership. Whether they serve as junior instructors in basic training or other schools, or they command small elements in their combat units, in each of these cases they are exposed to the daily challenges of leadership and caring for their troops. Occasionally, even at this early stage, they may be leading their men in combat. This is, in short, their on-the-job training in leadership, and for some of them it is their best introduction to their next phase as officer candidates.

It is during this phase that this corps of leaders is examined again for their potential as officers. The selection is made first on the basis of the initial quality classification. Only the highest Kaba categories (51 to 56) are considered for officer training. Far more important, however, are the additional means of selection. These include peer rating (sociometric evaluations), recommendations by the soldier's commander, and psychological evaluations by military psychologists. Among the personality dimensions which are evaluated during this psychological screening are found the following: sociability, social intelligence, emotional stability, leadership, devotion to duty, decisiveness, and perseverance under stress.[5] However, even after all of these selection procedures have been completed, the selected candidates will still undergo three to four days of situational screening procedures, called Gibush, which are conducted by the officers' school personnel themselves.

Those who fail to be selected, or refuse to volunteer for officer training after their selection (usually because they do not want to serve the additional year on active service that an officer's commission requires) remain as NCOs with their units until their three-year tour of duty is completed and they are assigned to a reserve unit.

The IDF officer courses for candidates from all corps and branches are conducted in one base, Training Base No. 1 (or "Bahad" 1). There are three types of courses: the Infantry course ("Kheer"), lasting six months and training officer candidates for all infantry and paratrooper units; the Combat Arms course ("Agam"), producing officers for the Armor, Artillery, Engineering and Air Defense corps; and the Basic Officers courses ("Basissi"), used for all the non-combat candidates.[6] These latter two types of courses last only three months, but are followed by more specific complementary courses (lasting an additional three months) conducted separately by each corps. By including candidates from all different branches of the military at the same base, the Bahad 1 is thus a most important unifying element for the IDF. The basic codes of the Israeli officer corps are implanted in all officer candidates, regardless of corps or specialty, by virtually the best personnel the IDF can provide. These instructors are all combat-experienced officers. They are guided by the most updated "lessons learned" derived from the most recent battle experiences of the IDF. Hence, firsthand combat experiences, rather than out-of-date military textbooks, are the grounds for the training of new IDF officers.

Israeli officer candidates undergo essentially the same kind of experiences and training found in most officer training programs: field maneuvers, map navigating, weapon systems utilization and tactics at the platoon and company levels. However, unlike the typical junior Western military officer, the Israeli counterpart already has almost two years of experience as a regular soldier and NCO prior to becoming an officer candidate. Consequently, the training in the officer course does not focus on technical or basic combat skills. Rather, the emphasis is on cultivating the young officer's cognitive ability to solve tactical as well as human problems and on his leadership ability to implement and pursue appropriate solutions. Both these aspects of command (tactical and human) are elicited rather than taught. The training methods most frequently used are practical exercises. Each begins with a team discussion, whereby the trainees, after being presented with basic facts about their mission, have to reach a solution to the given problem. Subsequently, one of the trainees will be nominated as the leader and will have to execute the plan, including making preparations, delegating tasks and pursuing the mission. Typically he will be confronted, during his performance, with some unexpected obstacles and be required to improvise on the spot.

Indeed, creative thinking and the ability to improvise and to accommodate to new, unexpected situations are the most important aptitudes fostered in the officer candidates trained in Bahad 1. But it is the leading from the front, the "follow me" dictum of the Israeli officer, which is certainly the motto most fervently preached in the socialization process of these young officers. This has been repeatedly observed by students of the Israeli military: "Since the approved style of combat leadership is based on personal example, problem-solving and 'leadership' interact: knowing that he will be able to 'pull' his men after him by being the first to advance, the officer can choose daring tactical solutions which he might otherwise have had to reject."[7] (Pp. 86–87)

Becoming an officer in the IDF is considered an extremely hard-earned accomplishment. This is reflected by the failure rate during the officers' course, an extremely high rate, sometimes as much as 50 percent. The evaluations of success or failure are done by the course personnel, based on continual observations of each candidate. An ongoing struggle among the training personnel in both Bahad 1 and the subsequent complementary corps' courses is whether their task is primarily to train or to assess their trainees. Knowing that both these aspects of their role may determine who will be the commanders on the future battlefield, these instructors operate with total awareness of their awesome responsibility. The emphasis, however, on both the training and the assessing aspects is made not just on the technical skills of the officer candidate but predominantly on his "human" skills as a leader.

In a recent interview with a company commander in the Armor officers' school, this commander described his perception of his responsibility:

"We have the power to make decisions as to who will become an officer in the IDF and who will not. Therefore, our main task is to assess his ability to be a commander. An officer is also a character: [possessing] integrity, fairness and diligence. If we do not know the candidate well enough, we may commission an officer who will perform his platoon maneuvers perfectly, but is not a human being. This is why we spend an enormously long time with them in the field, live with them as much as possible, and hence come to know them much better. . . . For us this means hard work, providing personal example on the assumption that whatever we are doing here, the candidate will try to emulate after he graduates. . . . We cannot make mistakes."[8] (P. 19)

Those who complete the officer courses will be commissioned as 2nd lieutenants and will then return to their units (generally the same units where they served as regular soldiers and NCOs) and will be assigned to the position of platoon commander.

The IDF officer is thus commissioned after twenty to twenty-four months of military service, and with his acceptance of his commission, he acquires an additional twelve months of active duty time beyond the usual three years of mandatory service. Accordingly, the IDF can count on having these new officers for approximately two years of active duty after commissioning; however, this period is seen only as an introduction for the many years of reserve service lying ahead.

Being an Officer

The transition from being an enlisted man to being an officer involves a major transformation in the Israeli soldier's life, not so much in terms of the physical setting of his service, but rather in terms of his expected behavior. The young officer's behavior is guided, first, by the high expectations held out for him, the sense of responsibility that he carries, the requirement for sound decisions, and the duty to set a personal example in whatever he does. As a platoon commander, he is responsible for the lives and activities of twenty to forty individuals, depending on whether it is an Army field unit, a Naval boat, or a support or service unit. In addition to his troops, the platoon commander is also responsible for several NCOs who serve as team leaders in his platoon. For them, too, he becomes a respected authority and identity figure, since some of them may be on the verge of also being selected for officer training; hence, they will try to learn from their lieutenant how to succeed as an officer candidate.

Here lies one of the unique differences between the IDF and many other Western militaries. The young Israeli lieutenant is not "taken under the wing" of his platoon sergeant; rather, the opposite generally occurs. He is the one who will tutor and supervise his NCOs. His ability to do that does not stem from longer service (quite frequently the young lieutenants may be the same age as their NCOs or even younger) but from two simple facts: first, they had been initially selected for officers because they were the best; and, second, because they have undergone that intensive program which makes the best soldiers into the best commanders.

This does not necessarily mean that platoon leaders operate completely independently. In fact, they continue their training immediately after their arrival in the unit by attending an orientation seminar to familiarize them with the specifics of their unit, especially the unit's weapon systems, missions and history. Occasionally, especially if their duties involve training others, they will also participate in instructor training courses which are mandatory for all instructor personnel in the IDF. Throughout their first tour of command, these young lieutenants will be closely supervised by their company commanders who may be only a year or two older but frequently have some combat command experience. And combat experience is the key word.

The time in grade for a 2nd lieutenant is one year, and this is roughly the period of time in which they serve as platoon commanders. At the end of that year, they are promoted to 1st lieutenant and frequently stay in the same unit, however, and will normally be assigned the position of deputy company commander[9] or executive officer. In these positions they will pursue their command tasks and further improve leadership and professional skills during the remaining conscripted service time. It should be noted that the IDF considers the regular service primarily as preparation for the extended reserve service that awaits every Israeli upon completion of regular service.

After forty-eight months of regular active service, the Israeli officer faces the termination of the compulsory phase of his active duty. During these past four years, he has mentally matured considerably beyond his chronological age. The stresses he has faced, the decisions he has made, and the human problems he has dealt with far exceed the usual experience of a young man in his early twenties. It is certain that he has had an actual battlefield experience, sometimes even more than one. At the end of these four years, he will be discharged along with many of the friends with whom he was originally drafted. In fact, with some of these friends he may have spent most of his service, sharing with them both the good times and the bad times. Quite frequently, alas, not all of these friends are still living. The frequency of casualties for junior officers (as will be discussed further in this chapter) is high. Many who survive will carry with them their scars from combat throughout their lives. Whatever the specific nature of their service, these twenty-two-year-old men will appear to be older and more concerned than their years. These matured and concerned faces express, better than anything else, the impact of their responsibility as officers in the IDF.

Approximately 90 percent of all officers, upon completion of their compulsory service, will leave active duty and join reserve units. They will be assigned to units comparable to those in which they served on active duty and will usually be given the position of platoon commander, hence beginning a long career as reserve officers which will continue to

THE LEADERSHIP CORPS 123

the age of fifty-five; until the age of forty or so, they will continue to serve in combat assignments. While the term "career" is indeed not the most exact term to characterize this type of military service, reservists, nevertheless, are promoted as well as schooled throughout this time. Though at a slower pace, they may be promoted from platoon commander to company commander and even, on rare occasion, to battalion commander. From time to time they are also sent to advanced military courses. However, most of those released from active service as lieutenants would not exceed the rank of major, and even that would not occur for quite a few years.

Their sense of responsibility, nonetheless, and their devotion to their command do not fade during their reserve service. As a matter of fact, the high frequency of their reserve call-ups does not permit them to "forget" their command skills, even though they have now been civilians for some time. Furthermore, in a time of need this pool of reserve officers can provide reinforcements for the regular component of the IDF. These reserve officers are often solicited by the IDF to return to active duty, this time in the permanent service corps (Keva) to fill manpower shortages. They are also called upon to volunteer for active duty at times of acute needs.

One of the classic examples of the IDF soliciting reserve officers was during the War of Attrition (1967–70) when, for approximately three years, the Israelis and Egyptians conducted what was almost a "stand-off" war along the Suez Canal. The Israelis suffered excessive casualties during this period, despite their fortified positions on the Bar-Lev Line along the canal. The increasing need for replacement officers to command the Bar-Lev strongholds generated the "tigers" phenomenon: a wave of reserve officers who volunteered specifically for assignment to these critical front-line positions, for a period of six months to a year. The continuing high rate of casualties among these front-line officers did not prevent additional tigers from requesting such an assignment. In addition to filling necessary positions, the appearance of the older and more mature reserve officers had the benefit of lessening the stress of the younger regular officers.

This phenomenon of reservist volunteers reemerged, though on a lesser scale, during the IDF occupation of Lebanon following the 1982 incursion. While at this time all-out combat was not involved, the long supply lines (in Israeli terms), and the frequent ambushes along the lines, made the transport drivers the real combatants during this period. Consequently, the IDF authorities turned again to the reserve corps and solicited volunteers for this duty. The first to respond were two reserve paratrooper captains in their late forties who had been "forced" to retire from their previous combat positions in the reserves and were willing to take on this task. As "greenies" on the job, these two were initially assigned as secondary drivers, under the supervision of the more experienced regular drivers, all of them NCOs. That did not prevent these two officers from performing this task as best they could. Indeed, these two set an example for other reserve officers to follow.[10]

About 10 percent of all the officers who have completed their required four-year service choose to join the permanent (Keva) service corps and will normally sign for an initial period of two to three years. While some may select the permanent service corps quite willingly, there are many others who will sign on only after a great deal of persuasion from their commanding officers. The predominant reason given for staying on active duty is normally reported as job satisfaction and the perceived challenge in one's job, while only in the background are the patriotic motives.

In recent years it has been noted with concern that not necessarily the cream of the crop has chosen to remain on active duty.[11] The strongest arguments made by those who refrain from joining the permanent service corps are related to the enormous stress these officers have already experienced. At the end of their four years, many of these officers have reached burnout, and most want to get away from it all and do some traveling or anything that does not involve the military. Other arguments may fluctuate according to the current political situation. Thus, for example, in the period following the 1982 War in Lebanon, which had become very unpopular, many young officers justified their objection to remaining in the military by stating their reluctance to serve in Lebanon. This was caused either by their political objections to Israel's involvement in Lebanon or simply by the fact that serving in Lebanon "had left them 'burned out,' caused by the nonstop string of combat alerts and their continual concern about their soldiers' lives."[12]

The ones who remain and join the permanent service corps will either be assigned directly to company commander positions or will be assigned first to staff or training positions and then assume a company command. In any case, however, they will command a unit within the same brigade or division in which they have been to that point. Thus it is common to see a company commander in the rank of lieutenant or junior captain, between the ages of twenty-two and twenty-four. A thirty-year-old lieutenant or a forty-year-old captain—frequent in other militaries—is almost unknown in the IDF.

At some point during this period, some of these young officers will attend the company commanders' course run by their corps. However, due to the officer shortage and the quick rotation, many will simply skip this course and instead make do with on-the-job training. As a result, the main bulk of the annual company commanders' courses is not regular officers but reserve officers, who will be assigned as company commanders in their reserve units.

Time in grade between 1st lieutenant and captain is normally three years, although exceptional officers may be promoted in two years. This is also the time when they will consider the possibility of a longer career and the planning of their career. Such planning may include a two- to three-year academic study period, after which they will return to regular active duty. It may also include a tentative commitment, on the part of the IDF, to assign the officer to the desired position of a battalion command.

The Command and Staff School (called "Poum" in Hebrew) is the first full-year course which most IDF officers attend after commissioning. The Poum course is designated primarily for majors (though many of the attendees are promotable captains) and is a prerequisite for promotion to lieutenant colonel. It includes officers from all branches and corps of the IDF, although the Navy and Air Force maintain a separate course structure within the Poum. As such, the Poum is again, as in the case of Bahad 1, an important interservices binding factor in the IDF. The course includes subjects such as IDF structure and organization, staff work, tactical and strategic exercises, and classes in psychology, resource management, statistics and economics.

The fate of the Israeli officer, up to this point (rank of major), has been determined primarily by his brigade or, if he is not a combat officer, by his professional unit. Brigade commanders are normally the ones who will assign company commanders and approve their attendance to Poum and even their assignments as battalion commanders. The General Staff, as well as the division and corps command, have minimal involvement in these decisions, and their required approval will usually be only a formality. The officers, too, consider themselves primarily to belong to their brigade. It is, for them, their predominant frame of reference. Indeed, in many cases when pondering whether to continue their career, their final agreement will be based on the condition that they remain with their brigade.

These are, then, the main ingredients in the career of the young IDF officer: rapid advancement from 2nd lieutenant through captain, in mainly command positions and the incorporation of some staff or instructor assignments, where learning is mostly on-the-job or within short seminars. However, he always returns to the same battalion or brigade; he also always returns to the same specialty: Armor officers will always be in Armor assignments, adjutants will always deal with personnel issues, and logistics officers will always be assigned to logistical commands. If there is a transition, it will almost always be from a combat position to a combat support or service position and normally for health reasons or unsatisfactory performance of duties. Only on rare occasions will the opposite transition occur (i.e., from service to combat position).

The above description has focused mainly on combat officers. This reflects the fact that the IDF, too, focuses on this core of officers and structures the rest of the IDF according to the model of the combat officer. It is necessary, nonetheless, to delineate some of the other officer models to complete the picture of the IDF officer structure.

Pilots

The Israeli Air Force pilots, as previously discussed, are screened prior to and during the first days of the induction process. They are then sent directly to flight school. The IDF's principle of first being a regular soldier has no relevance for pilots. Their intensive training is designed to make them, first and foremost, aviators. Flight school lasts for approximately two years. In spite of the rigorous screening processes, the attrition rate remains very high because of the particularly high and uncompromising standards required in the Israeli Air Force flight school.

At some point, approximately midway through flight school, the student pilots are categorized, based on their performance to date, into types of assignments (i.e., combat, transport, etc.). The very best will be selected for training as fighter pilots, the next best as fighter-bomber pilots, and the others as transport, helicopter and light aircraft pilots. Here, too, as in the Army, the policy is one of keeping the men[13] in the same squadrons as they progress in rank and position, even though they occasionally depart the unit for staff assignments. Promotion to the position of squadron commander is competitive and select. It is predominantly determined by the pilot's combat performance. Since there are many "aces" among Israeli aviators, the competition is not easy. An additional screening method for promotion is peer evaluation (the sociometric technique). This is used extensively in the Israeli Air Force for various purposes and at different levels.[14]

Pilots who complete their required five years of service and choose to leave will continue as reserve pilots and will be called frequently for refresher training. In all of Israel's wars, they have played a major role. Those pilots who opt to remain on active duty after their five-year obligation has been met will almost always pursue their academic education at this point, before returning to their squadrons. As a prerequisite to promotion to lieutenant colonel, these pilots will attend the Poum (Command and Staff School) where they will mingle with their colleagues from the Army and Navy.

Naval Officers

The majority of naval officers begin their careers at the Naval Officers School. As is the case for pilots, naval officer candidates report for training immediately after their induction. The Navy, however, also commissions a certain number of officers from the ranks. (This varies by year, sometimes accounting for almost one-third of the officers commissioned in a given year.) The naval officers' course lasts approximately twenty months and combines both classroom lessons and shipboard exercises. At the end of the course they are commissioned as 2nd lieutenants and are usually assigned to command small patrol craft, where they will practice their newly acquired skills as naval officers and commanders. Only in the following phase are they assigned to one of the naval missile ships, where they will serve as a gunner-officer, navigation and communication officer, or an engine-officer.

Those who choose to continue their naval career after completing their five years of required service will undergo an advanced course which will eventually qualify them as missile ship commander—the ultimate career goal of any Israeli naval officer. As in the case of the Air Force, the Navy also has its own branch in the Poum, and, like the Air Force, many of the naval officers will elect to pursue academic studies before reaching the rank of major.

Non-combat Officers

This category includes non-combat officers who fill support and service positions in the various branches of the IDF. There are two main sources of these officers: the first (which was described in Chapter 2) is the academic reserve officer program. These engineers, physicians, psychologists, attorneys, and so forth, because of their professional skills, are not usually required to serve as soldiers first in their professions. Rather, after completion of their short (one month) basic training and special officers' orientation training, they are sent to the officers' school at Bahad 1 for three months followed by an additional three months of specialized professional coursework, after which they are commissioned as officers. Their promotion, while normally similar to the rest of the IDF officer corps, will nevertheless always be at a pace slower than that of combat officers. For example, rarely will these non-combat officers be promoted ahead of the minimum time in grade requirement, a privilege reserved almost exclusively for combat officers. This is one of the means by which the IDF expresses its clear priorities regarding combat personnel.

The other main source consists of officers trained and promoted as non-academic specialists from the ranks. These officers have served first as regular soldiers in various non-combat specialties, have normally completed the NCO (or professional) training course and, consequently, were selected as officer candidates. The same medical profile which initially precluded their assignment to combat units now also dictates their assignment to "Basissi" (Basic Officers Course), which is not as physically demanding as the two combat versions of Bahad 1. Though not combatants themselves, the best of them will be assigned to combat units in combat support or staff positions. Most frequently their career will progress within their specialty, and it is uncommon for such an officer to be transferred into another specialty. Thus, an ordnance officer, for example, will never be assigned to a signal officer position though each may be assigned to a variety of different units during their careers.

In summary, the Israeli military has neither an Army officer academy, such as the British Sandhurst, the Canadian Military Colleges, or the American West Point, nor an equivalent naval or Air Force academy. Israeli officers, in all branches of the military, are drafted as conscripts and (with the exclusion of the academic specialists) are vigorously trained, continually selected, and additionally trained toward their profession— leadership. Being a "gentleman," an academician or an aristocrat has never been a prerequisite. In fact most Israeli officers place little value on such behavioral, educational or social attributes. While being a gentleman or an aristocrat is, indeed, alien to the Israeli culture and unnecessary for its military, the lack of higher education is becoming a problem for the Israeli modernized army. As a highly professional military which must keep up with the most recent developments in the modernization and sophistication of its weapon systems, the IDF can no longer afford to exempt the officers' corps from a requirement for early higher education.

While it is clear that the IDF is an officer-led (rather than NCO-led) military, there is nonetheless a continual struggle within the IDF regarding the size and scope of the officers' corps. On the one hand are those who urge the expansion of this corps (to the extent, as some senior generals claim, that every tank commander should be an officer). On the other hand are those who argue for a smaller corps of officers. The current proportion of IDF officer corps' strength to the IDF total strength (active and reserves) is less than 10 percent (in the front-line units it is even lower, about 6 percent).[15] However, when taken only within the standing army, it increases to approximately 14 percent, reflecting the nature of the infrastructure of the permanent service corps. The proportional size of the officer corps in a military organization sometimes is considered an indication of its strength and quality (the smaller the proportion—the better).[16] One is not surprised, then, that the traditional trend in the IDF has been to keep its officer corps relatively small. Whether this trend can continue, in light of technological advancements, remains to be seen.

Characteristics of Junior Commanders

Leadership is usually viewed as a behavior which has universal characteristics, not only across cultures but also across institutions and organizations.[17] Some organizations, however, develop leadership patterns which in turn affect the entire systems' functioning. Such is the case in the IDF. In fact, a common belief in the IDF is that "the effectiveness of the IDF *is* the effectiveness of its commanders."

This belief is also shared by authorities in the field of military history. In an attempt to account for the Israelis' superiority in combat effectiveness in all of their confrontations with their Arab adversaries, Trevor N. Dupuy, a prominent war analyst, stated: "In the first place, from company to top command the Israeli leaders were more flexible, aggressive and dynamic."[18] While such attributes may be conceived of as almost personality characteristics, they may be better viewed as the external expressions of some deeper characteristics of the IDF's combat leadership structure in general.

What are the unique characteristics of this leadership structure, and what makes them so critical to the IDF's total effectiveness? The following discussion identifies and delineates the most important of these.

Authority and Independence

The IDF is basically a decentralized military. The heavy involvement in operational missions virtually necessitates the downward delegation of command authority. When an officer deploys his unit on a mission, he knows not only that he is in charge, but also that he is free to make command decisions as necessary for mission completion, relatively free of the chain of command above him.[19]

> One of the most dramatic examples of a critical decision made by an on-site commander occurred during the Yom Kippur War. The commander of the "Quay" fortification, one of those on the Bar-Lev Line along the Suez Canal, was Lieutenant Ardinest. For the first five days of the war, despite their high casualty rates, he and his troops managed to stave off the advancing Egyptian forces. Despite the critical positioning of the "Quay" fortification, Ardinest was never directed in his many radio communications with his higher headquarters to either surrender or fight to the last man. This decision was left for him alone to make. On the seventh day of the war his concern for his seriously wounded soldiers, plus the total depletion of his ammunition, prompted him to surrender to the Egyptian forces in order to secure medical treatment for his troops.[20]

The extensive freedom of action enjoyed by on-site commanders derives from the Israeli belief that on the battlefield things seldom go exactly as planned, nor do they appear the same as they do in maps or aerial surveillance photographs. Therefore any senior commander who is not on location cannot make better command decisions than the on-site commander, regardless of the ranks involved. As a result, a junior lieutenant may have the authority to determine the fate of his assigned stronghold even though that stronghold may be the key to an entire region. Similarly, Israeli pilots are sent out on their missions after an identified target. It is left up to them to decide the details necessary to accomplish their mission. The IDF pilots are perhaps one of the least restricted of all Western pilots, definitely more than Soviet pilots[21] or Soviet-trained Arab pilots.

Reading the Situation and Improvisation

Since the early stages of his training, the Israeli junior commander is encouraged to improvise solutions to problems and to operate immediately upon situations when they alter unexpectedly from the proscribed plan. In short, he must continuously read the situation and react accordingly. Such an approach requires a great deal of initiative, creativity, and problem-solving ability. In fact, in the formal training doctrine of the IDF, it is emphasized that "the commander will accomplish his missions in accordance with the general 'spirit' of the command and based on his reading of the situation." The spirit of the command implies that the high headquarters only gives general directions, leaving to the commanders the translation of that spirit into action. More important though, the reading-the-situation component refers to the fact that more than any prior planning and instructions, it is the ongoing evaluation of current battlefield conditions that will ultimately determine the combat outcome.

Trust in Commanders

All of these characteristics could not exist without unconditional trust at the various command levels. Decentralized command is the privilege of trustworthy leadership, while leadership which cannot be completely trusted will consequently yield a centralized command. This perception, which is so deeply rooted in the IDF, is exemplified by the fact that, in general, orders and plans concerning operational missions are not dictated to a given unit by the higher command. Rather, each level, down to the battalion level, is required to prepare and submit its own plans for mission execution. The upper echelon only approves the plans and coordinates them with other participating units.

Furthermore, in the IDF's elite units, where trust in commanders and their men is complete, not only are the plans generated from the bottom up, but, on occasion, even questions of mission feasibility are addressed to the commander who may eventually be given the mission.

> In a recent symposium on international terrorism, one of the featured speakers was Benjamin Netanyahu, the younger brother of the late Lt. Col. Jonathan (Yoni) Netanyahu, who was killed while leading his special-operations unit on the famous rescue mission in Entebbe. Benjamin himself was also a member of an elite special IDF unit, usually called upon to react to terrorist situations. In his remarks to the symposium, he noted: "I served five years in such a special unit, first as a soldier, and then as an officer. I never heard once, not once, of a unit being simply told by the political leadership that it would *have* to accept a perilous assignment. Always the commanders of the unit were *asked*: Is it possible? Do you think you can do it?"[22]

Such an unconditional trust in commanders requires a close, virtually intimate, familiarity in order for a senior commander to almost blindly trust his subordinate commanders. While in the elite units this intimacy does exist, in the larger corps, for example the Armor corps, some of this has disappeared in recent years. Resulting from the IDF's enormous expansion in the years following the 1973 Yom Kippur War (some sources have estimated that the IDF has expanded from six divisions in 1973 to about eleven divisions in 1982),[23] the number of units has increased, as has the number of commanders; consequently, the sense of close familiarity has generally diminished. Among other things, the consequence has been a significant decrease in these commanders' independence, coupled with a significant increase in the command restrictions applied to them.

Accountability of Commanders

Each commander is highly visible, and all of his command actions (in terms of level of performance, execution of missions, accurate and prompt reporting, and combat discipline) are carefully scrutinized. This scrutiny focuses on the most vital aspects of his command. If an officer is found lacking in this regard, the consequences for him are severe. For example, it is not unheard of for a battalion commander to be relieved of his command because of a performance failure in one of his subunits.

One of the results of this doctrine of accountability (which reached its height during General Eytan's term as Chief of Staff—1978 to 1983) was the development of an attitude which was the opposite of the initiative, creativity and improvisation mentioned earlier. This attitude was known among Israeli troops as "small head" (in Hebrew, "Rosh Katan"), meaning someone who avoids taking responsibility, initiating actions, or diverting from proscribed procedures and instead maintains a "low profile." While the Rosh Katan attitude was somewhat expected among lower-ranking enlisted soldiers, it also began appearing in the IDF officer corps. Its causes were both the overaccountability of officers' actions and their exhaustion resulting from the extremely tense times prior to and during the War in Lebanon. The pendulum swing between "small head" and commanders' independence and initiative has become one of the IDF's most sensitive subjects. This will be further discussed in the last chapter which describes the IDF's current faultlines.

Direct Command

At all command levels—from squad leader to a battalion or even brigade commander—the commanders feel they are directly responsible for, and totally concerned about, their troops. Whether during periods of peace or war, the perception of these troops as the unit's key asset, who therefore must be carefully taken care of, is a central theme of the IDF's leaders. An interesting reflection of this can be seen in the soldier's viewpoint. In a field study[24] conducted by the IDF's Unit of Military Psychology, immediately after the 1973 Yom Kippur War, the sampled soldiers (all enlisted men who had actually participated in combat) were asked whom they considered to be their direct commander. Table 7.1 presents the response distribution for that question by corps and command positions.

While it is apparent that the greatest response frequencies are associated with platoon and company commander positions (and tank commander positions in Armor units), it is also apparent from the wide range of responses that all of the command positions from squad to battalion level (and even sometimes at the brigade level) may be perceived, on occasion, as "the direct commander" by their soldiers.

Military Proficiency

Since the road to becoming an officer or NCO in the IDF begins with being the best soldier in the unit, it is obvious that the junior commanders are highly proficient. A strong emphasis on military proficiency is quite apparent in all military units. Being proficient means not only having the knowledge and specific skills necessary to perform one's duties. It also means implementing these to effectively lead troops—in short, to act as a leader. Military proficiency, thus, is perceived by IDF

Table 7.1
Percentage of Soldiers (in Each of Four Main Ground Combat Corps) Referring to Various Levels of Command as Their "Direct Commander"

Levels of Command	Infantry (N=462)	Armor (N=1030)	Artillery (N=503)	Engineer (N=105)
Brigade Commander	1.3	2.3	0.5	0.0
Battalion Commander	10.7	14.4	8.8	3.8
Company /Battery Commander	21.3	28.9	19.8 (36.4)*	35.3
Platoon Commander	34.0	22.8	6.0	39.2
Squad/Section/ Tank Leader	18.7	27.4	14.3	15.7

*Refers to the deputy battery commander who, in the case of the artillery, is the officer in charge of the artillerymen at the battery position.

combat soldiers as part of their commander's leadership skills and accounts for their high degree of trust in their commanders.

The IDF's behavioral scientists studied this relationship between trust and commander's professional competence.[25] Using data obtained from twenty-six platoons (approximately 300 soldiers), all of whom had actively participated in the 1982 War in Lebanon, it was found that the perceived proficiency of the commander was the most important component in the Israeli soldiers' trust of these commanders. The other two components of that trust were the commander's credibility and the perception of how caring he was for his soldiers. All three components were found to be essentially equally important ingredients of trust in the commander while the troops remain in garrison. In combat, however, the perception of the commander's proficiency becomes the primary ingredient of trust. This perception is complex: it includes both the appraisal of the commander's overall professional competence and, more specifically, the appraisal of the thoughtfulness with which the commander tailors the missions he receives from higher command to the particular condition of the battle and of the men under his command. Specifically, in this survey the soldiers described the trustworthy commander in terms of his personal example (i.e., always being in the forward position, leading the charge, and risking himself first before ordering his men to take hazardous actions). These were seen by the soldiers as important components of commander competence and therefore of overall trust. Also seen as important in commander competence were good tactical and navigational skills and prior combat experience.

Although this perception of commander's proficiency is broad, there are those in the IDF who are concerned about the growing overemphasis on the technical component at the expense of the human component, in other words, the extent to which the commander cares for his troops. In a recent interview given by Brigadier General Zohar, Chief of the Educational Corps of the IDF, after the War in Lebanon, this concern was brought up:

> Today's IDF is a highly modern organization in which professional specialization and the knowledge required for it are increasing. A commander today requires much more knowledge than was required of him ten years ago. This pushes people toward the phenomenon of "overproficiency." The other areas which a commander may have emphasized ten years ago—the educational and ethical—he now leaves for others: educational specialists, psychologists, etc. He is uncomfortable trying to deal with these areas and therefore he creates an image of someone who is constantly preoccupied with technical and tactical matters and is not available for relationships beyond these matters.[26]

In spite of these concerns, the empirical data from the previously mentioned IDF study[27] demonstrate that combat commanders still earn a remarkably high level of trust from their troops. In the third week of combat engagement in Lebanon, these 300 soldiers were asked about their level of trust in their commanders. About 76 percent of the sampled soldiers indicated either "very high trust" or "high trust" in their commanders at that moment. When queried about any changes in this level of trust as a result of combat experiences, about 90 percent of these soldiers reported either the same or greater level of trust than before combat. Only 8 percent reported a lower level of trust after combat. (An identical phenomenon was found following the 1973 Yom Kippur War.)

The Israeli officer, then, is not only highly effective in mission accomplishment. Obviously he also generates a high level of trust among his men and in so doing elevates their combat motivation to remarkably high levels.

Motivating Power

The IDF is a conscript military; its soldiers serve without any real monetary compensation. The greatest proportion of the IDF is composed of reservists who, once again, do not receive any additional salary for their reserve service. Monetary gain, then, cannot be used by commanders as an incentive. Neither could physical punishment or threat of such punishment be used as a motivational force in the IDF, certainly not in field units. The main means used by IDF junior commanders in the IDF, whether squad leader, platoon or company commander, is himself—his leadership, his ability to persuade his troops, and their confidence in him. In the previously mentioned study, 81 percent of the soldiers stated firmly that in case of future engagement they would follow their specific platoon commander on "any mission"; 90 percent declared that they would perform "any job" given to them by their platoon commander.[28] When commanders enjoy such a high level of trust, they are not perceived as coercing or forcing their troops; rather, their men will choose to follow them wherever they take them.

Another motivational force is the unit. Here again, especially in the field units, the level of unit pride and the concern about "what will the others say" are so powerful that they too become motivating factors in activating individuals in the group for the most difficult and risky missions. Since the commander actually controls the unit dynamics and develops its cohesion level, he essentially has in his hands the key to the behavior of his soldiers by using peer pressure as a motivator. In fact, in many of the IDF's elite units, the most severe sanction that a commander might apply to his soldiers is to remove a member from the unit. Nothing is more threatening, especially in volunteer units, than the prospect of such an act.

But beyond anything else, the most effective leadership tool available to the Israeli junior commander is that leadership style which the Israelis have developed to an ultimate level—the "follow-me" style of leadership.

The "Follow-Me" Leadership

This leadership characteristic is so deeply rooted in the Israeli military that it has developed, beyond its daily practice, into an ethos. Indeed, the roots of this leadership style go back to the Palmach generation, prior to the establishment of the IDF, and continued to develop during the retaliation actions of the 1950s when General Dayan served as Chief of Staff.

Basically, this dictum says that commanders should not expose their men to any danger to which they are unwilling to expose themselves, and that in combat there is no better way of motivating your men to charge in the face of enemy fire than to lead the charge yourself with your men following behind. And so, since all commanders' training in the IDF is geared toward this moment of charging the enemy, the dictum "A'harye" (the Hebrew word for "follow me") is imprinted in all junior commanders from their earliest training. This dictum is not only "mouthed" but is actually practiced: in Infantry units, for example, commanders will always be located at the head of their troops, the squad leader at the head of his squad, the platoon commander at the head of his platoon, and so forth up to the battalion and sometimes even the brigade level. In the Armor, too, commanders are always located at the center and front of their "wedge." (The IDF's Armor corps is the only known army in the world where brigade commanders still lead their forces from their tanks.) They stand up in their open turrets, exposing themselves not only to get a clearer picture but also, sometimes primarily, to enable their men to see them at any moment. Among combat pilots, frequently the squadron commander himself will be in the lead plane in the formation. It is also a common practice that the commander of the Air Force, a general, will continue flying fighter aircraft quite frequently despite his high position.

> The rationale of the personal example (i.e., that as a commander you do not expose your men to any risk you would not expose yourself to) can result in paradoxical behavior on the part of IDF senior commanders, as demonstrated in the following story:
> In the summer of 1981 the Israeli Air Force was preparing, under close security, for a perilous mission of destroying a nuclear plant in Iraq. The geographic distance from the Israeli air base to the target location was approximately 500 miles, and the flight had to be very low altitude in order to evade radar detection. When the proposed plan was presented for approval by the Chief of Staff, then General "Raful" Eytan, he immediately recognized the extreme risk involved. Raful, an experienced combat commander himself, who had abundantly demonstrated on the battlefield the follow-me dictum, decided to personally test the feasibility of the mission before sending the pilots on it. He thus joined a night practice flight which was designed to test the practicality of this very risky mission. Only after being personally convinced of its probability of success, he reported to the Israeli Prime Minister that the mission was possible. On the next night the nuclear plant was destroyed by the Israeli Air Force.

Leading by personal example, then, exists throughout the IDF command structure, from the squad leader commanding his handful of men to the Chief of Staff commanding the entire army. Personal example, however, is not only required in combat, it begins with the relationship that exists between commanders and their men outside the combat arena—in training, in their accommodations and in their day-to-day activities. Officers live in the same billets as their soldiers, wear the same uniforms and eat the same food. Although in rear headquarters there are usually separate dining areas for officers and enlisted men, this is not the case in the field units: officers and non-officers dine in the same halls, attend the same military "cantina" (in the IDF there is no officers' open mess) and sleep in the same barracks. During training they do everything their men do—leading them from the front, whether it is a forced march, loading trucks, "carrying the wounded" or donating blood. They are expected, in short, to set a personal example in all areas of behavior, both combat and non-combat.

The Price of Leadership

The IDF's follow-me leadership does not come without a high price. An army which operates under a policy of commanders leading their men, thus exposing themselves first to enemy fire, will obviously have its commanders not only as heroes but also as casualties. The IDF has experienced in all its wars a substantially high casualty rate for officers. This rate has been as high as 20 percent of all its unit commanders, as compared to an expected international average of about 10 percent.[29] However, the figure that dramatized the significance of leading from the front is the number of officer losses as a percentage of total IDF casualties. This percentage in the Yom Kippur War was 28.5 percent, three times higher than their 9.5 percent strength within the IDF (or four and a half times their proportion within line units).[30] During that war some units had to replace a company or battalion commander three or four times because of extensive casualties; toward the end, sometimes lieutenants commanded battalions or sergeants commanded companies.[31]

In 1982, during the War in Lebanon, this phenomenon repeated itself. Out of 468 war fatalities, 111 (i.e., 24 percent) were officers from 2nd lieutenant through the rank of general, including one major general.[32] Table 7.2 gives a breakdown of total casualties for this war.[33]

To complete this picture, it is necessary to add figures for NCOs in command positions. These include the ranks from corporal to staff sergeant (in the IDF a corporal usually serves as a tank commander or squad leader). These junior leaders represented almost 50 percent of the total war casualties, obviously much higher than their proportionate representation in the fighting units.

It is interesting to note that the percentage of wounded officers (14.5 percent), which in theory should equal the percentage killed, is markedly less than the 24 percent of officer fatalities. There are two possible explanations for this. First, the front position in any charge always draws the most intense fire, thus is more likely to result in death rather than injury. The second explanation (although not exclusive of the first) lies in the fact that a larger number of officers (than enlisted men) with marginal wounds did not report them, in order to prevent being evacuated and thus separated from their men.

Similarly, the proportion of officers among psychiatric casualties was minimal. In the Yom Kippur War, for example, officers' ratio of psy-

Table 7.2
IDF Casualties (KIA and WIA) by Ranks in the Lebanon War

	Officers					Enlisted					Total
	2nd Lt–Captain	Major–Lt Col	Colonel–General	Total Officers		Private–PFC	Corporal–Staff Sgt	SFC–Master Sgt	Total Enlisted	
Killed in action	84	25	2	111		80	217	60	357		468
% from total KIA	(18%)	(5%)	(1%)	(24%)		(17%)	(46%)	(13%)	(76%)	
Wounded in action	34	67	6	420		566	1384	530	2480		2900
% from total WIA	(12%)	(2.3%)	(0.2%)	(14.5%)		(19.5%)	(48%)	(18%)	(85.5%)	

chiatric to physical casualties was five times less than the equivalent ratio among enlisted men.[34]

Regarding heroism, again commanders and officers have historically been overrepresented in all of the IDF's wars. For example, of the 283 heroism medals awarded after the Yom Kippur War, 64 percent were given to officers and another 24 percent to NCOs in command positions.[35] Furthermore, about half of these medals were awarded posthumously. Similarly, after the War in Lebanon, 54.5 percent of the citations for bravery were given to officers and about one-third to NCOs in command positions. Thus, in all Israel's recent wars, IDF officers have died at a rate four times their numbers in the fighting units and have also won bravery medals at a rate ten times greater. Their fellow NCOs have also demonstrated a combat behavior which was almost identical in gallantry.

The IDF has continued to lose its officers, sometimes even high-ranking ones, at a high rate, not only in full-scale wars but also in more limited operations. Between major wars, in the frequent low-intensity operations (such as routing terrorist teams) executed by small units, there were nonetheless senior officer casualties. These officers chose to lead these missions, albeit small unit operations, because they saw it as their responsibility.

The wisdom of such an expensive approach in terms of leadership cost has been strongly and repeatedly criticized, both by the public and within the IDF. More than once the concern was voiced that the IDF recklessly risked losing its most valuable officers. However, in all of these debates it became clear that there is no substitute for the follow-me leadership model on the battlefield and that the loss of officers and commanders was the necessary price the IDF had to pay for its victorious record. Thus "the 'follow-me' ethos has such a strong hold on the mentality of Israeli officers that it has been very difficult to restrain even the most senior from taking the lead in combat."[36]

Conclusion

IDF procedures for generating, selecting, and training its junior officers and NCOs ensure that the best and the most qualified are selected for leadership positions. The fact that these junior commanders have been soldiers first and are now competent leaders enables them to develop in their units—squads, crews and platoons—a high degree of military cohesion, to the point of total devotion of each unit member toward the unit's goals, its men and, above all, its leader. Furthermore, the "A'harye" leadership style allows these leaders to conduct daring tactics in combat "that few other armies are able to achieve."[37]

Essentially, the IDF is an officer-led, rather than NCO-led, army from its very lowest echelons up to the highest levels. In a unique way, the Israeli junior officer's model has developed in which the officer, at all different levels of command, plays the leader's role, both in leading his men in combat and in taking care of their personal needs at all other times. He is the one who will personally instruct his troops on proper weapon usage and two hours later will discuss with them the historical significance of the area in which they are currently located. He will also, for instance, check their physical condition from head to toe, caring not only for their combat readiness but also for their general health.

All of these qualities together form the foundation of the IDF's leadership, from its inception to the present time. This is not to imply that this foundation is without cracks (which will be further discussed in Chapter 13). Indeed, the leadership foundation will be sustained only as long as there is a high-quality officer corps, exemplary competence, complete trust and confidence, and the glamour of combat success. However, if the quality of the officer corps declines, trust and confidence gradually erode, and traditional combat successes sometimes intermingle with combat failures. Then these foundations may allow the formation of small cracks which may ultimately weaken the entire organization.

Notes

1. Pilot candidates are selected (as described in Chapter 5) prior to induction. Upon entry into active duty, they are assigned directly to flight school where they will undergo all their training, including basic training, as pilot cadets, until they are commissioned. Naval ship officers (as distinguished from those with shore duty) undergo a similar process.

2. Gabriel, R., & Gal, R. (1984). The IDF officer: Linchpin in unit cohesion. *Army*, 34(1), 42–50.

3. The "Oxford" of the armor corps. (1983, June 22). *Bamahane*, 41, 18.

4. Taken from *The Commander Training Institute of the IDF*. (1982, October 24). Pamphlet distributed as background information for visitors to the institute.

5. Gal, R. (1983). Courage under stress. In S. Breznitz (Ed.), *Stress in Israel* (pp. 65–91). New York: Van Nostrand Reinhold, p. 78.

6. For the infantry officer candidates, the Bahad 1 course, with its strong infantry orientation, trains them in their actual profession. For the other two groups, however, infantry training is mainly used as a vehicle for learning and practicing leadership. Therefore, the Kheer course lasts six months, while candidates in the other two courses split their training into three months of infantry and three additional months of specialized training.

7. Luttwak, E., & Horowitz, D. (1975). *The Israeli army*. London: Allen Lane, pp. 86–87.

8. *Bamahane*, The "Oxford" of the armor corps.

9. Deputy company commander is an established position in the IDF. While normally the deputy is primarily responsible for logistical and administrative

concerns, he also would assume command in combat if the company commander is killed or seriously wounded.

10. The "tigers" are back. (1984, May 30). *Bamahane, 37,* 22–23.

11. Pa'il, M. (1975, January). The Israeli defence forces: A social aspect. *New Outlook,* 40–44.

12. Garti, M. (1984, July 27). The young ones abandon the IDF. *Ha'aretz,* p. 7.

13. Not since the War of Independence has the Israeli Air Force had women pilots.

14. See Ravid, Y. (1984, May). Sociometric pilot testing saves time, lives, and money. *Defence Systems Review,* 44–45.

15. It is rather difficult to compare Israeli percentages with those of other militaries. From available information, the Soviet Army, for instance, has a comparable percentage of 14 percent, and the U.S. Army approximately 11.5 percent. (These figures were provided to the author by an official from the National Defense University, Research Directorate, Washington, DC.) R. Gabriel and P. Savage (in *Crisis in command.* New York: Hill and Wang, 1978) indicate 13.8 percent for the entire U.S. military for 1974. A more recent report specifies that the U.S. Armed Forces of the mid–1980s have 2.1 million personnel, of which 300,000 (i.e., 14.29 percent) are officers. See Doering, Z. D., & Grissmer, D. W. (1984, May). What we know and how we know it. A selected review of research and methods for studying active and reserve attrition/retention in the U.S. Armed Forces. *Proceedings of the Second Symposium on Motivation and Morale in the NATO Forces* (pp. 251–299). Brussels: NATO.

16. See Gabriel & Savage, *Crisis in command.* This viewpoint is also reflected in van Creveld, M. (1982). *Fighting power: German and U.S. Army performance 1939–1945.* Westport, CT: Greenwood Press.

17. See for example, F. Fiedler's approach which typifies this viewpoint. Fiedler, F. (1967). *A theory of leadership effectiveness.* New York: McGraw-Hill.

18. Dupuy, T. N. (1984). *Elusive victory: The Arab-Israeli wars, 1947–1974.* Fairfax, VA: HERO Books, p. 335.

19. An interesting comparison can be made in this regard to the "Auftragslaktik" (translated as "mission-oriented command system") which characterized the German military in World War II. See van Creveld, *Fighting power.*

20. Herzog, C. (1975). *The war of atonement: October, 1973.* Boston: Little, Brown and Company.

21. Donnelly, C. (1982). The Soviet attitude to stress in battle. *Journal of the Royal Army Medical Corps, 128,* 72–78.

22. Netanyahu, B. (1984, June 26). Statement prepared for the *Jonathan Institute: Second Conference on International Terrorism,* Washington, DC.

23. *The Military Balance, 1982–83.* London: The International Institute for Strategic Studies.

24. Zvulun, E. (1974, April). *The reactions of the Israeli soldier in the Yom Kippur War* (Research Report). Unit of Military Psychology, IDF, Israel.

25. Kalay, E. (1982, July). *Confidence in commanders* (Research Report). Department of Behavioral Sciences, IDF, Israel. A summary of this study was also reported in *Skirra Hodsheet.* (1983, February-March), *30*(2–3), 82.

26. Inspector, Y. (1983). The commander in combat: Part I. *Bamahane, 13,* 17.

27. Kalay, *Confidence in commanders*.
28. Ibid.
29. Rothenberg, G. E. (1979). *The anatomy of the Israeli army*. New York: Hippocrene Books, Inc., p. 117.
30. U.S. Army and Air Force officers formed 13.9 percent of their total units' KIA in World War II. (In the land forces alone, officers constituted 6.6 percent of those KIA.) At the time of VE Day the percentage of officers in the U.S. Army was 9.6.

In the German Army, officers accounted for about 4 percent of total casualties. Their proportion within the Army was, in 1944, about 2.5 percent. See van Creveld, *Fighting power*, pp. 127–162. Gabriel and Savage report the percentage of officers KIA in Korea to be 5.45 percent (officers' strength was 10.5 percent); in Vietnam, officers' deaths accounted for 10.7 percent (8.4 percent when warrant officers are removed), while their proportion in the total strength was 14.97 percent. See Gabriel & Savage, *Crisis in command*.

31. Herzog. *The war of atonement*.
32. Major General Yekutiel ("Kuti") Adam was, during the War in Lebanon, the Deputy Chief of Staff. He was killed by PLO soldiers at close range in the second week of the war.
33. IDF Spokesman press release, February 1983.
34. Levav, I., Greenfeld, H., & Baruch, E. (1979, May). Psychiatric combat reactions during the Yom Kippur War. *Am. J. Psychiatry*, 136(5), 637–641.
35. Gal, R. *Courage under stress*.
36. Luttwak & Horowitz, *The Israeli army*, p. 116.
37. Henderson, W. D. (1985). *Cohesion: The human element in combat*. Washington, DC: National Defense University Press, p. 201.

1. An Israeli tank on parade.

2. A squad leader (corporal) checking his men's weapons.

3. Night river crossing.

4. A tank crew, belonging to one of the "Yeshivot companies," taking their prayers during a lull in training.

5. Practicing "carrying the wounded."

6. Basic training: the trainees and their instructor.

7. Instructing a fresh group of conscripts in "Bakum" (Induction Base).

8. IDF female soldiers in the Artillery School.

9. Paratrooper trainees receive their personal weapon during a night ceremony near the Wailing Wall, Jerusalem.

10. A group of "miluimmniks" (reservists).

11. Impromptu command briefing in the field. (Sitting on the Jeep is Major General "Yanoush" Ben-Gal.)

12. "Nahal" commanders during training lull.

13. An Infantry unit reviewing a just-completed exercise. (Lieutenant General Moshe Levi is sitting on the left.)

14. Aboard a naval gunboat.

15. Two Israeli combat pilots on their way to their aircraft.

16. Air Force air traffic controllers.

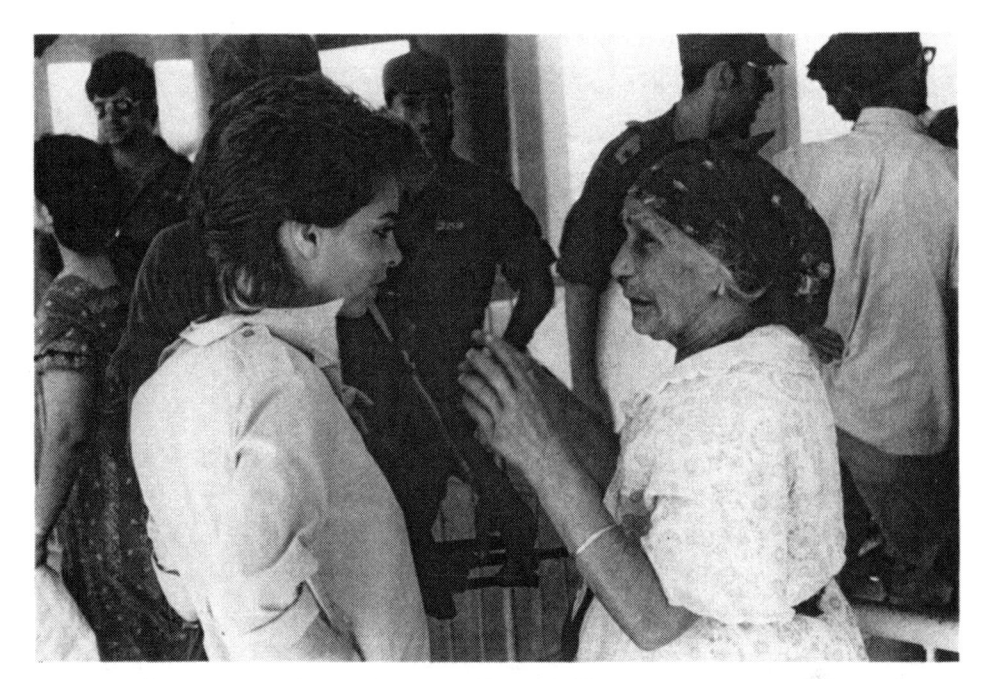

17. IDF soldiers in Kiriat Shmona (a town in Upper Galilee) after massive PLO bombardment.

18. Infantry troops patrolling in Lebanon.

19. IDF soldiers upon return from night operation in Lebanon.

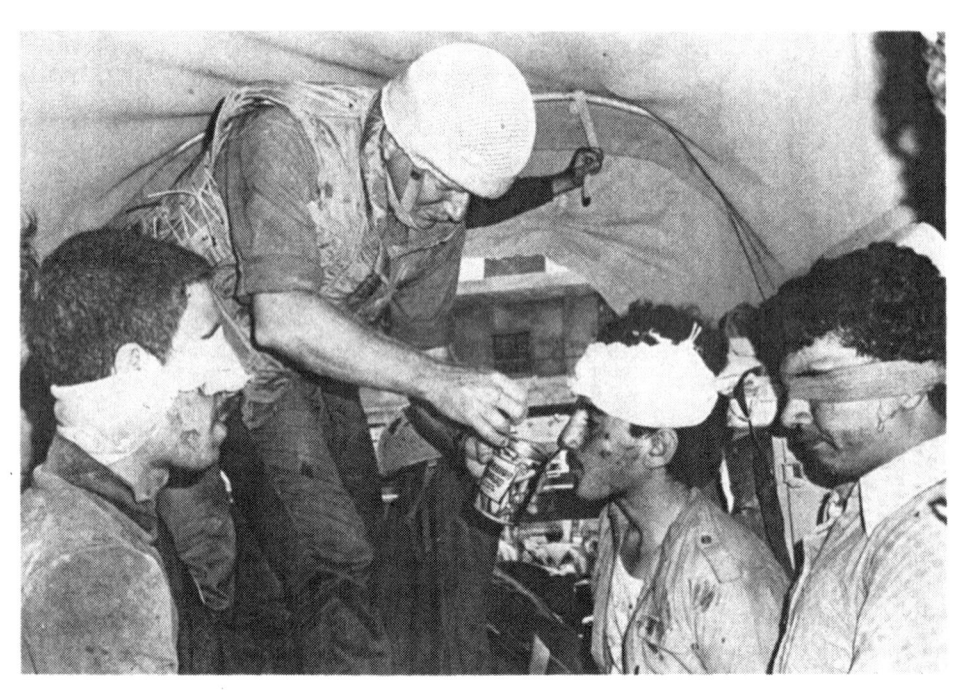

20. An Israeli soldier feeding PLO POWs.

8

THE FIGHTING SPIRIT

Many attribute the high level of effectiveness of the Israeli Defence Forces to its vast history of combat experience. While this is unfortunately true, it cannot be the entire explanation. The Egyptian and Syrian armies, to mention just two of Israel's traditional adversaries, have at least the same amount of combat experience. And obviously there are many nations with long military histories whose accumulated combat experience is greater than that of the three-and-a-half-decade-old IDF.

Almost since its inception, the IDF has always inspired and emphasized the offensive spirit of its forces. In the absence of a long military tradition this spirit had to be conceived, developed and quickly implemented. In a very interesting way, the IDF's fighting spirit has been drawn from certain individuals who played key roles during the formative years of the IDF. Thus, for example, though each one of the first Chiefs of Staff made his own contribution to the IDF, the most important emphasis, that of the offensive combat spirit, was permanently stamped on the IDF by its fourth Chief of Staff, General Moshe Dayan (1953–58). Dayan "wanted officers who were fighting men rather than managers in uniform; he wanted training which stressed combat skills rather than parade-ground drills, and he wanted a maximum of 'teeth' units with an absolute minimum of 'tail.'"[1]

The contemporary IDF is not only a "military of teeth," but the combat units are its overriding emphasis and focus of concern. They always receive the highest priority in every aspect of military life. Their members are always accorded the highest prestige. The spirit of the combat forces has pervaded the rest of the IDF. They set the standard for the entire Israeli military. Thus, this fighting spirit of the fighter pilot, naval gunboat teams, and the ground combatant accounts for the IDF's superior combat effectiveness. This spirit is the "secret weapon" of the IDF. While

Chapter 4 dealt with motivation to serve in the IDF, this chapter will be an attempt to reveal the origins of the IDF's battlefield fighting spirit.

Combat Unit Organization

A word must be said at this time to reacquaint the reader with the structure and formation of the IDF's combat units before we discuss their fighting spirit. The basic Israeli combat formation, among the ground units, is the "Ugdah," which is translated loosely as a division. It is, however, closer in nature to the German "Battle Group" (Kampgruppen) or task force group.[2]

An Ugdah may be composed entirely of regular units or partly of regular, partly of reserves or totally of reserves. Subunits within the Ugdah may be identical (in size, structure and weapon) or different from each other. Above all, these units are only a basic formation for peacetime activities. However, in time of war they may be separated and then reconfigured into various formations. The IDF has a strong inclination to tailor its combat formations relative to the particular task at hand.[3] In all such cases, however, the subunits comprising the new configuration and their leaders or commanders will retain their original identity and structure. This fluid nature of the Ugdah has led most analysts of the IDF to the conclusion that the brigade is actually the fundamental unit of the Army.[4] Elements of the regimental system, if present at all in the IDF, exist at this brigade level.

IDF brigades are triangular in structure: they contain three combat battalions, a reconnaissance unit, and artillery, signal and engineer elements. Battalions are also configured the same way (i.e., with three companies, along with a few support elements). Artillery battalions (five in each artillery brigade) have three batteries, each of which has four guns.[5] Typically, the Israeli units at all levels are small in size, much smaller than equivalent Western units. Thus, for example, an Infantry battalion will contain approximately 400 to 500 men. Each of its three line companies will be made up of about 100 combatants. Infantry companies are subdivided into three platoons, each of which is further divided into three squads, each of which has seven to ten members. Armored battalions, likewise, are small and contain as few as thirty-five tanks.[6]

Units are usually designated with numbers. Though brigades and occasionally battalions also have names (for example, Golani brigade, OZ battalion), these names are never used operationally. Publicly, the unit names are carefully concealed. In fact, when mentioned by name in any other context, units of all sizes are always called forces ("Utzba") for obvious security reasons, about which the IDF is very vigilant. Only occasionally will a certain task force be named after its commander. In the Lebanon War, for example, there were "Yosi Force," "Vardi Force," etc.—all ad hoc task forces. They were led by commanders specifically assigned to them.

In any case, however, regardless of the larger formation, it is the smaller units—the company, battalion and brigade—with which the individual identifies and from which, as will be shortly shown, he will be imbued with his fighting spirit.

In the present chapter, we will explore the characteristics of the fighting spirit along three dimensions. First, we will uncover the sources of combat motivation of the IDF soldier. Second, the components of the fighting spirit itself will be discussed. And finally we will describe how these units, in actuality, apply this fighting spirit on the battlefield.

Sources of Combat Motivation

When discussing sources of combat motivation, it is necessary to distinguish between root sources and acute sources. The former are deep-rooted, operate on the long term and reinforce affiliation with the unit, while the latter are immediate and operate predominantly in combat, under fire, facing the enemy. The two are not identical. Thus there is the need to discuss them separately.

Root Sources

Although the IDF is a new and modern military, the product of a country which has yet to celebrate its fortieth anniversary of statehood, it is nonetheless an army based on the historical and cultural roots of the entire Jewish history.

> In describing IDF soldiers immediately after the Six Day War (although this description has relevance for each of Israel's wars), Ruth Bondy, an Israeli author, has portrayed the image of the IDF soldiers as seen though the eyes of the everyday Israeli citizen. "They all have a great name now—*Giborei Israel*—the heroes of Israel. Zahal is the modern name. *Giborei Israel*—those were the warriors under King David, those were the Maccabees, those were the people of Masada and the rebels of the Warsaw Ghetto. That is what we call them today."[7]

The contemporary Israeli soldier is a combination of various historical ingredients. He has the self-determination, that dauntless spirit of resolution, coupled with a "sense of having his back to the wall," characterized by Elazar Ben-Yair and his followers at the Masada. He carries with him that perception of "the whole world is against us" as epitomized by the survivors of the Holocaust. He also has that special combination of "chutzpah" and courage which characterized the Palmach youngsters prior to the establishment of the State of Israel. And yet, along with all of these ingredients, he also retains the Western orientation which makes him well adapted to the modern weapons and technologically sophisticated equipment of the contemporary Israeli army. This unique combination renders him a particularly effective combatant who clearly knows what he is fighting for.

This knowledge of what he is fighting and dying for exists in the consciousness of every Israeli soldier. In fact, the underlying theme of "Ein Breira" which means "no alternative" is typical not just of soldiers but of the entire Israeli populace. The Ein Breira concept is a result of the combination of two collective memories shared by the people of Israel. On the one hand, there is the vivid memory of the Holocaust and the systematic extermination of 6 million helpless Jews. On the other hand there is the realization that the State of Israel, the only sovereign home for the Jews, is surrounded by Arab states, who are waiting to take advantage of any Israeli weakness. Although there are currently very few Israel soldiers who are actual survivors of the Holocaust, this combined collective memory is foremost in the mind of every Israeli soldier, regardless of his or her age, and translates into this sense of Ein Breira—there is no alternative.

Against the heavy burden of repeated wars, continual casualties, demanding and repeated military service, Ein Breira constitutes the only counterbalance for the Israeli populace—that is, between Israel and survival there is only the IDF. As a matter of fact, in most of the past Israeli wars this was indeed the case. From the 1948 War of Independence through the 1973 Yom Kippur War, the Israeli soldier who was fighting on the front literally knew that he was fighting for the defense of his own home and family. Even those fighters in the remote Sinai who were desperately trying to stop the massive Egyptian force crossing the Suez in 1973 could still see the threat that these forces might reach the heart of Israel, if they were not stopped in their tracks. This vivid sense of "fighting for your home and country" is not just a patriotic slogan for the Israeli soldier.

> During the Six Day War, I participated as a combat officer in the battles in Jerusalem. My house then was located less than two miles from where I was fighting with my company (which was composed of men also from Jerusalem). When I paid a quick visit to my home on the eve of June sixth to say goodbye, it was quite clear to all of us where and why I was going.

This sense of no choice is as essential for the soldier as it is to his family members. It was Ben-Gurion, the first Prime Minister of Israel and the founder of the IDF, who once said: "Every Israeli mother should know that her son is in the hands of reliable commanders. They may indeed be compelled to send him to his death, but only if it is vital for the survival of the state."[8]

The 1982 War in Lebanon was a deviation from this concept. For the first time in its history, the IDF launched an offensive attack from a position of numerical superiority and not in response to an actual threat to the very existence of Israel. The IDF soldiers who fought that war with the same decisiveness demonstrated in previous wars now found themselves in a quandary. This was especially the case for many of the reserve soldiers who recalled a much different sense of urgency in their previous wars.

The sense of Ein Breira has not only been a motivational source for the Israeli soldier, but it has also always been the moral justification for all of Israel's wars. It was this sense of being forced by the enemy to defend himself, rather than any hatred for the enemy, that characterized the Israeli soldiers' motivation throughout all times. As in most Western countries where hatred toward an enemy has never been a predominant motive,[9] it was likewise very rare in all of Israel's wars. In fact, in none of the IDF's studies of combat motivation was hatred found to be a significant factor. In an anthology published after the Six Day War, containing conversations with young kibbutz members who had been in the war, the general consensus was that there was no hatred for the Arabs.[10]

The same conclusion was drawn by Rolbant[11] regarding Israeli society in general at that time. His suggested explanation for what some might consider a surprising attitude was twofold. First, he attributes this attitude to the Israeli educational value system. Second, Israel is a state in which Jews and Arabs live together, generally tolerant of one another. These observations may have been accurate in 1967 and may still be essentially the case for most Israeli Jews today. For many other Israelis, however, there has been a decrease in that tolerance of the Arabs. In fact, recent years have seen the emergence of a few, sometimes underground, radical anti-Arab groups.[12] In general, however, this deterioration in tolerance has not manifested itself in the overt actions of Israeli soldiers. During the involvement in Lebanon, once again the general lack of hatred toward the enemy was frequently discussed. A typical expression of this was found in an Israeli book, written by Igal Lev, an author and a reserve officer, a seasoned combat veteran of all of Israel's wars from 1956 to 1982.

In a chapter titled "To Kill without Hatred," Lev notes the moral problem facing the Israeli soldier: "To go into a war without hatred.

To kill with no hatred. At the end of everything, when I try to summarize my feelings throughout all the wars I have been in, it comes to me that this is perhaps one of the most painful and difficult problems that a combatant faces: to kill your enemy without hating him."[13]

Within the IDF, whatever hatred toward the Arab enemy there is may be found among Sephardic soldiers, particularly those whose families came from Arabic countries. These soldiers, some of whom had personally suffered atrocities from Arabs in their countries of origin, carry within them a deep animosity that the Ashkenazi Jew cannot possibly comprehend. There were, indeed, a few incidents where Israeli soldiers used excessive force against Arab civilians. These events have generally occurred in the course of police-type activities conducted in areas heavily populated by Arabs. These incidents of hatred and revenge as a source of motivation notwithstanding, they constitute only a negligible part of the combat motivation of the Israeli soldier.

Acute Sources

It is not collective memories nor patriotism nor moral concerns nor even emotional outbursts that motivate the soldier in the midst of combat. Israelis in this regard are no different than any other soldier. As was observed by an expert student of battlefield behavior, S.L.A. Marshall noted: "When fire sweeps the field, be it in Sinai, Pork Chop Hill or along the Normandy coast, nothing keeps a man from running except a sense of honor, of bound obligation to people right around him, of fear of failure in their sight which might eternally disgrace him."[14] (P. 304)

Even factors such as unit pride or regimental spirit fail to drive men on in the face of battle "because in the crisis of battle the majority of men will not derive encouragement from the glories of the past but will seek aid from their leaders and comrades of the present."[15]

The Israeli experience is similar. Though as described earlier, the Israeli soldier has in his background ideologic and patriotic motives, in the terror that is battle, such motives are of limited importance.[16] The acute and immediate sources of combat motivation which will drive the combatant to fight in the face of battle are threefold.

First and foremost, there is self-preservation. The strong urge to survive is the force that, perhaps paradoxically, drives the soldier to fight rather than flee. This instinct of self-preservation will force the combatant not merely to defend himself but to fight more effectively and more fiercely, and thus ultimately to be victorious.

Second, there is the soldier's small unit which is a forceful motivating factor.[17] The group has its impact in two different ways. On the one hand, the strong bonds that a soldier feels for his buddies are expressed during combat in his deep commitment to them. He is ready to do anything for them, just as he believes they are ready to do anything they can for him. On the other hand, the group influences the individual's expected behavior by means of a sense of shame, a sense of "what will the others say if I fail?" (This is apparently what S.L.A. Marshall meant by "fear of failure.")

And last, but certainly not least, there is the leadership factor. The motivating power of the leader in combat is critically demonstrated in his ability to inspire his men to charge even in the face of heavy enemy fire, in spite of their fears, their fatigue or the horror of combat itself.

There is certainly nothing innovative in this nor is it particularly unique to the IDF. However, a careful observation of the training, organization and leadership characteristics of the Israeli military shows the various methods by which the IDF maximizes the effectiveness of these three components of combat motivation. The IDF's training methods place a great deal of emphasis on realistic training using live fire and combat-simulated conditions. These methods are designed to increase the soldiers' level of both competence and self-confidence to the point where he can use his instinct for self-preservation and respond effectively and virtually automatically to a variety of combat situations. Hence, the high level of soldiery competence of the IDF soldier becomes not only a necessary skill but also a powerful psychological defense mechanism under the stress of battle.

The personnel stability of the IDF's combat units greatly contributes to soldiers' bonding and unit cohesiveness. Whether it is the sense of commitment, or the fear of shame in the event of failure, the fact that the Israeli combat soldier has served with the same team from the beginning of his military service—and at times (in the reserve units) has been with them for many more years and through several wars—all make the unit a major factor in combat motivation. This closeness, which is enhanced by the compact nature of the State of Israel, has been clearly described by Rolbant in a section entitled "Deep Sense of Brotherhood":

> Men said that what worried them most during combat was what others would think of them, or what their friends and families would feel about them when they came home. The vague fear of shame, of possible ostracism or disapproval they might experience on getting home alive unscathed, featured prominently in the boys' answers about their behavior on the battlefield. Everybody knew where you were, in what outfit you served, what you did or failed to do, so that it was imperative to return with a clean bill of moral health, morality in this case being judged by standards of selflessness.[18] (Pp. 161–162)

In addition to training and personnel stability, which are important sources of enhancing combat motivation, it is also the IDF's leadership style, based on the follow-me dictum, which ensures that even under the heaviest fire soldiers will follow their commander, not just because he gave them the order but rather because he is leading them by his example.

And so, if the history of the Jewish people and the State of Israel provide the root sources of motivation of the Israeli soldier, then the IDF's training methods, its structure, and its leadership model provide the immediate and acute sources of motivation of the combat soldier.

Continuity

To conclude this section on the combat motivation of the Israeli soldier, it is necessary to place it in a time perspective. The Israeli public, at different times in the history of Israel, has expressed deep concerns regarding the readiness of Israeli youth to sacrifice themselves in future wars. Whether these concerns stem from a general sense of burnout from the ever-present threat of war or overconfidence in the military or a lack of public consensus, the question always resurfaces: will our next generation of soldiers still be as decisive and motivated as our previous ones?

Fortunately, the answer has always been positive, sometimes surprisingly so. Whenever called upon, Israeli youth, throughout the history of the State of Israel, have repeatedly demonstrated that they could meet, and even exceed, the hopeful expectations of their elders. The youth which were labeled in the 1960s as the "expresso generation" fought vigorously in the Six Day War; the youngsters of the 1970s called the "discotheque generation" are the ones who sacrificed themselves in the 1973 Yom Kippur War; and the last generation, the "punks," have again proven themselves in the War in Lebanon.

The usual explanation regarding this phenomenon—that of generation distrust and misjudgment—is not sufficient. Every generation of fathers discovers, to their surprise, that their children are capable of meeting the challenge. But the Israeli army has, in fact, suffered from morale and motivation problems at various periods during its history. In the early 1950s, for example, troop morale and combat motivation were extremely low, and commanders frequently refrained from engaging in combat operations. "Even the special night-fighting skills ... had apparently been lost and Israeli task forces frequently failed to find their objectives when engaged in night operations."[19] Again, during the War of Attrition, combat troops (especially in Army and Air Force line units) were morally and physically exhausted "often near the breaking point."[20]

The Lebanon War and occupation era (1982–85) certainly was another period of decline in the IDF's combat motivation.

Yet, each decline was always followed by a revival. In the Israeli case, this perseverance of fighting spirit is perhaps a reflection of the fact that combat motivation and its components are more prevalent than any of the temporal fluctuations inflicted upon Israeli youth and society. This is a very important point to remember by anyone who analyzes fluctuations in the fighting spirit of the IDF.

Components of the Fighting Spirit

Unit Morale

In the third week of the War in Lebanon the IDF's military psychologists administered a morale survey to the combat units positioned inside Lebanon.[21] A "very high" or "high" level of morale was reported by two-thirds of the surveyed soldiers—both regular and reserve soldiers who had actively participated in the incursion into Lebanon. Surveys of this sort are conducted regularly in the IDF, reflecting the deep awareness by the IDF's commanders of the importance of their unit morale. Commanders of combat units, in particular, spend a great deal of their time on, and give great attention to, increasing and maintaining the morale level of their troops. Indeed, morale is sometimes referred to as the "secret weapon" of the IDF.[22] Historically, this level of morale (60 to 70 percent reporting "high" or "very high" morale) has been found in all of the IDF's surveys since its early years.[23]

What is the meaning of morale for IDF units? What are the ingredients of unit morale? The answers to these questions have been provided by the published results of a field survey, the Golan Heights study, which was conducted by the IDF's Behavioral Sciences Department in May 1981.[24] This study involved a sample of 1,250 enlisted soldiers assigned to various combat units in the Golan Heights, while the units were on alert, preparing for a possible operation against PLO terrorists operating from Lebanon. The soldiers responded to an attitude questionnaire—the Combat Readiness Morale Questionnaire (CRMQ)—which includes questions dealing with morale, cohesion, and readiness. Two items in the CRMQ pertain directly to morale levels: the first item inquires about the soldier's personal level of morale, while the second refers to his perception of his company's morale. Figure 8.1 is a schematic presentation of the most significant correlations for the Golan Heights data among these two morale items and nine other items included in the CRMQ.

Two variables were found to be most strongly associated with both personal level of morale and the perceived company morale: these were

Figure 8.1
Correlations Between Morale and Other Variables

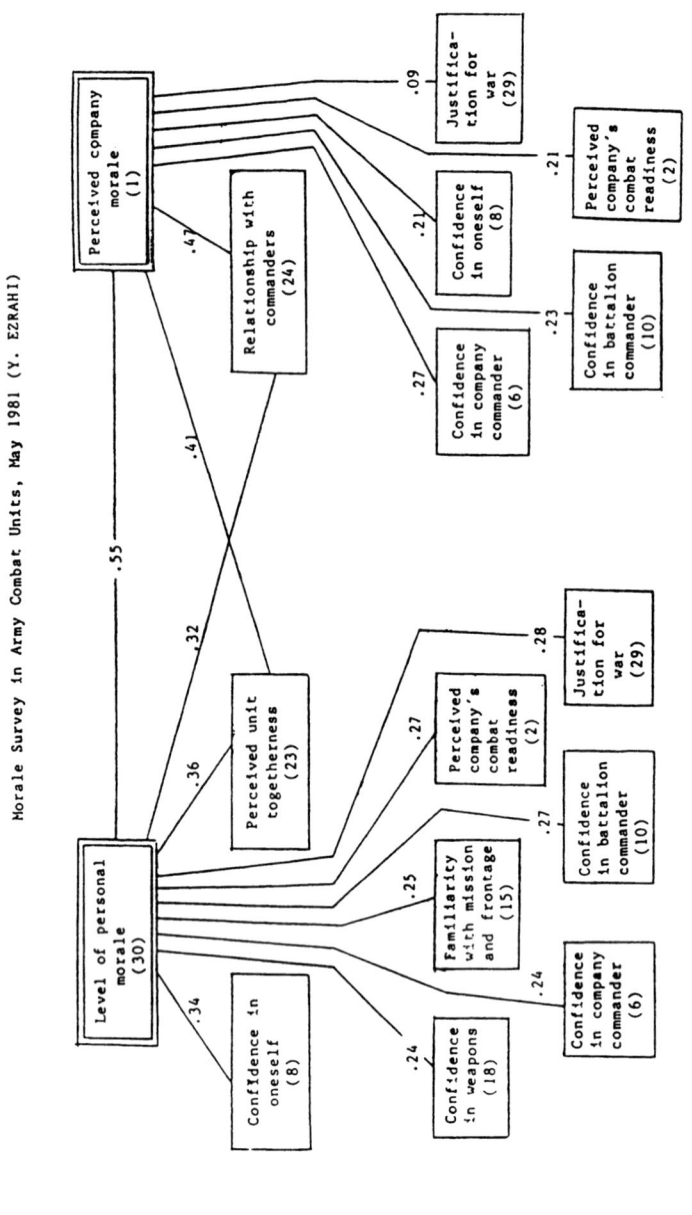

Morale Survey in Army Combat Units, May 1981 (Y. EZRAHI)

N=1250   All correlations are significant (p <.01)

Note: The numbers in parentheses refer to the CRMQ items.

perceived unit togetherness (a subjective evaluation of the unit level of cohesion) and relationship with commanders. Other variables which correlated positively with the personal level of morale were (in a descending order of correlations): the perceived justification for the anticipated War in Lebanon; the perceived combat readiness of the company; the level of confidence in the battalion commander; the familiarity with the unit's missions and frontage; the level of confidence in the company commander; and the level of confidence in one's weapons or weapon systems (i.e., tank, APC, artillery battery). Similarly, the perceived company morale variable correlated positively with confidence in company commander; confidence in battalion commander; confidence in one's self; and the perceived company's combat readiness.

It is interesting to note how the Israelis differ from comparable American troops responding to the same CRMQ items.[25] While the Israeli soldier derives his perceptions regarding unit morale and cohesion basically from the human components of the unit climate (i.e., cohesion, relationships, and confidence in commanders), the American soldier's perception of his unit morale is strongly associated with his appraisal of the technical and operational aspects of the unit.

Thus a number of factors are associated with the soldier's level of morale, the most central of which are unit cohesion, confidence in commanders, self-confidence and the perceived legitimacy of the expected military operations. Let us examine more carefully these correlates of morale.

Unit Cohesion

As has been detailed earlier, the organizational structure of the IDF insures highly cohesive units both in the regular forces and among the reserves. This level of cohesion is experienced in a sense of brotherhood, especially among members of front-line units, hence its extreme impact on unit morale and combat effectiveness.[26] However, the prevalence of cohesion in the IDF's units is not just a result of the military organization. Above all, it reflects the nature of educational and societal values in Israel. Israel is basically a group-oriented society, certainly not an individual-oriented one. Not only in the kibbutz, but also in cities and townships, life centers around groups in the community. The Israeli schools, for example, are structured around stable home rooms, with student cohorts remaining together throughout their years of school. Youngsters are socialized from their early years to develop strong friendships which will continue throughout their lives with a deep sense of commitment. Youth movements flourish in Israel, and, indeed, recreation activities are always carried out in groups.

On the battlefield, this gregarious nature of the Israelis becomes an implicit factor "which may be crucial in achieving superiority over their adversaries. In contrast, it has been noted that in combat situations, the Arab soldier, rather than becoming a team member and deriving confidence from it, instead becomes an isolated individual."[27]

This is the background from which the Israeli youngster comes when he joins the military. The army, by its very structure, reinforces the importance of the group. This explains why the cohesion items in the CRMQ were so closely associated in the Golan Heights study with morale level. Unit cohesion is the source of the soldiers' high morale particularly in combat situations. Furthermore, the bonds and familiarity among the men influence their capability to cope with the horror of battle. Some observations during the Yom Kippur War demonstrate this point. Since the 1973 war caught the Israelis by surprise, tanks from several of the IDF reserve Armor units were sent expeditiously to the front lines as soon as reservists arrived to man them, rather than waiting to form their usual long-standing combat teams. Hence, army tank crews found themselves fighting the battle without even knowing each other's names. When psychiatric casualty figures were subsequently compared, they were profoundly higher among such crews than among "organic" crews, fighting under identical circumstances.[28]

At the other end of the spectrum, the relationship of unit cohesiveness to heroism under fire has also been demonstrated in the Israeli military.[29] A study of combat heroism during the Yom Kippur War showed that more heroic acts were performed among cohesive and "intimate" units than among units with a lower level of cohesiveness. Thus, unit cohesion is not only associated with the unit's current level of morale but also may serve as a powerful preventive measure against psychiatric breakdown in battle and as a "generator" of heroic behavior among the unit's members.

The strong sense of cohesion and mutual support among Israeli troops has, at times, mistakenly led to an underestimation of the perseverance of the individual Israeli soldier. Thus, Dupuy, for example, has stated that while the Israelis' combat performance as a group was more effective than their adversaries, "individually they do not seem to have been braver, more intelligent, or more highly motivated" than the Arab soldiers.[30] Group cohesion is, indeed, an important element in Israeli combat effectiveness; however, individual combatants have also demonstrated their high effectiveness under the most extreme battle conditions. The best example has been given throughout the years by the Israeli Air Force pilots in their combat performance. While training and technology may account somewhat for their unequivocal effectiveness, it is predominantly their fighting spirit which made them by far superior to their Arab counterparts in the hundreds of one-on-one "dog fights" which have occurred in recent years. On the ground, too, there have been countless instances throughout the different wars where individuals, who found themselves separated from their own units, nonetheless performed heroic acts.[31]

The observed discrepancies between Israeli and Arab soldiers are also reflected in the Israeli approach concerning individuals in combat. For example, it is known that the Arabs follow the Soviet doctrine of having their infantrymen dig two-man foxholes.[32] The Israelis, on the other hand, on those rare occasions when they dig foxholes, opt for individual ones (though always with direct eye contact between soldiers). This is based on the Israeli assumption that a single soldier is quite effective as an individual fighter.

Confidence in Commanders

The critical role of the Israeli field commanders leading their troops to combat has been discussed already (see Chapter 7). The impact of this factor (confidence in senior commanders and confidence in immediate commanders, combined) on the Israeli soldiers' level of morale was also clearly demonstrated in the previously mentioned Golan Heights study. As shown in Figure 8.1, both individual level of morale and the perceived unit's morale were significantly correlated with the degree of confidence in the battalion commanding officer and in the company commanding officer. However, an even higher correlation was found between self and unit's levels of morale and the perceived relationships with the commander. Thus, morale in the IDF combat units is strongly related to both the troops' confidence in, and relationships with, their commanders.

Another Israeli study[33] has further shown that the soldiers' trust in their commanders depends on the commander's proficiency, his credibility as a source of information and the amount of care and attention that he pays to his men.

The Golan Heights study, however, revealed two different factors for the confidence-in-commanders issue. It distinguished between confidence in senior commanders (which appears as the leading factor, accounting for 19.2 percent of the common variance) and confidence in immediate commanders (the fifth factor, accounting for 4.3 percent of the variance). This finding reveals yet another characteristic of the nature of the relationships between Israeli troops and their leaders. Reviews of Israeli morale surveys during both the 1973 Arab-Israeli War and the 1982 Lebanon incursion[34] showed marked differences of soldiers' levels of confidence in their officers at various command levels, from platoon to division. While assessments before combat (see Figure 8.2) showed an almost linear increase of confidence of troops in their commanders with increasing levels of command (i.e., relatively lowest at the platoon

Figure 8.2
Level of Confidence in Commanders

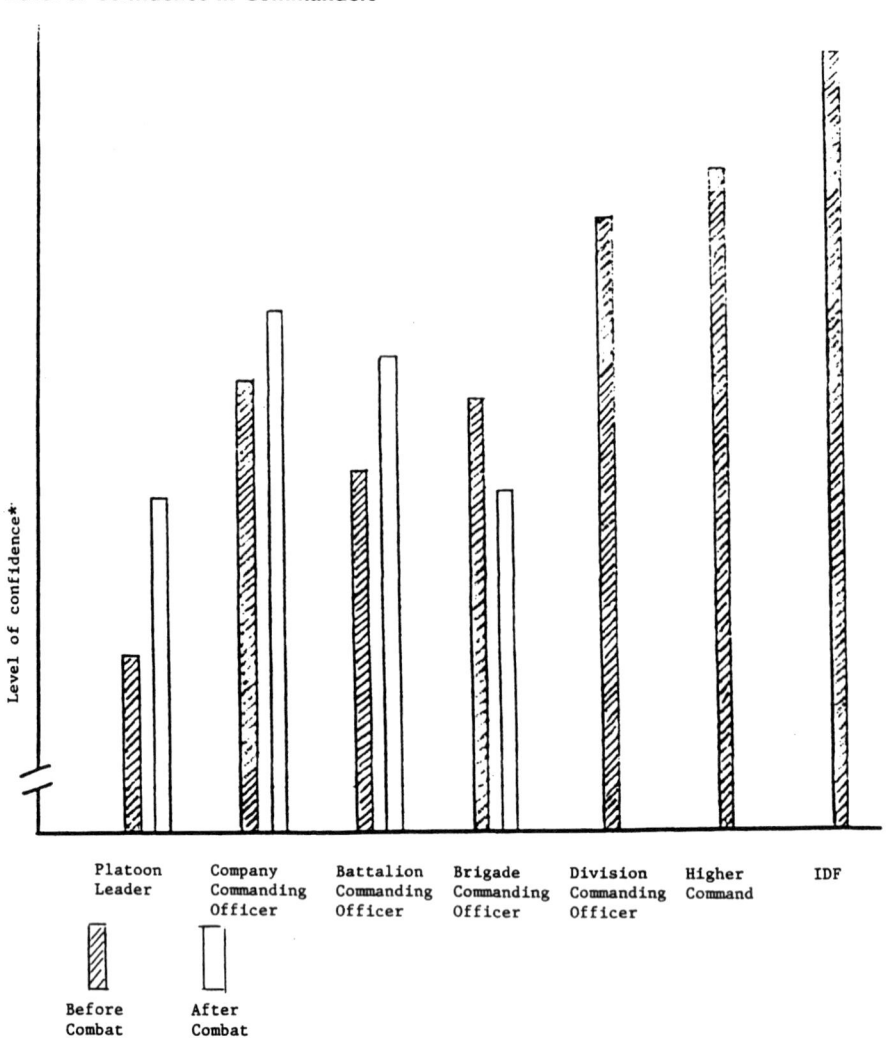

| | Platoon Leader | Company Commanding Officer | Battalion Commanding Officer | Brigade Commanding Officer | Division Commanding Officer | Higher Command | IDF |

Before Combat

After Combat

*Note: The actual figures are classified

leader and highest at the division and higher command levels), after combat the trend was generally reversed, with increasing levels of confidence shown now in the more immediate commanders (platoon, company, and battalion) and relatively lower confidence at more remote levels of command (e.g., brigade level). (After-combat confidence levels for higher echelons are, unfortunately, unavailable.) This difference may be accounted for by postulating that prior to battle the soldier perceives his welfare and success as being dependent mainly on higher command plans and decisions, but in actual combat he finds that his very survival depends mainly on the actions of his more immediate leaders. The Golan Heights findings are a typical example of troops' attitudes in a prewar situation, when ambiguity is maximum and much trust is placed in high-level commanders.

Confidence in Oneself, Team and Weapons

Various Israeli observations, covering a span of about thirty years and five wars, clearly (though, regretfully, not empirically), reveal a gradually increasing effect of the soldier's trust in the weapon he uses—whether it be his personal weapon or his crew's—on his self-confidence and, subsequently, on his morale level and sense of well-being as a combatant. Apparently, the augmentation of this factor is influenced by the increasing sophistication of the weapons systems and other related modern auxiliaries of the war machine. It is, in any case, a significant component in troops' morale, as the Golan Heights study has shown.

These three aspects are indeed interrelated: the soldier's self-evaluation and self-confidence as a professional combatant, his confidence in his team (whether a tank crew, an Infantry fire-team, a gunboat crew, or an aviator wing), and his confidence in his weapon system. On the modern battlefield one never fights alone, nor does one fight bare-handed. For the Israeli soldier, his combat team, his weapon, and his sense of competence may frequently be the determinants of his own survival on the battlefield. The higher his confidence in these factors, the higher his morale, hence his combat readiness.

It is interesting to note (from Figure 8.1) that confidence in one's self and the unit's cohesiveness reveal the two highest correlations with the individual's level of morale. This finding is in accordance with a recent, and widely accepted, definition of "individual morale."[35] It thus provides empirical support for the view that individual morale in military units is characterized by "a sense of well-being based on confidence in the self and in primary groups."[36] (P. 6)

Legitimacy of War

It is a general rule, known in social and organizational psychology, that the perceived legitimacy of goals affects the group's efforts to achieve them. As long as the unit's goals are accepted as legitimate, the hardships and cost are minimized, the necessity is of prime importance, and the readiness for sacrifice is enhanced. Yet, the legitimacy of any war is not always apparent, and, furthermore, it is not always free of value judgments and moral considerations.[37]

The Israeli soldiers who were abruptly mobilized and thrown into dreadful battles in the middle of Yom Kippur in 1973 had no doubts about the legitimacy of the war for which they were called up. Many of those soldiers who were fighting then in the Golan Heights against the flood of Syrian tanks needed only to look over their shoulders in order to see their homes and remind themselves that they were fighting for their very survival. But when circumstances are different, as in the case of the 1982 War in Lebanon—when the cause of war is not a sudden attack and the course of war carries you far away from your country's borders and from your own home, when the justification of such a war becomes questionable—then the issue of the perceived legitimacy of that war by the soldier becomes a crucial factor concerning morale and combat readiness. The positive correlation ($r = .28$) between the IDF soldiers' morale during their alert calls in the Golan Heights in the spring of 1981 and their perception regarding the justification of the pending incursion into Lebanon could have served as an early indication of the serious legitimacy problems that indeed arose later in the Lebanon War.

The legitimacy item in the Combat Readiness Morale Questionnaire correlated strongly with soldiers' levels of confidence in their commanders, especially in the high echelons. One may assume, then, that the extent to which the perceived legitimacy of a military operation will affect the morale of its operators is mediated by the level of their leaders' trustworthiness. This has indeed been found in the Israeli case. Several morale surveys (using questionnaires similar to the CRMQ) that have been conducted among the Israeli troops in Lebanon immediately after the first cease-fire between the fighting parties have shown only sparse indications of decline in units' morale, despite the increasing debates and objections among both civilians and soldiers against further deployment of Israeli forces in Lebanon.

The explanation for this discrepancy was found within the arena earlier labeled confidence in commanders. The units which preserved high morale, notwithstanding the increasing erosion in the legitimacy question, were the ones which also showed high and stable confidence in their immediate and senior commands. Soldiers in such units would trust their commanders to assign them their immediate missions, without allowing their doubts about the general goals of the war to affect their morale. Hence, when the order comes from the commander to move, these soldiers will accept his order as a legitimate one only because they have full confidence in that commander. Thus their high level of morale had not been weakened.

One should not confuse this complete trust in commanders with total obedience. The issue here is not that of blind obedience,[38] for in a case where a commander does not have the full trust and confidence of his soldiers, they will, indeed, start to question his orders. In the case of blind obedience, the orders could come from someone remote and abstract and still be followed without question. In our case the doubts exist and the ambivalence and conflict are there, too. But as long as the direct commander is trusted, the doubts and conflicts are resolvable.

Operational Behavior in Combat: Combat Decisiveness

Let us turn now from motivational and attitudinal surveys to the actual behavior of Israeli troops in combat. How do they fight? How is the IDF's fighting spirit translated onto the battlefield? What are the distinguishing characteristics of the Israeli combatant as an individual and within his group?

From this complex social and historical background, including the socialization of Israeli youth, emerges the actual behavior of the Israeli combat soldier. Perhaps more than anything else, it is the aggressiveness, "hawkishness," combativeness—in short, the combat decisiveness—of the Israeli soldier that best characterizes his operational behavior in combat.

This decisiveness is apparent even before the first combat engagement. When facing the enemy, the Israeli military tries to deliver the first shot rather than be on the receiving end of it. At the unit level, with the first indication of a pending operation, the various units involved will begin vying for selection as the unit to carry out the operation. Participating in and proving oneself during a combat operation is the ultimate goal of every combat soldier and of every commander for his unit.

During the Yom Kippur War, there were innumerable examples of Israeli commanders directly initiating combat missions, sometimes bypassing the chain of command, in order to react immediately and most forcefully to the enemy thrust into Israel. The Israeli Navy, for example, persistently operated in a very aggressive manner during these weeks. In several self-initiated raids against both the Syrian and Egyptian navies, the Israeli Navy sank eight Syrian and ten Egyptian vessels without any Israeli vessel even taking a hit.[39] The "ferocity, daring and dash" of the Israeli attacks overwhelmed the Syrian and Egyptian navies, causing them to retire all their vessels to their own harbors in order to take shelter against the Israeli attacks behind breakwaters and beside merchant ships in these harbors. This, however, did not stop the Israeli Navy. IDF naval commando units were activated to perform underwater raids into the protected water of the Egyptian harbors, causing additional losses to the enemy navy.

The same decisiveness characterized the Israeli Air Force in the Yom Kippur War. Herzog, in his book, *The War of Atonement*, offered this description:

The Israeli Air Force fought a desperate battle, flying into the teeth of one of the most concentrated missile systems in the world. . . . In the first phase of the fighting—the holding phase—the Israeli Air Force was unable to attack as planned and was obliged to throw caution to the winds and give close support (a good proportion of the sorties made were in close support of ground forces), without dealing adequately with the missile threat and achieving complete air superiority. Consequently losses were comparatively heavy. . . . Despite the losses sustained, the Israeli Air Force persevered in its attack and at no point relented.[40] (Pp. 256; 258–259)

There is not adequate space to delineate all the available examples of this decisive characteristic as it was also exhibited by the ground forces, especially the Infantry and Armor during the battles of the Yom Kippur War. One example, however, of the extreme determination of the Israeli ground forces in that war can be drawn from the comparison of the Syrian and Israeli forces in the northern front. The balance of forces in the Golan Heights during the first twenty-four hours of the war were as follows: a combined force of five Syrian divisions with approximately 1,500 Syrian tanks had attacked roughly 177 Israeli tanks[41] from two Israeli brigades, the Barak and the Seventh. During the first night of combat the Barak brigade fought with 60 tanks against 600 Syrian tanks.[42] Their fighting was so desperate that by noon of the following day this entire Israeli brigade was virtually decimated: 90 percent of its commanders were wounded or dead; only one of the original deputy commanders and two platoon commanders remained functional. And yet, on the fifth day of this battle, it was the remnants of the Barak brigade who led the Israeli counterattack on the Syrians, stopping only twenty-five miles short of Damascus. Likewise, the Seventh brigade had 40 tanks[43] with which to engage 500 Syrian tanks. On the morning of the fourth day of fighting, this brigade was left with only 7 functional tanks.[44] However, the Seventh brigade had managed to block the Syrian attack and had destroyed more than 260 Syrian tanks in the process.[45]

Similar combat situations occurred, as well, on the southern frontier in the Sinai. Many of them have also been documented by various military observers.[46] All of these combat instances (from both the northern and southern fronts) clearly portray the determined and resolute behavior which characterizes both the troops and their leaders on the battlefield.

This extreme combat decisiveness of the IDF has been met more than once with severe criticism: such battles as Ammunition Hill in Jerusalem during the Six Day War, the battle in the city of Suez during the Yom Kippur War, and the battle of the Bofour Castle during the Lebanon War, to mention just a few, have been post facto assessed by many authorities, including Israeli military experts, as being non-vital and their casualties as inexcusable. The counterargument for all of these cases, however, centers around the very essence of combat decisiveness. A nation under siege cannot expect to maintain its fighting spirit without paying a heavy price.

Combat support units, too, have their share of combat decisiveness. These individuals, like their combat counterparts, have also emerged during wartime as heroes. During the Yom Kippur battles, for example, 150 out of a total of 250 damaged Israeli tanks were repaired and returned to the ongoing battles within a few days.[47] These repairs were actually performed in the midst of the fighting by the ordnance crews who, under fire, searched out the damaged tanks and either towed them away for repair or, if possible, repaired them on the spot.

In a similar vein, Air Force ground crews have also exhibited exemplary performance of duty. According to published figures, the Israeli Air Force, during the Yom Kippur War, launched four times as many sorties as in the 1967 Six Day War. This frequently involved four or five or even six sorties a day for an individual pilot. This strenuous task was given not only to the pilots but the ground crews as well. Again, it was this decisiveness, the determined resolution of the Israeli troops—both combatants and non-combatants alike—that made these tasks possible.

The reader may attribute a great deal of this behavior during the Yom Kippur War to the concept of "no alternative" which so characterized this particular war. In fact, one will find this argument in the early part of this chapter. However, combat decisiveness also characterized the more recent War in Lebanon, a war which was fought for the first time without this sense of "no alternative." This time, again, there were commanders who took the initiative, sometimes by manipulation, to ensure that their units were actively engaged on the battlefield.[48] This time, too, there were battles in which soldiers fought decisively to their death. This was seen in all the different branches of the IDF.

To minimize Lebanese civilian casualties and to reduce unnecessary Israeli military casualties, the IDF, for the first time, adopted in the Lebanon War, a policy of moderating both the nature and the pace of assaults. This policy change involved sometimes using indirect as opposed to direct assaults. While such an approach undoubtedly prevented many casualties for both sides, it evoked considerable disapproval from officers in the field.

This disapproval increased during the long months of the IDF's occupation of Lebanon when it was forced to adopt a more passive and defensive posture. Many concerned IDF officers reacted with alarm to the probable psychological detriment of this policy on the fighting spirit of the IDF. More than anything else, these concerns reflected not so much what was already damaged but rather what is perceived as so critical for the IDF.

Conclusion

The operational behavior of the Israeli combat soldier, whether a regular or a reservist, is a reflection of the behavior of the typical Israeli citizen. The latter, though generally gregarious, seldom chooses to be an acquiescent follower. In any case, the typical Israeli does not like to be driven. In contrast to a psychological analysis of the Russian soldier which concluded that "the Soviet [military] system is a 'driven' system, not a self-motivated one,"[49] the exact opposite can be said of the Israeli soldier.

The typical Israeli citizen is often seen as arrogant, aggressive and determined. When this same citizen dons a uniform, these characteristics translate into military combat decisiveness. The IDF, by its very structure, leadership style, realistic training and exacting performance standards, transforms the basic Israeli nature into a highly motivated, quite aggressive, yet distinctly moral, effective fighting machine.

This effectiveness of the Israeli military has been systematically studied by international experts. Colonel Trevor Dupuy, for example in his analyses of the Arab-Israeli wars between 1947 and 1974,[50] quantified Israeli military superiority as being two to three times greater than its main Arab adversaries.

Accurately enough, Dupuy has presented this comparison under the title "The Human Element in War." The Israeli advantage in all its wars was never in number of units or quantity of weapons. This advantage is solely attributed to the human element in combat—the troops, their leaders and their fighting spirit—that's where the Israeli soldier proves his superiority.

Notes

1. Luttwak, E., & Horowitz, D. (1975). *The Israeli army.* London: Allen Lane, p. 117.
2. van Creveld, M. (1982) *Fighting power:* Westport, CT: Greenwood Press.

3. This has been done quite frequently including, for example, during the 1982 Lebanon incursion. See, for example, Gabriel, R. A. *Operation peace for Galilee*. New York: Hill and Wang.

4. Nyrop, R. F. (Ed.). (1979). *Israel: A country study*. Washington, DC: American University Press, p. 257.

5. Keegan, J. (Ed.). (1979). *World armies*. London: McMillan Press.

6. Ibid., p. 366.

7. Quoted in Glick, E. B. (1974). *Between Israel and death*. Harrisburg, PA: Stackpole Books, pp. 24–25.

8. Quoted in Gavron, D. (1984). *Israel after Begin*. Boston: Houghton Mifflin Company, p. 46.

9. Kellett, A. (1982). *Combat motivation*. Boston: Kluwer Nijhoff Publishing, pp. 190–193.

10. Shapira, A. (Ed.). (1970). *The seventh day: Soldiers talk about the Six Day War*. New York: Charles Scribner's Sons.

11. Rolbant, S. (1970). *The Israeli soldier: Profile of an army*. New York: Thomas Yoseloff Publishing.

12. In the July 1984 elections in Israel, Rabbi Meir Kahane campaigned calling for the forcible eviction of all Arabs from Israel. While he was elected with the vote of less than 2 percent of the total population, when the soldiers' vote was tallied, he received almost 4 percent of their total votes. Though still negligible, this figure of 4 percent alarmed both the civilian and IDF educational systems.

13. Lev, I. (1984). *First night without mummy*. Rechovot, Israel: Adar Publishers.

14. Marshall, S.L.A. (1957, April). Combat leadership. In *Symposium on Preventive and Social Psychiatry*. Sponsored jointly by the Walter Reed Army Institute of Research, Walter Reed Army Medical Center and the National Research Council.

15. Montgomery, V. (1946). *Morale in battle: Analysis*. Germany: British Army of the Rhine.

16. This is true also with regard to American soldiers. In *The American Soldier*, a study of American enlisted men during World War II, it was found that only 5 percent reported fighting for idealistic reasons. See Stouffer, S. A., DeVinney, L. C., Star, S. A., & Williams, R. M. (1949). *The American soldier, volume II*. Princeton, NJ: Princeton University Press, p. 109.

17. For an excellent review on this issue, with a special reference to the Israeli military, see Greenbaum, C. W. (1979). The small group under the gun. *Journal of Applied Behavioral Science*, 15(3), 392–405.

18. Rolbant, *The Israeli soldier*, pp. 161–162.

19. Luttwak & Horowitz, *The Israeli army*, p. 107.

20. Ibid., p. 332.

21. Kalay, E. (1982, July). *Confidence in commanders* (Research Report). Department of Behavioral Sciences, IDF, Israel. Figures from this report were published in *Skira Hodsheet*. (1983, February–March), 30(2–3), 82.

22. Gal, R. (1983, January). *Unit morale: The secret weapon of the Israeli Defence Forces*. Presented as a major address in the Third International Conference on Psychological Stress and Adjustment in Time of War and Peace, Tel-Aviv.

23. Ibid. Such a level of morale (60 to 70 percent) can be frequently found only among elite units of most Western forces. The usual expected level among regular combat units is in the area of 40 to 50 percent. Figures averaging at the

40 to 50 percent level were reported at the Second Symposium on Motivation and Morale in NATO Forces (1984, May), Brussels, Belgium.

24. The Golan Heights study was conducted and reported by Ezrahi, Y. (1982). *Morale survey in combat units: Golan Heights, 1982* (Research Report). The Department of Behavioral Sciences, IDF, Israel. Subsequent papers and presentations have been based on Ezrahi's report. See, for example, Gal, R. (in press). Unit morale. *Journal of Military Psychology*.

25. The CRMQ was translated into English and administered to several combat units in the U.S. Army. Basically, similar factors emerged from the American samples although there were some differences in the order and inner structure of these factors. These comparative analyses have been reported by Gal, R. & Manning, F. G. (1984). *Correlates of unit cohesion and morale in the U.S. and Israeli armies*. Paper presented at the Annual Convention of the American Psychological Association, Toronto.

26. Greenbaum, C. W., The small group under the gun.

27. Harkabi, Y. (1967, Fall). Basic factors in the Arab collapse. *Orbis*, a Quarterly Journal of World Affairs.

28. Steiner, M., & Neumann, M. (1978). Traumatic neurosis and social support in the Yom Kippur War returnees. *Military Medicine, 143*(12), 866–868.

29. Gal, R. (1983). Courage under stress. In S. Breznitz (Ed.), *Stress in Israel*. New York: Van Nostrand Reinhold.

30. Dupuy, T. N. (1984). *Elusive victory: The Arab-Israeli wars, 1947–1974*. Fairfax, VA: HERO Books, p. 335.

31. Chaim Herzog, in his account of the Yom Kippur War (1975), *The war of atonement: October 1973* (Boston: Little, Brown and Company), has described several such incidents, for example "Force Zwicka" and the "Tiger Force," to mention just two of many.

32. Donnelly, C. (1982). The soviet attitude to stress in battle. *Journal of the Royal Army Medical Corps, 128*, 72–78.

33. Kalay, E. *Confidence in commanders*.

34. The following data, as well as the data on which Figure 8.2 is based were taken from two studies conducted by the IDF's Department of Behavioral Sciences: Ezrahi, Y. Morale survey in combat units; Ezrahi, Y. (1982, August). *"Operation Peace for Galilee" operation—Main results from the fighting units* (Research Report). Department of Behavioral Sciences, IDF, Israel.

35. Ingraham, L. H., & Manning, F. J. (1981). Cohesion: Who needs it, what is it, and how do we get it to them? *Military Review, 61*(6), 2–12. Ingraham and Manning identify three different concepts which refer to the different levels (individual, small group and large group) of analyses of military groups. "Individual morale" is defined as "a psychological state of mind characterized by a sense of well-being based on confidence in the self and in primary groups." "Cohesion" is defined as "feelings of belonging, of solidarity with a specifiable set of others who constitute "we" as opposed to "them." And, they define "esprit" as "characterized by pride in group membership and by unit of purpose and devotion to the cause."

36. Ibid.

37. Gal, R. (in press). Commitment and obedience in the military. *Armed Forces and Society*.

38. Milgram, S. (1965). Some conditions of obedience and disobedience to authority. *Human Relations, 18*, 57–75.
39. Herzog, *The war of atonement*, pp. 264–266.
40. Ibid.
41. This is according to Herzog's numbers; Dupuy's assessment indicates approximately 200 Israeli tanks: some 105 with the Seventh brigade and nearly 90 with the Barak brigade. See Dupuy, *Elusive victory*.
42. Ibid. Dupuy still refers to the 90 tanks of the Barak brigade defending along a front of 40 kilometers.
43. Herzog, *The war of atonement*; less than 60 according to Dupuy.
44. Herzog, *The war of atonement*, p. 113.
45. Herzog, *The war of atonement*. A firsthand account of the battle of the Seventh brigade is by Avigdor Kahalani, one of the brigade's commanders. Kahalani, A. (1984). *The heights of courage*. Westport, CT: Greenwood Press.
46. Dupuy, *Elusive victory*; Herzog, *The war of atonement*.
47. Herzog, *The war of atonement*, p. 145. In fact, Herzog reports that during the Golan Heights battle, virtually every Israeli tank suffered some damage at least once.
48. Schiff, Z., & Ya'ari, E. (1984). *Israel's Lebanon war* (Translated from the Hebrew by Ina Friedman). New York: Simon and Schuster. See also Gabriel, *Operation peace for Galilee*.
49. Donnelly, The Soviet attitude to stress in battle, p. 78.
50. Dupuy, *Elusive victory*.

9

Senior Leadership

Perhaps more than any other aspect of the human side of the Israeli Defence Forces, the character of the senior leadership corps has undergone major changes in the period since the Yom Kippur War. The young men who served as battalion or brigade commanders in the early years of the IDF were not professional soldiers who regarded their service as a military career but rather were elite leaders who responded to patriotic duty. This founding generation has gradually disappeared. During the Six Day War many of the generals were still from this generation of Independence War soldiers. By the time the Yom Kippur War broke out in 1973, only a few of them remained. In the late seventies and early eighties virtually none remained in the leadership corps. From the Chief of Staff through the entire general officer corps, a new generation of military professionals has emerged from within the Israeli military.

The continual involvement of the IDF in frequent wars or military operations throughout its four decades of independence has generated a unique breed of new, senior commanders. They have, without exception, a rich array of combat experience acquired during three or four wars and innumerable combat operations. The IDF places great emphasis on combat experience. This is exemplified by the IDF's formal policy of promoting everyone one rank after each war.[1] Indeed, combat experience is the most important criterion for both future promotions and assignments. The richer the record of combat command, the more likely the promotion or assignment to a desired position.

The combination of frequent wars and the policy of accelerated promotion after each war has served to compress the length of the Israeli military career, resulting in the IDF's senior officer corps being one of the youngest in the world. Hence the 1984 General Staff of the IDF is composed primarily of men who were privates (or not yet drafted) during the Sinai campaign of 1956, were company commanders during the Six Day War of 1967 and brigade commanders in the 1973 Yom Kippur War (see Table 9.1).

While these senior officers bring with them vast combat experience, many of them lack both a broad academic background and professional management training. In fact, almost by definition, those officers involved in combat engagements with their accompanying demands and promotions are the ones who have few, if any, opportunities to pursue educational or professional training. The result: a senior leadership corps with incomparable combat experience, but suffering from "tunnel vision" in regard to the broader intellectual aspects of life.

The IDF, however, is not unaware of this shortcoming. In recent years several attempts have been made to correct this situation. In the early 1980s a promotion policy was adopted by the General Staff which required a university degree as a prerequisite for promotion to the rank of colonel. However, implementing such a decision is not easy in an army continually involved in fighting and consistently experiencing officer shortages. The 1982 Lebanon War again postponed rectifying this problem.

In this chapter, portrayal of the Israeli senior leadership corps will focus on career progression and motivation characteristics of behavior and leadership styles and the dilemmas facing the corps.

Career Progression

In Chapter 7 we discussed Israeli officers up to the point of completing Poum (Command and Staff School). As he enters into the ranks of lieutenant colonels, the IDF begins to view him as a senior officer. His promotions and assignments are no longer determined by his division but rather are made at the corps and General Staff level. In the ground forces he will serve first as a battalion commander, then as a deputy brigade commander or as a staff officer at the division headquarters. If in the Navy or Air Force, he will likewise command an independent unit, whether a vessel, a small base or, if in the Air Force, a squadron. Since in most cases he has not yet completed his academic studies (except for the short university exposure in Poum), officers are encouraged, at this point, to attend universities to pursue academic studies of their own choosing. While such an academic experience is of value in the long run, in the short run it may appear to be disadvantageous. This is because while he is in school, his contemporaries are acquiring the assignments and experiences which are so essential in the IDF. At this stage, the number of available combat commands for each rank becomes smaller and smaller. However, the pool of qualified officers also shrinks with each rank because of the rigorous selection process and the never-

Table 9.1
The 1984 IDF General Staff Members

General Staff Position/Name	Date of birth	Drafted (date)	Sinai Campaign (1956)	Six Day War (1967)	Yom Kippur War (1973)	Lebanon War (1982)	Joined G.S./Age
Chief of Staff/ Moshe Levi	1936	1954	Battalion Operation Officer	Staff Officer/ Paratrooper	Chief of Staff, Central Command	Deputy Chief of Staff	1977/ 41
Depurty C of S & Operations Chief/ David Ivri	1934	1952	Combat Pilot	Commander, Flight School	Deputy Chief of the Air Force	Civilian	1977/ 43
Northern Command/ Ori Or	1939	1957	------	Company Commander	Brigade Commander	Commander, Central Command	1981/ 42
Central Command/ Amnon Shahak	1944	1962	------	Company Commander	Deputy Brigade Commander	Territorial Commander, Beirut	1983/ 39
Southern Command/ Moshe Bar-Kochba	1930	1947	Company Commander	Brigade Commander	Deputy Division Commander	Chief Armor Corps	1979/ 49

Commander Air Force/ Amos Lapidot	1934	1953	Combat Pilot	Squadron Commander	Wing Commander	Chief, "Lavie" Project	1983/ 49
Commander Navy/ Ze'ev Almog	1935	1952	Frogman	Flotilla Commander	Red Sea Front Commander	Chief, Israeli Navy	1979/ 44
Commander Ground Forces/ Dan Shomron	1937	1956	Paratrooper	Company Commander	Brigade Commander	General Staff Position	1978/ 41
Chief, Intelligence/ Ehud Barak	1942	1959	------	Company Commander	Battalion Commander	Chief, Planning Division	1982/ 40
Chief, Planning/ Menachem Einann	1939	1957	------	Company Commander	Chief of Staff, Northern Command	Division Commander	1982/ 43
Chief, Logistics/ Haimm Erez	1935	1954	Platoon Commander	Battalion Commander	Brigade Commander	Commander, Southern Command	1982/ 47
Chief, Personnel/ Amos Yaron	1940	1957	------	Brigade Chief of Staff	Deputy Brigade Commander	Chief, Infantry & Paratroopers	1983/ 43
Chief, Training/ Yosi Peled	1941	1960	------	Company Commander	Brigade Commander	Commander, "Yosi" Force	1981/ 40
Assistant to Operations Chief/ Uri Saguie	1943	1961	------	Company Commander	Battalion Commander	Head, Operation Division, GS	1983/ 40

ending casualties. Thus the number of qualified officers is as limited as the available slots.

A critical point is reached when a small group of officers are carefully selected as brigade commander candidates and sent to a brigade commander's course. Frequently, these commanders already know what assignments and rank they will hold—removing enormous career pressures—enabling them to devote their time fully to the study of the arts of war at the brigade level.[2]

From this point on (rank of colonel), assignments and promotions are determined by a central board, chaired by the Chief of Staff or his deputy. This group of colonels is so small and well known that decisions made at that echelon are on a personal basis and in a centralized form.

An analysis of the factors bearing on these selections would convey a great deal of insight into the IDF's personnel policies. An officer who has served most of his career in a given brigade will eventually be assigned to be that brigade's commander. The one who fought one or more wars in a specific frontier will be assigned to be the commander of that frontier instead of any other. A pilot who was "brought up" in a given base will one day return as that base commander, etc. This aspect of identification with a certain framework (a unit, region or base) is a central component in the decision-making process concerning senior assignments. Thus, some aspects of regimental character exist within the IDF, though not formally.

Toward the end of their thirties, the most talented and combat experienced of these officers may join the exclusive family of IDF generals. Beginning as brigadier generals these officers are surprisingly young, highly ambitious and very professional. Above all, they bring to this rank their extensive combat experience. With fewer than twenty years of military service, each one of them has had numerous combat involvements and battlefield command experience. This cohort of commanders has served together at various stages of their careers, and they know each other very well, as they likewise know well their superiors and their subordinate officers. Typically, these careers will be characterized by a relatively small number of assignments (sometimes fewer than ten). Moreover, they have spent almost no time in staff or "professional development" schools and only minimal time in mandatory "staff tours" at various headquarters. Instead they served with their units in combat or combat support roles most of the time, taking time off only to be sent to schools which are directly related to the combat command role.[3]

The highest military school in the IDF is the National Defence College (in Hebrew "Michlala Lebitachon Leumi"—with the acronym "Mabal"), a one-year intensive course of military, strategic, and management-related subjects. Students are brigadier generals or promotable colonels. Some of the students, however, are civilians: senior civil servants in

Senior Leadership   171

various government positions frequently associated with defense concerns. This mixture enables the two parties to acquire a certain amount of familiarity and understanding between each other. Though the academic quality of Mabal is excellent, this one year of study cannot be considered equivalent to regular university work. For many senior officers, however, this is the only "equivalent" coursework they receive.

Throughout the years, a few of the IDF's senior officers have been sent to various staff colleges abroad, mostly in France, Great Britain and the United States. These select few are sent to broaden their military knowledge base beyond that available in Israel. While these IDF students usually graduate near the top of these classes, they carefully maintain their military integrity, adhering to their own Israeli combat training and experience.

> Barbara Tuchman, in her perceptive portrayal, "Israel's Swift Sword," has also noted this trait of the Israeli senior officers:
> "These officers have in common a self-assurance so confident that it can afford to be quiet, if not exactly modest. There is no reluctance whatever to acknowledge, in the most charming and friendly way, that 'we're *good*.' . . . One theme they notably and unanimously maintain is refusal to acknowledge any debt to foreign methods or doctrines and insistence on their independent development. There are no foreign experts or advisers in the IDF."[4] (P. 178)

One of the typical results of this career progression is the extreme youth of the senior officer corps. The dynamic nature of the IDF, the accelerated promotions resulting from frequent wars, the mentality which rewards improvisation over traditional methods, combat experience over age—all of these combine to result in quality officers progressing rapidly through the ranks. No less important is the casualty factor: during each war the IDF loses a significant portion of its command staff.[5] These officers must be replaced as quickly as possible. Since the replacement pool is quite limited, those who only yesterday were company commanders may now find themselves battalion commanders, already on their way to higher ranks.

> An indication of the youth of the IDF's senior officers is found in the age (upon entering office) of Israel's number one senior officer, the Chief of Staff. In the last two decades Israeli Chiefs of Staff have been appointed when they were in their forties. Prior to the Six Day War, however, they were even younger (see Table 9.2).

Table 9.2
Israeli Chiefs of Staff: 1948 to 1983

Chiefs of Staff	Period in office	Age upon entering office
Ya'akov Dori	1948-49	49
Yigael Yadin	1949-52	32
Mordechai Makleff	1952-53	32
Moshe Dayan	1953-58	38
Haim Laskov	1958-60	39
Zvi Zur	1960-63	37
Yitzak Rabin	1963-67	40
Haim Bar-Lev	1968-71	44
David Elazar	1972-74	47
Mordechai Gur	1974-78	44
Rafael Eytan	1978-83	49
Moshe Levi	1983-	47

In the contemporary IDF, it is common to find battalion commanders between the ages of twenty-seven and twenty-nine, and division commanders (with the rank of brigadier general) at the age of thirty-five. And in the exclusive family of the General Staff, the average age is only forty-five.

There have never been any reservations, on the part of the Israeli public, about the fact that the IDF is led by such young men. The Israelis have full confidence in these military leaders who have repeatedly proven themselves capable of preserving Israel's security. The reservations expressed by the public regarding the IDF (for example, after the Yom Kippur War) have not focused on age. Within the military, however, one may occasionally hear complaints regarding the contemporary commanders being "just kids." However, the complaining generals usually forget that they themselves were in the same position at the same age, or perhaps even younger.

One area in which reservations do surface is when one such young general ends his career and retires from the military. On several occasions during the history of the IDF, those generals who were in competition for the position of Chief of Staff, but were not selected, chose to retire. In most of these cases many Israeli citizens felt this was a waste of valuable experience and leadership. The waste, however, is not that severe. First, these generals will still have major command positions in the event of war since they are now in the reserves. Second, the civilian job market will gain from these early retirements. Typically these retired generals are recruited by various governmental, industrial or political organizations even before they take off their uniforms. While their success in these civilian organizations reflects their managerial skills which they have developed throughout their military careers, their overrepresentation in the political arena is, no doubt, an indication of the close association between the IDF's senior officer corps and the political milieu.[6] Thus, for example, of the eleven Chiefs of Staff who have retired between 1948 and 1983, six (Yadin, Dayan, Rabin, Bar-Lev, Gur and Eytan) have ultimately become either Prime Ministers, government ministers, or parliament members.[7]

The abilities and skills of the IDF's senior officers are thus utilized not only while they are in uniform but also in their second, civilian, career which normally begins at a comparatively young age.

Characteristics of Behavior and Leadership Style

The IDF is a relatively small military in global terms. Furthermore, it has a unified structure (i.e., all services are under one Chief of Staff). Consequently, senior officers have great influence on their areas of command.

More than any of the others, the Chief of Staff has an enormous impact on the Israeli military. Throughout the history of the IDF, the Chiefs of Staff have each shaped the military according to their own priorities. Lieutenant General Mordechai ("Motta") Gur (1974–78), for example, was the driving force behind the expansion of the IDF after the Yom Kippur War to almost double its previous size. Raful Eytan as Chief of Staff (1978–83) decided to reintroduce "spit and polish" into the military, consequently implementing increased discipline and strictness in the IDF. (One of his methods to achieve that was to expeditiously relieve the commander of any unit which failed to meet his strict standards; the price for this policy, in turn, was a growing tendency among senior commanders to go by the book rather than take the initiative or be innovative.)

Raful's successor, Lieutenant General Moshe Levi, also imprinted his own personal preferences on the IDF. He called upon IDF officers at all levels to take the initiative, to assume responsibility and authority and to make autonomous, though prudent, decisions. On one occasion he even set a precedent by rejecting the recommendation of the IDF's Judge Advocate General to take legal action against the officers who were in charge of security at the IDF headquarters in the city of Tyre in Lebanon which was bombed by terrorists in 1983. Using his prerogative as Chief of Staff, Levi explained his exceptional action by stating that commanders who are required to have ultimate responsibility cannot be expected to function without any mishaps. If you punish commanders for unavoidable mishaps, he claimed, they will refrain from exercising their responsibility in future situations. Since the legal report did not indicate any failure in the decisions of those commanders, Levi preferred to use that occasion to deliver a clear message to the IDF's commanders, to reestablish their sense of autonomy. Both the clear content of that message as well as the act of overruling the Chief Judge Advocate reflect the strong emphasis given in the IDF to the independence and authority of senior officers.

> The IDF's Supreme Court of Military Appeals is an institution which interprets the legal basis of the IDF's doctrine of autonomy for its senior officers. It also reflects the great emphasis the IDF places on the fighting spirit. This court, which is the equivalent of the civilian Supreme Court, determines to a great extent behavioral norms and codes of desirable and non-desirable military behavior. The Chief Justice of this court has always been a senior combat officer, major general in rank, who did not necessarily have a legal background. In 1979, in response to a public dispute over one of the court's decisions, a special commission was appointed to study the military legal system. Its major recommendation was that the Chief Justice of the Military Court of Appeals must also have legal training. This recommendation was not implemented. The main objection came from the Chief of Staff and the IDF's general officer corps who always considered that position to be not only a legal one but also a source of determining behavioral norms.
>
> It should be noted that both the Chief of Staff and the chief regional commanders have the legal authority to modify, to a limited degree, decisions made by the military legal system.

Not only the Chiefs of Staff but also corps commanders may, and do, imprint their personal leadership philosophy on their corps during their commands. The IDF's development is so dynamic, its considerations so pragmatic, that a single senior commander may have a great impact on these developments for an extended period. It thus happens that a certain Armor corps commander will determine for years the tactical doctrine of the entire Israeli Armor corps. Another one may dictate, by virtue of his own determination, the conception and development of a new Israeli-made tank. A given Chief of Naval Operations may mandate the direction of the Navy's next generation of combat vessels. And an Air Chief General may personally select the quality standards for Air Force pilots. Though comparable examples may have occurred in other militaries, it would appear that the IDF's rapid changes coupled with its lack of tradition, on the one hand, and the relative autonomy of its senior officers, on the other hand, make this phenomenon much more frequent in the IDF.

Foreign military experts usually point to the IDF's capability to absorb new weapons and get maximum usage out of them. Dupuy, for example, has noted that the Israelis, by virtue of being more cosmopolitan and Western-oriented than their Arab adversaries, have adapted better to the technologically sophisticated weapons and equipment they have been provided.[8] The IDF's senior officers' approach to new technology is nonetheless somewhat ambivalent: on the one hand, they are always eager to acquire the latest equipment, always be one step ahead of other militaries, particularly those of their adversaries who historically have always received the latest Soviet technology. On the other hand, however, there is a certain amount of skepticism concerning overreliance on technology, seen as a possible threat to the importance of the essential human component. When these officers finally do decide to acquire a new weapon system, they will, almost always, modify it slightly so that it better suits the "Israeli mind."

Barbara Tuchman, in her observation of the Israeli military immediately following the victories of the Six Day War, gave a classic example of the phenomenon of Israeli equipment adaptation, still practiced today in the IDF.

"In negotiating with the French, for instance, for purchase of Mirages (fighter aircraft) . . . the Israelis insisted on the plane's having two cannon built into it although it was designed to carry only missiles. The French argued that with new sophisticated developments only missiles were needed in air-to-air combat, but the Israelis had a dual purpose in mind. They wanted to use the planes not only to intercept bombers and fight Mig 21s, which carried missiles plus one cannon, but also to destroy planes on the ground, the essence of their strategy. Weizmann (Major General Ezer Weizmann, the Air Chief General of the Israeli Air Force) stuck to his guns and got them. 'I wouldn't have bought the planes without them.'

" 'We were fanatics in the Air Force,' he says. 'We knew exactly what we wanted. We meant to rely on our own ideas and not be prisoners of computers.' This was the secret of their ultimate supreme confidence that 'we could clobber the enemy,' even though the enemy represented the combined air forces of Egypt, Syria, Jordan, and Iraq. Why? 'Because the military world has become a victim of its own sophistication in weaponry, bewildered by the technology of the atom age. It has forgotten that brains, nerve, heart, and imagination are all

> beyond the capacity of the computer. No computer can go "beyond the call of duty," but that is what medals are given for."'[9] (P. 181)

This is the reason senior Israeli commanders have historically objected to the utilization of simulators and simulated training techniques such as the MILES[10] system commonly used in the U.S. Army. Though simulators are not unheard of in the IDF, their use is less frequent than in most other Western militaries. This is especially true with regard to the ground forces, most notably the Infantry corps. The Air Force and the Navy more frequently use simulators, for individual and team training. But they too will always remind their trainees of the critical difference between training in an air-conditioned simulator and the real horrors of the battlefield. Despite all of its sensitivity to the loss of human life, the IDF seldom prefers machines to men.

The most critical impact that senior commanders in the IDF have on their troops, however, is in the realm of their leadership. The follow-me dictum does not cease at the level of lieutenant colonel or colonel. Brigade commanders within the line units still lead their units from the front and expose themselves to enemy fire alongside their soldiers. The IDF is perhaps the only military where Armor brigade commanders, for example, lead the unit from their own tank. During the Yom Kippur War, there were a great many incidents in which commanders at the battalion or brigade level critically affected the battle outcome by providing personal example and taking personal risks in leading their exhausted troops. The loss of these senior commanders was also critical to the IDF. During the 1973 war, a division commander, several brigade commanders and scores of battalion commanders were killed in action during fire engagement with the enemy. In Lebanon in 1982 it was again brigade and battalion commanders who often led their troops into battle, and likewise the casualties in this war included senior officers: five lieutenant colonels, one colonel, and a major general.[11]

> Of the numerous examples of cases involving senior officers actually directly leading their troops in Lebanon, the following description refers to the final stage of fighting between Israeli paratroopers and Syrian forces scattered around the perimeter of Beirut.
>
> "The Brigade commander, Yair and his deputy Arik were now at the spearhead and were each leading a squad of paratroopers. The two squads now charged forward.... The residuals of the Syrian forces were now withdrawing, while the Brigade Commanding Officer and his deputy were leading the charge of these two squads through the entire (Shemlan) village. Shemlan was now captured by the paratroopers."[12] (P. 234)

Table 9.3
1973 Yom Kippur War and 1982 Lebanon War Fatalities and Bravery Awards

	Yom Kippur War (1973)		Lebanon War (1982)	
	Fatalities	Medals	Fatalities	Medals
TOTAL	2523	216	468	55
Brigadier General/GEN	1	0	1	0
Colonel	2	3	1	1
Lt. Colonel	25	20	5	2
These officers as % of total	1.1%	10.6%	1.5%	5.5%

The direct involvement of the IDF's senior officers in combat is also seen in their acts of bravery. The IDF is extremely tight-fisted and conservative in the awarding of medals for heroic acts. Furthermore, the IDF expects higher standards of behavior from its officers than its enlisted men because of the very nature of leadership. Nonetheless, of the 216 medals for bravery awarded immediately after the Yom Kippur War, twenty-three (10.6 percent) were given to senior officers; and of the fifty-five medals awarded in the Lebanon War, three (5.5 percent) were awarded to colonels.[13]

Table 9.3 summarizes IDF senior officers' participation in the last two wars in terms of fatalities and medals. Keeping in mind that senior officers constitute a tiny portion of the IDF, their rate in terms of fatalities and bravery medals is quite notable.

What drives these senior commanders to continually be along the front, exposing themselves to the certain risks? First, in order to understand these commanders' behavior, one should remember that it is part of the follow-me leadership style which characterizes the entire Israeli leadership corps. As brigade or division commanders, these officers do not cease to be leaders. They certainly do not consider themselves to be managers in their command positions. And, as leaders during war, they ought to lead. So they do, in spite of the risks involved. Even at the highest echelons of ground commands, there is no such thing as commanding your forces from the safety of the rear, in a secure headquarters or a remote helicopter. Second, this behavior stems from the great sensitivity Israelis have to casualties. There is nothing that affects the national morale more than the number of fatalities in each of its wars. The senior commanders of the IDF consider themselves to be personally responsible for the lives of their men and totally committed to the goal of minimizing casualties. They live with the knowledge that their decisions will determine how many of their men may die in battle. This knowledge drives them to personally shoulder as much of the risk as possible and to be where the action is in order to make the best decisions. Although this approach extracts a high toll from the senior officer corps, it has never been challenged.

But there is yet a third, though less desirable, reason for this daring behavior of the IDF's senior officers. It is sometimes difficult to distinguish between these officers' decisiveness, courage and mission completion motto, on the one hand, and their desire to achieve success, at any price, to enhance their military careers, on the other.

Such phenomena occurred, on occasion, during the Lebanon War. At the same time that many commanders demonstrated great courage in battle, there was sometimes the impression that various other senior commanders who lacked distinct or "glorious" missions were actively seeking "better" missions for their units. Sometimes these commanders even generated the conditions under which such missions could evolve; hence, in Lebanon at times there were too many units and commanders crowded into a relatively small area. Some of these commanders created their own formations, thus adding to the confusion and interfering with the traditional chain of command.

Whatever the reasons for this extravagant behavior, the IDF's senior commanders are just as decisive and courageous in their leadership as are their younger counterparts. Furthermore, they provide a model for the younger ones in their determined leadership style.

The relatively small size of the IDF, coupled with the fact that line commanders continuously interact with one another within the same parent units, provides yet another advantage to the senior leadership corps. Anyone who has ever commanded a unit in war knows that what is important for the decision maker is not only information about the terrain, enemy and location of friendly units, but also exactly who his subordinate commanders are, along with the strong and weak points of each. This is, indeed, the situation in all of the IDF's combat units: both in regular and reserve units, brigade and division commanders personally know their subordinates well. They know exactly what they can expect from each of them on the battlefield, and they take full advantage of this knowledge.

The famous battle of the Seventh brigade during the Yom Kippur War, commanded by Colonel Avigdor ("Yanoush"') Ben-Gal, has been extensively described in the military literature.[14] There was widespread recognition by military experts of the exceptional nature of his feat: with less than a full strength brigade to begin with, Colonel Ben-Gal managed to block a continual onslaught of more than 500 Syrian tanks who had penetrated the Israeli border in the Golan Heights and were on the move into the heart of Israel. He managed to accomplish this despite the fact that at times during the non-stop three-day battle his unit had fewer than ten operational tanks. However, only a postbellum detailed analysis of Yanoush's command conduct, made by a young military correspondent who became an expert on this battle of the Seventh brigade, revealed the real secret of how he was able to achieve this great victory.

"The uniqueness of Yanoush's operation in that chess game which turns on October 9th to an open poker game when you put everything—his men's lives and the fate of Israel—into the pot is in his absolute knowledge of who is who amongst his subordinate commanders. His precise judgment based on his personal and professional familiarity with each one of his subordinates . . . enables him to decide exactly whom to throw into the battle, at what time, with how many tanks, and at which exact point. In this risky poker game he must know precisely what his cards are, competing against the stronger cards of his adversary.

"This is, it is now very clear to me, the key to the better understanding of that battle. This was the secret."[15] (P. 66)

This sense of intimacy is characteristic of the entire senior leadership corps of the IDF. Though the IDF is predominantly a reservist military, most of its senior officers are in the permanent service corps (commanders of reserve divisions, their staff officers and some of their brigade commanders and their staffs are all permanent service officers). With the relatively small size of the standing army, by definition the group of officers at the rank of colonel and above is quite small. From brigadier general and above they all know each other, and on the General Staff, one finds comrades who have fought side by side. These groups are not free from competition, power struggles and "political" considerations (on the contrary, sometimes such elements flow over onto the battlefield as for example happened in the Southern command during the Yom Kippur War between the generals Adan, Gonen, Bar-Lev, and Sharon).[16] Despite this, the predominant characteristic of staff work in the IDF's high echelons is that of teamwork based on personal familiarity of each one of the participants with one another's capabilities.

One of the symbolic expressions of this command intimacy is the relative lack of formalities between these top ranks. The General Staff meetings, for example, are usually conducted in an open forum where any subject is open to discussion and sometimes deteriorate into rambunctious exchanges. The word "sir" ("Adoni," in Hebrew) is seldom used in the IDF. Instead the word "Ha'mefaked" ("the commander" or "mon commandant") is used with senior officers, and even that is not always the rule.

The IDF's officers are known for having nicknames. Their colleagues call them by these nicknames even when they become generals. Raful, for example, is hardly ever addressed as General Eytan. Only a few know the real name of Yanoush, and the present Chief of Staff is known to all as "Moshe and a half" ("Moshe vahetzi") due to his height.

This lack of formality at the senior officer level certainly does not stop there. It also transfers into relationships with subordinates. The rank and file can always interact with their senior officers without the restraints of a formal setting. This is especially true of the reserve units. However, the lack of formal distance by no means reflects a lack of respect.

> *The Jerusalem Post's* military correspondent, Hirsh Goodman, accompanied Lt. General Moshe Levy to Lebanon on one of his frequent visits to an IDF unit stationed there.
>
> "It was not a visit of top brass to make sure that the tents were clean and the kitchen kosher, but a dialogue between the chief of staff and his senior aides, and the men in the field.
>
> "Rav Aluf (lieut.-gen.) Levy did not inspect their weapons, or their uniforms. He did not cast a glance in the direction of the dining hall. He sat down opposite the 30 or so men who would be in Sidon for some time, on exactly the same hard bench as the men were sitting on, and began to talk to them. He listened to their questions, and it was clear to all present that the chief of staff had come to listen. One could speak openly. . . .
>
> "Levy listened both to the problems and to the solutions that had been applied, made a few suggestions and found himself contested on several ideas he put forward. The discussion around the table was a discussion of equals, where those with rank seemed to respect the practical experience of the men in the field; while the junior com-

> mander in the field seemed more than willing to learn from the experience of those who have been in similar situations in the past."[17] (P. 14)

When discussing the characteristics of the IDF senior commanders' daily routines, one cannot escape discussing their workload and work values. If service in the IDF for the enlisted men and junior officers is seen as demanding, then service for the senior officers, especially in line and command positions, is extremely wearing. The operational activities and extreme responsibilities, in addition to the frequent separations from family, make military life a great personal sacrifice for the senior officer. The sacrifice not only involves the officer's family but also particularly impacts on the officer himself in terms of his own personal growth. Under such circumstances, then, it is not surprising that some of these officers have serious doubts about their commitment to the military. Furthermore, when discussing commitment to national and public service, one should also take into account the changing times in Israeli society. In the early years in the State of Israel, the general atmosphere was that of the pioneer spirit. Then the highest value was given to public service and unconditional commitment to the country. Prominent public figures who devoted their lives to serving their country received the highest appreciation from their fellow countrymen. Financial success, career success, comfortable life-style or self-indulgence all carried negative connotations in those days. Since then, things have changed considerably. The Israeli society has absorbed many of the values and norms of Western industrial cultures and in some areas even exceeded them. The average Israeli today prefers personal success to public service, and a comfortable life to a life of sacrifice for society.

The IDF's officers reflect Israeli society, even while being the elite of that society. They are not immune to these changing norms. Some of those senior officers who make military service their entire way of life still believe in the old values and norms regarding serving your country; many others, however, have chosen this career for other, more material, reasons.

Dilemmas

In the period following the Yom Kippur War, the IDF has gone through a process of self-scrutinization, as a part of the shake-up of the military hierarchy after the war. The process included also the investigation of the role played by the senior officers of the IDF permanent corps in the "blunder" of the 1973 war. This part of the self-examination was also the most difficult. What made it particularly difficult was the fact that the senior officer corps was both the investigator and the object of the investigation. In this regard, the Israeli officer corps is no different from any other officer corps when it comes to receiving criticism.

No wonder, then, that some who have expressed the most extreme criticism quickly found themselves socially expelled from their peer group. Two of these individuals were Ya'acov Hasdai and Meir Pa'il. Colonel Hasdai, a well-known paratrooper officer, who participated in a great many military operations through his twenty-two years of excellent service, resigned from the military after the Yom Kippur War, with the image of being an overly critical officer. In a series of articles, Hasdai continued to warn against the dangers evolving in the IDF, especially with regard to the quality of the senior leadership corps.[18] He detailed dangers in the following areas: first, the deterioration of military values as reflected in the life-style of the IDF officer corps in the years before the Yom Kippur War; second, the deterioration in the overall quality of the senior officer corps; and third, the deterioration of creative, abstract and critical military thinking of the senior officers corps.[19]

Likewise, Meir Pa'il[20] has pointed with alarm at the fact that those who remained in the Keva corps in the 1960s and eventually became senior officers were not necessarily the cream of the elite but rather could be characterized as those "who were of high professional but mediocre intelligence and spiritual level."[21] (P. 41)

With the passage of several years since Pa'il and Hasdai leveled their criticism at the IDF, it is possible to better assess the validity of their arguments and also to observe whether the situation has changed since then. With regard to the life-style issue, it seems that the IDF's officer corps was cured to a great extent of the ostentatiousness which had characterized it before 1973. Senior officers in the contemporary IDF keep a relatively low profile, do not seek out the media and, in general, maintain strict and high standards of behavior. It is still doubtful (as was discussed earlier in this chapter) if their value system and the depth of their commitment is comparable to that of the IDF's founders. However, in this regard, the IDF is not unique. Rather it shares this problem with the rest of Israeli society.

The quality of officer personnel, as questioned by both Pa'il and Hasdai, is still apparently a central problem for the IDF. The IDF of the 1980s is a large and complex organization. In terms of size, it is larger than it has ever been. Its increased quantity of troops and materiel has, by definition, rendered it more difficult to maintain quality. Not necessarily the best ones remain in Keva. Those who choose to remain do not always have the will, or the opportunity, to further their personal development. This does not mean that there are not officers of excellent quality in the IDF. Nor does it mean that the selection process for the top positions does not choose the best of those available. It is the overall average that is not as high as the IDF has had in the past and, indeed, presently needs.

Consequently, the third area of concern, that of critical military thinking, is still problematic for the IDF too. Various observers[22] have noted, for example, that the Lebanon War did not match Israel's previous wars in terms of creative planning and innovative tactics (this argument is directed particularly toward the IDF's ground forces operation, as compared to the striking success of the Israeli Air Force in destroying the Soviet-made missiles emplaced by Syria in the Bekka Valley). Other critics have pointed to the fact that the IDF presently utilizes, to a lesser extent than before, night combat operations, indirect approach operations and improvised maneuvers—tactics which have always been the strong side of the IDF. And yet other critical observers claim that the senior officers of the IDF did not play their expected crucial role with regard to the War in Lebanon and accepted, almost without reservation, the dictation of the Lebanon operation by the political administration.

The Lebanon War of 1982, indeed, added more sticks to the increasing pile of problems for the senior officer corps of the IDF. On the one hand, these officers found themselves for the first time in the situation of fighting a war not completely supported by the Israeli public. To make matters worse, their role has subsequently degenerated into that of an occupation force, further involving questions of legitimacy and justification. As compliant soldiers, they are expected to ignore the moral and political issues. However, as human beings, citizens of a democratic society, and perhaps even as senior officers who feel a responsibility beyond mere compliance with orders, they cannot remain indifferent to these problems.[23]

On the other hand, the long duration of the Lebanon incursion has increased the already heavy burden laid upon these senior officers because of the continual terrorist activities in the Israeli-occupied parts of Lebanon. Not only do they have to take care to protect the lives of their soldiers, they also have to continually be vigilant to preclude any mishaps which might occur under their command.

The combination of all these problems has placed the IDF's senior officer corps in the mid-1980s under tremendous pressure. Perhaps never before had these officers been as exposed to criticism as they have been in recent times. As one of the General Staff officers remarked: "I have to prove myself again and again every day."[24] (P. 21)

These pressures have generated various reactions among the IDF senior officer corps: some are expressions of protest; others involve feelings of worry and concern; some senior officers opt to lower their profile and adopt the "Rosh Katan" syndrome, while others try hard to improve the system.

The most extreme expression of protest seen in the senior officer corps of the IDF occurred in the midst of the actual fighting in Lebanon and developed into the most controversial issue in the senior officer corps. This was the case with Colonel Eli Geva,[25] an armored-brigade commander in the Israeli Army, who was released from service in the middle of the recent War in Lebanon, after requesting to be relieved of his command position. During the siege that the IDF laid on the PLO fighters barricaded within the city of Beirut, Geva's brigade was tasked with the mission of being the first brigade to enter Beirut should the order be given. Eli Geva, one of the youngest full colonels in recent times in the IDF, was known as a decisive young officer, with General Staff potential. He found himself in deep conflict between his military commitment to carry on his assigned mission and his moral commitment to object to a mission he believed to be illegitimate. His moral reservations finally outweighed his military obligation. He requested that his superiors relieve him from this particular assignment.

Though he offered to stay in this unit and participate in the continuing battles as an ordinary tank-driver, his request was denied. His case was referred through the channels all the way to the Office of the Chief of Staff of the IDF, General Raful Eytan. Geva was also called before Prime Minister Begin to explain his actions. However, within a few days of Geva's initial request, General Eytan personally ordered Colonel Geva's complete release from the military.

As could be expected, Geva's behavior led to a wide range of reactions. The rarity of similar cases in the history of the Israeli Army made Geva's demonstrative action both controversial and unique. Among critics of his decision, some blamed him for shirking his obligations as an officer and as a commander to his men. Others considered his act as clear insubordination and regarded his denial of any intent to disobey orders as untenable, since a request "to be relieved of command" at such a high rank is equivalent to a soldier's refusing to fight.

There were many others, however, who supported Geva's decision. Several other high-ranking officers had also voiced their reservations during that time concerning both the military wisdom and the political legitimacy of the IDF's operational plans concerning the siege on Beirut. One of them, Brigadier General Amram Mitzna, even expressed openly his lack of confidence in Israel's then defense minister, Ariel Sharon.[26] However, none of these incidents developed into a military protest on the group level. Nor was there any other case, besides Geva's, of a demonstrative protest leading to resignation among the senior officers of the IDF. But even among those officers who had rejected Geva's act, there were nonetheless those who agreed that the IDF was fortunate to have a Geva of its own. The most significant contribution of Geva's act was perceived as reminding his fellow senior officers that their military service does not involve unthinking compliance, since their profession is also based on commitment, constant examination and questioning.

Another type of reaction to the pressures from the senior officer corps involved the expression of worries and concerns. These expressions came from officers who believed that the IDF was receiving too much criticism and that most of that criticism was without justification. They felt that the IDF had turned into a national scapegoat by Israelis who expressed their frustrations about matters completely unrelated to the military.

In the Israeli magazine *Yedi'ot Ahronott* of February 1983, a short time after the findings of the Kahn Commission regarding the Sabra and Shatilla massacres were published, an article was published by a senior officer in the IDF. The author, "Colonel A," was a thirty-four-year-old permanent service officer, who had participated in the battles in Lebanon. Such an article by an active duty officer is very rare in Israel. From his remarks, which follow, it appeared that he expressed the sentiments of many other senior officers as well:

"I walk around very frustrated. Everyone in the country expresses his opinion and only we military personnel are prohibited from expressing ours. I am a senior officer in the military with rich combat experience and yet I have to walk around apologizing for sins I have never committed. . . .

"I live in an extreme contradiction and I don't know how to resolve it. On the one hand I believe in democracy and recognize all of the democratic processes. On the other hand, I feel terrible when judgments concerning me, my colleagues, and my superiors are made without any proportion, with no knowledge of the real situation out there in the field. And this is very frustrating. . . .

"I have the feeling that the military has become a punching bag, that everyone can hit and blame everything on it. The army, they believe, is strong . . . and it will recover. I have no doubt that it will recover, but the army is also me and you and now I am afraid there will be more fear of taking responsibility, people will think twice before giving an order, will question everything, etc. . . .

"This time I cannot be silent any longer and so I urge through you: we have a wonderful army and excellent commanders. Please don't blame us for everything that's happening in the Israeli society. We have enough to cope with ourselves and we do cope with it successfully and I can say with perfect conviction—we have the most moral military that I know. Don't undermine it."[27] (P. 10)

There are others, however, perhaps not the best of the officer corps, for whom the pressures and frustrations they experience in these senior positions lead to the development of withdrawal behaviors. These behaviors are characterized by maintaining a low profile and only doing exactly what they are told, thus adopting the Rosh Katan (small head) syndrome. This was a new phenomenon at this high level of the senior officer corps—a behavior which is the antithesis of what had always been the arrogant, entrepreneurial, innovative style of IDF leadership.

But there is also the opposite reaction to these pressures: to shake things up, to improve them, to rise above mediocracy and to actively cope with everyday difficulties. Thus in the daily grind of work, without the glamour of publicity, the majority of the IDF's senior officers are waging a campaign to preserve the IDF's high standards and, in areas where it deteriorated, to return it to its desired levels. These officers feel a strong commitment to this effort. Whether in the area of training, personnel policy, logistics, or operational planning, these senior officers attempt to reinstate the former brilliance of the IDF. The trying conditions facing the IDF in the 1980s—Lebanon, serious budget reduction, continual task overload—make it all the more essential to move in this direction. Leading this resurgence are the top leaders of the IDF—the senior officers of the permanent service corps, who are all aware of the current deficiencies and are committed to overcoming them.

> In the summer of 1984, the IDF marked the first anniversary of its newly founded Ground Forces Command. In addressing the senior officers of this command, Major General Dan Shomron, Chief of the Ground Forces Command, urged his officers:
> "Don't be 'small heads.' Don't wait for the orders to be given. All of your initiatives will be welcomed. Just go ahead and start it. Begin your initiative the bottom on up and don't wait for orders to come down from above."[28]

Conclusion

The Israeli military is, in many ways, rather unique. Its senior officer corps exemplifies this uniqueness. One aspect of this is the surprising dualism in many areas. These officers can be tough and decisive as generals and yet emerge as doves the minute they become civilians.[29] They may be aggressive commanders on the battlefield, in relentless pursuit of their enemy, and yet a moment later be the first to offer water to a wounded enemy soldier. These commanders can also be involved in destruction one minute, and repairing the results of this destruction shortly thereafter. The same officers, for example, who in the Six Day War led the capture and partial destruction of the West Bank were also the ones who supervised the complete reconstruction of all that had been destroyed by the battle. The same thing has happened in Lebanon. Even while the siege of Beirut continued, IDF officers were involved in repairs of damaged structures in towns elsewhere in Lebanon. They also provided shelter for homeless Palestinian refugees.

To an extent, these officers reflect, in their behavior, the spirit of the IDF in general: a military which was established for defense and development and was instead forced to conquer and destroy. These officers carry with them in their day-to-day duties their great responsibility to keep this military not only moving but also to determine in which direction it will move and the character it will possess in the future.

Notes

1. It is interesting to compare this policy with those of the U.S. Army and the Wehrmacht during World War II. In the U.S. military, promotion continued to be tied to time in grade; whereas, the Germans implemented a policy allowing for speedy promotions for officers in combat units. See van Creveld, M. (1982). Leadership and the officer corps. In *Fighting power* (pp. 127–162). Westport, CT: Greenwood Press.

2. Gabriel, R., & Gal, R. (1984). The IDF officer: Linchpin in unit cohesion. *Army*, 34(1), 42–50.

3. Ibid.

4. Tuchman, B. W. (1981). *Practicing history: Selected essays*. New York: Ballantine Books.

5. In the Yom Kippur War alone, close to 1,300 officers were killed or wounded in action.

6. Peri, Y. (1983). *Between battles and ballots: Israeli military in politics*. London: Cambridge University Press. This recent book by an Israeli scholar presents the thesis that the Israeli military enjoys a close partnership with the civilian political structure. This partnership is based on three sources. First, the IDF has become a critical avenue to top political jobs. Second, the political means for controlling the military are extremely weak, resulting in the military having a strong impact on political decisions. And third, the IDF's responsibility for the occupied territories (including, most recently, Lebanon) has expanded the sphere of influence into the political arena.

7. Another example is that of the 1967 General Staff which conducted the Six Day War. To date, one (Rabin) has been Prime Minister, three (Rabin, Weizmann and Sharon) have been defense ministers, and several others have been government ministers, parliament members, or prominent members of other institutions.

8. Dupuy, T. (1984). *Elusive victory: The Arab-Israeli wars, 1947–1974*. Fairfax, VA: HERO Books, p. 335.

9. Tuchman, *Practicing history*.

10. MILES (Multiple Integrated Laser Engagement System) is a training system for ground forces which uses low-powered laser transmitters, detectors, audio alarms, and visual cues to simulate live weapons and their effects. The

U.S. Army uses MILES at the National Training Center to simulate realistic battlefields. Source: Chaney, M., & Cannon, M. W. (1981, March-April). Improving combat skills: The National Training Center. *Armor*.

11. IDF Spokesman press release. (1982, September 16), Tel-Aviv.

12. Schiff, Z., & Ya'ari, E. (1984). *Israel's Lebanon war* (in Hebrew). Tel-Aviv: Schocken Publication.

13. These awards were given immediately after the war. An additional seventy-five medals for bravery were awarded at a later date (see Chapter 10).

14. The Battle of the Seventh brigade was described in varying length by the following authors: Dupuy, *Elusive victory*; Herzog, *The war of atonement*; Kahalani, A. (1984). *The heights of courage*. Westport, CT: Greenwood Press; and Kellett, A. (1982). *Combat motivation*. Boston: Kluwer Nijhoff Publishing.

15. Shurr, R. (1983, September). Back to the valley of tears. *Monitin, 61*, 61–68.

16. Dupuy, T. (1984). Sinai standoff. In *Elusive victory*, pp. 470–484.

17. Goodman, H. (1984, July 22–28). Face to face. *The Jerusalem Post*, pp. 14, 17.

18. These articles were published as a collection in Hasdai, Y. (1979). *Truth in the shadow of war* (translated from the Hebrew by M. Kohn). Tel-Aviv: Zmora, Bitan, Modan Publishers.

19. Ibid., pp. 13–27.

20. Colonel (Ret.) Meir Pa'il was also a highly respected combat officer. Among his IDF assignments were command of the Golani brigade and the officers' school (Bahad 1).

21. Pa'il, M. (1975, January). The Israeli defence forces: A social aspect. *New Outlook*, 40–41.

22. Sherwood, C. (1984, August 27). Israeli 'ineptitude' blamed for 'friendly fire' casualties. *The Washington Times*, pp. 1-A, 12-A; van Creveld, M. (1982, December 12–18). The war: A questioning look. *The Jerusalem Post "International Edition,"* pp. 12–13; Gabriel, R. A. (1984, August). Lessons of war: The IDF in Lebanon. *Military Review, 64*, 47–65.

23. This issue of commanders' conflict between obedience and commitment has been addressed by the author in Gal, R. (in press). Commitment and obedience in the military: An Israeli case study. *Armed Forces and Society*. The case study of Colonel Eli Geva is discussed in the following pages.

24. Habber, E. (1984, September 26). The general staff 1984: A portrait. In Seven Days, the weekend magazine of *Yedi'ot Ahronott, 1078*, 20–21.

25. Gal, Commitment and obedience.

26. Erez, Y. (1983, May 13). Mitzna: Learning from experience. In Weekend, the weekend magazine of *Ma'ariv*, p. 23.

27. Amikam, Y. (1983, February). They have turned the army into a punching bag. *Yedi'ot Ahronott*, p. 10.

28. Tal, O. (1984, July 18). General Shomron: Do not wait for orders, take the initiative. *Bamahane, 44*, 7.

29. Rabin, Bar-Lev, Gur, and Ben-Gal, to mention just a few, were all known as assertive generals during their military careers; yet after retirement they all

became known for their moderate political attitudes particularly regarding the use of force and maintaining control of the occupied territories. See also Peri, Y. (1977). The ideological portrait of the Israeli military elite. *The Jerusalem Quarterly*, 3, 28–41.

10

HEROISM: THE ROOTS OF BRAVERY

"Valor is still value." This thesis forcefully stated by Thomas Carlyle in the middle of the nineteenth century[1] seems to best describe the IDF in the latter part of the twentieth century. Indeed, to the student of the Israeli soldier's combat behavior, it may seem that courage and valor are common, albeit sacred, values rather than exceptional behaviors.

Historical Roots

The roots of Israeli heroism are found throughout the ancient history of the Jews. In biblical descriptions, the term "hero" was attributed not only to acts of courage in war but also to acts of leadership, authority, and righteousness. Characteristics of heroism were attributed to judges, leaders, and kings, not necessarily for battlefield occurrences but rather to recognize desirable behavior.

> The word hero ("Gibor") in Hebrew derives from the same root word ("Gavor") from which the words man ("Gever"), to overcome ("Le'hitgaber"), a master ("Gvir") and a synonym for God ("Gevura") also derive.
>
> Approximately twelve synonyms exist in Hebrew for the concept of heroism ("Gevura," "ometz," "haill," "ruach," "oz," "heruff-nefesh," "ta'tzumott"—to mention only the most commonly used). Most, if not all, of these words are found in the Old Testament and yet are still commonly used in Hebrew today.

In the periods of oppression that the Jewish people have known throughout their history, the concept of heroism was intermixed with that of martyrdom and self-sacrifice—the willingness to suffer death rather than renounce one's religious beliefs. This type of heroic behavior has been sanctified in the Jewish tradition to the point of becoming the ultimate act of heroism, known as "Kiddush Hashemm" (i.e., "sanctifying the lord"). In all of the times when the Jewish people had no homeland, from the days of the Roman occupation and the Masada epic through the atrocities of the Spanish Inquisition and the pogroms in Europe directed against the Jews, to the horrors of the Holocaust, the common expression of courageous behavior demonstrated by Jews was that of martyrdom. This heroism did not stem from hopes for any possible future changes but rather was driven by their adherence to past beliefs.

Only with the establishment of the State of Israel as a homeland for the Jewish people has there come the sense of something tangible and worth dying for. A new kind of heroism has emerged with the birth of Israel—the heroism of those who defend their homes and "wouldn't let it happen again." Indeed, for many of the young native Israelis (Sabras), who very distinctly perceived themselves as so different from their ancestors in the Diaspora, accepting that type of passive martyrdom as heroism was incomprehensible. They certainly couldn't identify with it because they felt their ancestors had allowed themselves to be led like sheep to the slaughter. For this young generation of Israelis, the association of Holocaust and Heroism (as the Holocaust Remembrance Day for the victims of Nazism is called in Israel) is not evident. For them the new Israeli image of the tough, non-capitulating Israeli hero is actually an antithesis of, and even perhaps a reaction against, the old stereotype of the weak Jew who responded with helplessness and passivity to adversaries.

Whether as a continuation of, or a reaction to, these past behaviors, with the beginning of the resettlement of Jews in Palestine, a new spirit of heroism welled up and burst forth from the new Israelis. The Hashomer, Palmach, and other pre-Israel paramilitary organizations were full of heroic incidents by both individuals and small teams who exhibited new, strong and decisive resistance to their traditional Arab adversaries. Typical of these incidents is the legend about Yosef Trumpeldor, a Russian-born Jewish pioneer who immigrated to Israel and was killed in 1920 by Arabs while leading the defense of a small settlement called Tel-Hai in the Upper Galilee. His dying words, according to the legend, were: "It's good to die for our land." These words have turned into a national motto under which the children of Israel have been reared all these years. Every year, on the Trumpeldor Memorial Day, thousands of elementary school students visit his burial spot in Tel-Hai and recite these famous words which exemplified the new Israeli heroism.

The Palmach, with its emphasis on socialistic-humanistic ideology, further sharpened the focus on the human aspects of heroism in its new Israeli version. This is reflected in the words of Yitzhak Sadeh, the first commander of the Palmach:

Heroism, which is a form of sacrifice, is not aggressive in its nature. Neither is it degrading; rather it is the ultimate form of service. In its essence it is altruism. Heroism is a positive human trait. There is no heroism without a human goal and without humanity since its main objective is preserving human life.... It is, therefore, why it is so difficult for the genuine hero to kill. He will commit this act only when there is no other alternative, when there is absolutely no doubt regarding the justification for the killing, when this act is absolutely necessary to save a life.... Neither can the ignorant be a hero since ignorance is lack of involvement in what's surrounding you; lack of involvement is lack of love and where there is no love there is no sacrifice and no heroism.[2]

The Heroism Ethos

With the formation of the IDF in 1948 as the official military framework within Israel, an appropriate "home" was created for the spirit of heroism which had been kept in the souls of the young Israeli generation. From the War of Independence, the first war for the IDF, there emerged numerous opportunities for the occurrence of this new Israeli bravery. Most of these courageous acts were performed under conditions of "the few against the many," a situation which typically characterized the Israeli perception of that war. Indeed, without these acts of courage in the face of overwhelming odds, Israel as a nation would not have survived this first war. These exceptional acts of courage by the IDF's first soldiers forged the mold of the heroism ethos in Israel.

The War of Independence was for Israel a war of survival in the strictest sense of the word. Acts of sacrifice and extreme courage on the battlefield were frequent and became almost expected and normative behavior. Indeed, only acts which were greatly beyond those expected and which involved extreme risk and sacrifice were subsequently awarded; thus the War of Independence set the standards in the IDF for all future citations for heroism. According to these standards, an act of bravery which is recognized with the awarding of a medal must be exceptional. Consequently, medals are rarely awarded in the IDF.

From the days of the War of Independence to the present time, the heroism ethos has become an integral part of the IDF and in fact Israeli society in general. Books, stories, and songs have been written about those IDF figures who have become heroic legends during their own lifetimes or unfortunately, but more frequently, have become legends posthumously for the very deeds which caused their deaths. The common theme running through these various literary expressions was that of valorous behavior in battle. From "Dodo," the heroic Palmachnik, to

Yoni Netanyahu, the hero of the raid on Entebbe; from Meir Har-Zion, the legendary paratrooper of the 101st strike unit to Avigdor Kahalani, the "Saviour of Israel" in the Golan Heights tank battles of the Yom Kippur War, the personal stories and descriptions of their heroic deeds are well known to even the smallest of Israeli children and serve as role models for them. Such models, admirable as they may be, are obviously not easy for everyone to emulate.

> A series of Gestalt group-therapy sessions conducted with combat veterans of the Yom Kippur War was described in a perceptive document written by the Israeli psychologist Amia Lieblich.[3] In a summary report detailing her work, called "Between Strength and Toughness,"[4] Lieblich illuminates the extreme social-normative pressure placed upon the Israeli youth, especially the men, to always be "tough, strong and a hero." This pressure, says Lieblich, is so demanding that in many cases it becomes a "personal value guiding one's life." To illustrate this, Lieblich cites one of her many subjects (Sol), who searches for an explanation for this demanding value: "I don't know. Just this country, I guess, being born in Israel and educated this way. We are all born to be heroes, to fulfill all the expectations of generations and generations of Jews out there."[5]
>
> Lieblich hence concludes her observations of these youth by pointing at the price these young Israelis pay for this strong norm expecting them always to be "tough, strong, and heroes." The price of heroism is apparent mainly in a certain emotional bluntness, in respect for doing rather than feeling, in lack of sensitivity to oneself and others, and in an excess of so-called objectivity in one's life.[6]

Students of the military institution frequently consider bravery awards not only as an act aimed toward an individual who deserves recognition, but also, perhaps even more important, as an organizational attempt to strengthen, by means of rewards, the desired principles of military ethics and its professional value system.[7] In the case of the IDF, an examination of the types of combat behavior which have been awarded since the IDF's early years reveals distinct patterns of behavior. Among them are assuming command in a leaderless situation, rescuing the wounded or trapped fellow soldiers, staying behind to hold off the enemy while the unit changes position, and taking an offensive initiative in seemingly hopeless situations.

> A sociological analysis that explores the latent function of military citations illuminates yet another implicit aspect which was addressed in the IDF with these awards—the "melting pot" issue.

The early 1950s, the peak years of immigration to Israel, were also the most difficult period for the absorption into the IDF of these newcomers, especially the Sephardic (Eastern) Jews. During those days the heroic story of Private Nathan Albaz became well known throughout Israel. Albaz, a Moroccan-born Sephardic who had just immigrated with his family to Israel and been drafted was busy one day in basic training with his peers cleaning weapons, when the pin on a hand grenade was accidentally pulled out, in the midst of a crowd of soldiers. Without any hesitation Albaz threw himself onto the grenade, which exploded under him. By his act he sacrificed his life for those of his friends and consequently became a legendary figure in the IDF. The ethos which developed from the story of Albaz not only helped establish the desirable norm of the "grenade act" but it also made it clear that such acts were not necessarily the sole property of senior soldiers, Sabras or Ashkenazi, but could also come from the Sephardic rank and file.

Awards and Decorations

Israeli soldiers, including high-ranking officers, wear few ribbons on their uniforms. A colonel, for example, a veteran of three wars (Six Day War, Yom Kippur War and the Lebanon War) and no doubt several other combat operations, will usually have just three campaign ribbons and perhaps another small medal indicating extensive service in frontline units. It is the scarcity of these awards and decorations that makes them so valued in the IDF. This is especially true with regard to bravery decorations. The total number of decorations awarded to IDF soldiers, of all ranks and branches, throughout the history of the IDF (from the War of Independence in 1948 through the 1982 Lebanon War) barely exceeds 1,000![8] Looking at Israel's three most recent wars in the last two decades and the numbers of killed in action, the distribution of medals was as follows:

Six Day War	258 medals; 810 killed in action
Yom Kippur War	291 medals; 2,690 killed in action
Lebanon War	55 medals; 400 killed in action

Prior to 1973, bravery decorations were categorized simply by the level of command awarding them. Thus, the highest level of awards were those given by the Chief of Staff, the next highest were those awarded by region or service commanders, followed by those awarded at the division, brigade and battalion level. However, no matter what the level of award may have been or the war it followed, the total number of these awards has always been limited. For example, after the Six Day War, a total of 258 decorations were awarded, of which only 52 were from the Chief of Staff, and 84 were awarded by the chief territorial or corps commanders. The rest were awarded by the lower-level commanders.

In 1973 the IDF implemented a revised system of military decorations retroactive to the 1948 War of Independence. All soldiers decorated since 1948 were awarded one of the three new medals established for outstanding deeds in the IDF. The three medals, ranging in order of increasing prestige, are these:

Exemplary Award ("Ott Hamoffett"): awarded for behavior that is an example of excellent soldiery.

Bravery Award ("Ott Ha'oz"): awarded for deeds of extreme bravery performed under fire.

Gallantry Award ("Ott Hagvurah"): awarded for extraordinary acts of heroism performed under fire with extreme risk to one's own life (equivalent to the Congressional Medal of Honor awarded U.S. servicemen).

The highest of these, the Ott Hagvurah, has been awarded to fewer than thirty IDF soldiers throughout the history of the Israeli military. Though these medals are relatively scarce, unit commanders may, by means of a letter of recognition, unobtrusively recognize service which is outstanding but not sufficient for one of these medals.

Other ribbons and medals in the IDF are limited to campaign ribbons awarded for service in the following: the War of Independence (1948); the Sinai campaign (1956); the Six Day War (1967); the Yom Kippur War (1973); and the Lebanon War (1982). In addition, soldiers are awarded a special emblem, worn on their uniforms representing six months or more of hazardous service on a front-line combat unit. The IDF also recognizes, by means of a badge, those who served in the Palmach and other prestate military groups. And finally, each Independence Day, Israel's president awards a hundred outstanding soldiers, chosen from both conscripts and careerists, with a placard.[9]

Awards in the Yom Kippur War: The Heroism Study

The following section delineates characteristics of heroism and heroes as seen in the Yom Kippur War. This description is based on a study I conducted while I was still on active duty in the IDF.[10] The study was prompted by a number of questions concerning heroic behavior: Are

Table 10.1
Distribution of Medal Recipients According to Types of Military Service

Type of military service	N	%
Compulsory service	80	28.3
Permanent service corps	90	31.8
Reserve service	113	39.9
TOTAL	283	100.0

there any specific characteristics which distinguish the heroic individual from his peers, and, if so, what are these characteristics? Are these heroic acts related at all to personality predispositions, or do they evolve from the specifics of the situation? If the latter is the case, what are these specific situational circumstances that generate heroic acts?

Subjects for this study were Israeli soldiers who received bravery decorations at the conclusion of the Yom Kippur War. The procedure for determining the allocation of these awards was as follows: An IDF committee representing the various services was appointed to examine the written information provided by unit commanders regarding exceptional acts of their soldiers and to carry out a preliminary selection of candidates. The candidates selected for further consideration (if alive) and other eyewitnesses were then interviewed by members of the committee. Subsequently, the members of the committee determined whether the deeds were worthy of decoration and, if so, what level of decoration should be awarded.

A total of 283 medal recipients comprised the final group of subjects in this study—all 194 soldiers who received the Ott Hamoffett (third-level award), and all 89 soldiers who were decorated with the Ott Ha'oz (second-level award). The studied sample did not include holders of the highest level decoration—the Ott Hagvurah—since they constituted a very small and exceptional group (only 8 cases).[11]

Background Variables

Tables 10.1, 10.2, and 10.3 provide some background information on the soldiers awarded these medals. This information includes (1) type of military service; (2) branch of service at the time of the action; and (3) military rank at the time of the action.

The distribution of the medals according to the type of service only slightly resembles the real proportion of these three components of the IDF: the permanent (Keva) category is overrepresented, while the re-

Table 10.2
Distribution of Medal Recipients According to Branch of Service

Branch of service	N	%
Armor	152	53.7
Infantry (including Paratroopers)	51	18.0
Air Force	22	7.8
Medical Corps	18	6.4
Navy	7	2.5
Engineering Corps	6	2.1
Ordnance	5	1.8
General Staff *	4	1.4
Other	18	6.4
TOTAL	283	100.0

*Officers with the rank of colonel and above

Table 10.3
Distribution of Medal Recipients According to Military Rank

Military Rank	N	%
Lower rank enlisted (Private, Private 1st Class, Corporal)	35	12.4
Noncommissioned officers (Sergeant, 1st Sergeant, Regimental Sergeant)	67	23.7
Junior officers (2nd Lieutenant, Lieutenant, Captain)	106	37.4
Senior officers (Major, Lieutenant Colonel, Colonel)	75	26.5
TOTAL	283	100.0

serves are somewhat underrepresented. Yet, the high proportion (about 40 percent) of reserve soldiers among the medal recipients certainly demonstrated that heroic behavior on the battlefield was not only exhibited by professional soldiers but also by ordinary civilians who had been called to fulfill their national military duty.

More than half of the decorated soldiers belonged to the armored units, thus reflecting the basic nature of the Yom Kippur War which involved primarily intensive tank battles. However, within the Armor corps group, most of the medalists were either tank commanders or members of tank crews which are normally characterized by very high cohesion. Being part of a highly cohesive group was also typical of medalists from the infantry and paratrooper units in this war. Indeed, these units too had a relatively high rate of recognized heroic behaviors.

The distribution of the medals ranged along the entire scale of military ranks—from privates to colonels. However, there is a clear overrepresentation of officers (mostly commanding officers) in this list. Officers (both reservists and permanent service corps members) comprised about 64 percent of the entire list of decorations[12] (about ten times their proportion in line units). Furthermore, if one adds to this figure the number of decorated NCOs (most of whom also served in junior command positions), one gets essentially an inverted ratio of leaders to led. The exemplary behavior of the Israeli combat leader, thus, is readily apparent from these figures.

Comparative Procedures

In order to compare the group of medalists to an equivalent group of combatants who were not awarded (control group), a carefully conducted procedure was applied. First, only those IDF units in which three or more individuals had received awards were selected for the comparative phase of the study. (This was done to eliminate situations in which only one or two individuals were in the position to perform an extraordinary act of bravery.) Second, for each medal recipient in those units, a group of matched pairs was allocated, resembling the medal recipient in three aspects: serving during the war in the same unit, having the same rank, and performing an identical duty. Although the number of the matched pairs (or rather the counterparts) varied for each single medal recipient, the final control group was composed of groups of three subjects randomly chosen for each subject in the experimental group. These two selection procedures significantly reduced the study sample size. Thus the final comparison was made between 51 medal recipients in the medal-awarded group and 153 individuals (matched by unit, rank and task) in the control group. However, statistical analysis showed that this final group of 51 recipients accurately represented the entire group.

Table 10.4
Distribution According to Age Groups of Medal Group and Control Group

Age Groups	Medal Group N	%	Control Group N	%
19-22	19	37.2	53	34.6
23-25	15	29.4	47	30.7
26-30	13	25.5	42	27.5
31-36	4	7.8	9	5.9
37-47	--	--	2	1.3
TOTAL	51	99.9	153	100.0

t-test: t=0.35; p, N.S.

The comparisons between these two groups, with regard to various background variables, are presented in Table 10.4. The mean age of the award recipients as well as that of their counterparts was relatively low, approximately twenty-four years of age. It should be recalled that more than 70 percent of the award recipients were reservists or permanent service corps members and thus of necessity older than twenty-one. There was no significant difference, however, between the mean ages of the experimental and control groups.

Table 10.5 shows the distribution of the countries in which the subjects were born (birth), as well as those in which their fathers were born (origin). Since Israel is a nation of immigrants whose Jewish population has come from the four corners of the earth, it is interesting to look into the differences which can be found among various ethnic groups. Specifically, the comparison between the Ashkenazi (mainly European) and the Sephardic (Asian and African) groups is meaningful. Within the population of Israel as a whole, the Israeli-born accounted (at the time of the study) for 55 percent of the total population. Those born in Europe and America constituted another 25 percent of Israeli citizens, and the remaining 20 percent were born in Asia and Africa. In terms of country of origin, the ratio between Ashkenazi and Sephardic was about 50:50 in 1973.

The figures in Table 10.5 indicate that the great majority of the medalists were Sabras (Israeli-born) and of European origin. Only a few of the medalists were of Middle-Eastern origin (that is, they or their parents had immigrated to Israel from Islamic countries). However, in this regard the medal recipients did not differ significantly from their fellow nonmedalist counterparts. For more insightful conclusions about the relationship between socio-ethnographical variables and the combat behav-

Table 10.5
Distribution by Countries of Birth and Origin of Medal and Control Groups
(Numbers in parentheses represent frequencies)

Country	Birth		Origin	
	Medal Group	Control Group	Medal Group	Control Group
Israel	84% (43)	75% (114)	14% (7)	14% (21)
Europe	10% (5)	12% (18)	75% (38)	62% (91)
Asia-Africa	6% (3)	13% (20)	11% (6)	24% (36)
TOTAL	100% (51)	100% (152)	100% (51)	100% (148)
chi^2	$chi^2 = 2.35$	(N.S.)	$chi^2 = 3.83$	(N.S.)

ior of Israeli soldiers, one would require a much more detailed analysis. From the present analysis, however, it can be concluded that in the Israeli Defence Forces of the Yom Kippur War era, it was much more likely for Israeli-born individuals of European origin to perform an extraordinary act of heroism on the battlefield than it was for any other ethnic group. However, this was essentially because this reflects the nature of the ethnic distribution in the IDF combat units in general. Within that distribution Ashkenazis and Sephardics performed basically the same.

The medal and control groups were also compared with regard to the quality score (Kaba) and other military indices. As can been seen from Table 10.6, the group of medal recipients clearly represents a high level of the Israeli soldiers in terms of their general quality. Their mean Kaba scores (based on their levels of intelligence, education and motivation) fell at the ninety-third percentile of the total population. The mean score of the motivation-to-serve (Tsadach) index alone was even higher, at the ninety-fifth percentile. Their achievements throughout their military training courses also reflected their military proficiency. The Israeli medalists also demonstrated a high degree of intellectual ability (although not significantly above the control average). The mean score of the intelligence indices (Dapar) of the medal recipients in the present study was at the eighty-sixth percentile of the entire IDF population. Although the mean scores of the three quality variables were slightly higher in the medal group, they did not differ significantly from the corresponding

Table 10.6
Means of Indices of Military Background

Indices	Medal Group Mean	N	Control Group Mean	N	t	p
1. Quality Score ("Kaba")	53.97	29	53.20	136	1.33	N.S.
2. Primary Psychotechnical Rating ("Dapar")	71.81	51	69.23	150	0.94	N.S.
3. Motivation to Serve Index ("Tsadach")	29.1	40	28.56	115	0.72	N.S.
4. Number of Military Courses	2.93	44	2.82	127	0.40	N.S.
5. Mean Score of Courses	79.86	44	74.58	127	3.85	0.001

means in the control group. Only with regard to performance in military courses were the medalists significantly better than the non-medalists.

Personality Evaluations

Because of limited data availability, the examination of personality variables and their relationship to the behavior of war heroes in this study included only part of the medalist sample and was confined to general personality evaluations. Of the original 283 medalists from the Yom Kippur War, only those 77 who had files at the IDF central Officers' Selection Board (OSB) were included in this phase. The mean scores of seven personality evaluations taken from these subjects' OSB files were computed. These personality evaluations included the following characteristics: sociability, social intelligence, emotional stability, leadership, devotion to duty, decisiveness, and perseverance under stress. Scores on these characteristics were determined by trained psychologists who had interviewed and otherwise assessed the candidates during their OSB procedures.

These scores taken from the medalists' files were subsequently compared to data obtained from a random sample of nearly 300 soldiers, who had also passed the OSB examinations in 1975.[13] Table 10.7 includes the mean scores of the subjects in this OSB group and those of the comparison group.

The medal recipients scored significantly higher—relative to the comparable group—on four out of the seven personality characteristics: lead-

Table 10.7
Mean Scores of Personality Evaluations

	OSB Medalist Group		Comparison Group		t	p
Personality Evaluations (range)	Mean	N	Mean	N		
Sociability (1-5)	3.94	77	3.96	273	0.57	N.S.
Social Intelligence (1-7)	4.06	77	3.90	273	0.44	N.S.
Emotional Stability (1-5)	3.20	77	3.12	273	1.02	N.S.
Leadership (1-7)	3.31	77	2.34	273	6.13	0.001
Devotion to Duty (1-5)	4.19	77	4.01	273	4.45	0.001
Decisiveness (1-7)	3.24	77	2.34	273	12.32	0.001
Perseverance under Stress (1-5)	2.94	77	2.18	273	11.81	0.001

ership, devotion to duty, decisiveness and perseverance under stress. No statistically significant differences were found with regard to the other three personality dimensions: sociability, social intelligence, and emotional stability. While these findings are not definitive (due mainly to an inherent inability to compare the OSB medalist group with a matched non-medalist control group), one may speculate, nonetheless, that the Israeli heroes of the Yom Kippur War (more accurately, those in the group who were officers or had been officer candidates) were slightly more devoted to their duty, more decisive, more persevering under stress, and showed slightly higher leadership capability when compared with their peers of the same population.[14]

Except for the above differences regarding the four personality characteristics, the study failed on the whole to identify any distinct properties which distinguish the heroes from the non-heroes. Israeli heroes, then, are not a distinct species. Apparently they are not *born* heroes; they *become* heroes. Based on the results of the present analysis, it seems that there is little chance of predicting who among a defined group of individuals, and in a given set of circumstances, will become a hero. True, the medalists represent extremely top-level quality in terms of their intelligence, skills and motivation. But so did their matched counterparts—fellow soldiers from the same units, same ranks and same military specialties. Hence, the least that could be concluded from this first part of the study is that we can perhaps distinguish some qualitative categories in which there is relatively greater probability to find potential heroes.

Situational Characteristics

The second part of the heroism study focused on the analysis of the situational and circumstantial characteristics of the settings within which the heroic acts occurred. Prominent students of heroism[15] have suggested that situational rather than personality factors may indeed be more useful in describing, perhaps even predicting, the emergence of extraordinarily gallant behavior.

The situational analysis which was applied in the Yom Kippur study[16] revealed four relatively specific situations, each characterized by a particular combination of several variables, accounting for the majority of heroic acts. These four categories were subsequently labeled as follows, using soldiers' parlance:

1. "With your back to the wall"
2. "The last remnant and saviour"
3. "Self-sacrificing"
4. "Fighting to the last bullet"

The first category of heroic situation occurs when a group of soldiers is surrounded by the enemy, outnumbered and engaged in a desperate defensive action and/or retreating. The act of heroism is carried out in most cases by the assigned leader or in his presence. Typically, the heroic behavior does not occur in isolation but rather occurs with the participation of some other members of the unit. About 28 percent of the awards fell into this category.

The second type of heroic situation—"the last remnant and saviour"—was characterized by face-to-face fighting during an offensive battle. In most of the cases, there had already been many casualties, many wounded in need of assistance, and in fact the commanding officer himself had usually been injured. Only a score of functional combatants are left in this situation, and they act in a state of psychological isolation. One individual takes command spontaneously and assumes leadership—ultimately remaining alive to save his fellows' lives. This category accounted for about 18 percent of the heroic cases.

The "self-sacrificing" situation is the third of these four identified situational profiles and accounted for 10 percent of the awarded acts. In this situation a small unit is encircled by the enemy. Although it is the hero's regular unit, the assigned commanding officer is not necessarily present, nor are there necessarily casualties involved. The heroic act comes at a critical moment, saving the lives of the unit's members and generally resulting in the death of the hero himself.

The fourth heroic situation was called "fighting to the last bullet" and included 14 percent of the cases. In this situation, a single soldier (or a crew) remained alone in an offensive battle, acting neither under direct orders nor in an attempt to save the lives of others, but to accomplish the assigned mission. Typically the encounter continued until his(their) death(s).

In the interviews conducted with combat medalists after the Yom Kippur War, the awarded soldiers tended to express their doubt as to whether they had been more worthy of the medals than some of their peers in the same unit. The question: "Why *me* in particular?" was often raised—not necessarily out of humility. In light of the present study it seems that in many of the given cases it was predominantly the specific constellation of the situational circumstances that evoked the exceptional behavior, while the determination of the particular individual who would accomplish this behavior was almost by chance.[17]

A further examination of the characteristics of the heroic acts revealed the predominance of the "social" (or "group") element in these events. In three out of the four situational categories, the acts were carried out not while the hero was alone or disconnected from his unit, but in the presence of others, most frequently his unit members. Almost half of the cases involved the risk of one's life for the sake of others' survival. In many instances the heroes said in later interviews: "I did it for my friends because I was convinced that they would have done the same for me." It seems that group morale and cohesion, as well as the sense of commitment to one's unit and friends, played a major role in instances of combat gallantry among the Israeli combatants, as it has throughout history among many other combatants.

Awards in the Lebanon War

The 1982 War in Lebanon, the most recent all-out war Israel has fought, also generated instances of heroism on the battlefield. This war, in contrast to Israel's previous war, was not a war which threatened Israel's very existence. Most of its battles were conducted with relative caution, lacking the sense of urgency and critical need which had so characterized the Yom Kippur War. There were nonetheless situations in which heroic acts effected a victory or a rescue.

Active combat in the Lebanon War lasted approximately three weeks, involved a cross-section of most of the IDF's different units and resulted in more than 3,000 casualties. Despite the intensity of the war, only six medals for heroism were awarded; another forty-nine citations were given by commanders from the brigade level all the way to the Chief of

Table 10.8
Distribution of Medal and Citation Recipients Following the Lebanon War According to Military Rank

Military rank	N	%
Lower rank enlisted (Private, Private 1st Class, Corporal)	7	12.7
Noncommissioned officers (Sergeant, 1st Sergeant, Regimental Sergeant)	18	32.7
Junior officers (2nd Lieutenant, Lieutenant, Captain)	21	38.2
Senior officers (Major, Lieutenant Colonel, Colonel)	9	16.4
TOTAL	55	100.0

Staff. Thus the total number of recognitions for bravery in the Lebanon War at all levels was fifty-five.[18]

It is not readily clear why the number of awards in this war was so few, relative to former Israeli wars. In an interview with Major General Nadel,[19] Chairman of the Awards Committee after the Lebanon War, the general admitted: "The IDF's criteria for bravery acts in combat are becoming stricter and stricter from war to war. What had been considered in the Yom Kippur War as an extraordinary act of courage has become now a standard [behavior] expected from any soldier in given situations.... Much of what was once exceptional is now routine." Notwithstanding the general's assessment, one may also speculate that the relative scarcity, even by the IDF's standards, of recognized awards following the Lebanon War was an unintentional indication of the ambivalent feelings that this war generated among many Israelis, including military personnel. If this was the case, then the Israeli soldiers of 1982 were unjustifiably penalized for the politicians' decisions.

The distribution by rank of these fifty-five awards and citations follows the pattern of those awarded after the Yom Kippur War (see Table 10.8). The combined percentage of officers (54.6 percent) among those recognized for heroic acts is once again almost eight times greater than their representative numbers in line units. Adding to these the NCOs recognized, most of whom were in command positions at the time of their heroic deed, the percentage of leaders among this group rises to 87.3 percent. The predominance of leaders in recognized heroic acts, as in previous wars, is obvious. Also, from other aspects, even though there has yet to be a systematic study, it appears that the characteristics of heroic behavior in the Lebanon War are similar to those of the Yom Kippur War.

Conclusion

While all the above studies and figures analyzed "heroes" by virtue of some predefined categories (i.e., individuals who had already been awarded a medal), a serious problem remains concerning the definition of real heroism on the battlefield. There is no easy way to distinguish between an act which is "above and beyond the call of duty" and one which, albeit courageous, is nevertheless within the framework of normal combat duty. Where does one draw the line between what is expected of a soldier on the battlefield and what constitutes extraordinary performance? The bravery medal is a symbol which is sometimes assigned to events and people not necessarily according to objective or tangible criteria. Certainly there are some acts of heroism which have been recognized as such in a given military unit, but which would not have been considered equally heroic if performed by members of a different unit. Indeed, some of the elite units of the IDF have refused for years to accept such medals (with the exception of some posthumous awards). In these units, it is maintained, heroic behavior is the standard. Similarly, rank differences may also complicate definitions of heroism. The same heroic acts performed by an enlisted man might not be regarded as being particularly heroic had it been performed by an officer or even an NCO.

With much caution and within a non-absolute framework, these numbers of awarded medals should be taken as an estimate of actual heroic behavior among Israeli combatants. For the reasons already mentioned, these numbers may certainly be an underestimation of Israeli bravery in combat.

Perhaps more than any other aspect of recent Israeli history, those frequent bursts of heroism of IDF soldiers may be seen as highlights of the metamorphosis of the stereotypical passive Jew of ancient times into today's modern and assertive Israeli. But this conception is superficial. The frequent wars, the repeated terrorist attacks and the permanent threat to the existence of the State of Israel provide all-too-frequent opportunities for heroic behavior. The roots of this heroism, however, did not begin with the formation of the State of Israel. They extend back through the entire history of the Jewish people.

Notes

1. Carlyle, T. (1946). *On heroes, hero-worship and the heroic in history*. London: Oxford University Press.

2. Sadeh, Y. (1961). Trails of heroism. In *Around the campfire*. Tel-Aviv: Marachot Publications.

3. Lieblich, A. (1978). *Tin soldiers on Jerusalem Beach*. New York: Pantheon.

4. Lieblich, A. (1983). Between strength and toughness. In S. Breznitz (Ed.), *Stress in Israel* (pp. 39–64). New York: Van Nostrand Reinhold Company.

5. Ibid., p. 58.

6. Ibid., pp. 53–54.

7. See for example: Blake, J. A., & Butler, S. (1976). The medal of honor, combat orientations and latent role structure in the United States military. *Sociological Quarterly*, 17(4), 561–567.

8. Nyrop, R. F. (Ed.). (1979). *Israel: A country study*. Washington, DC: American University Press, p. 267.

9. Ibid., pp. 267–269.

10. This study was reported at several professional conferences and was published in Breznitz, S. (Ed.), *Stress in Israel*. New York: Van Nostrand Reinhold.

11. Preliminary statistical checks showed no significant differences on several major variables between those awarded the Exemplary Conduct Medal and those receiving the Bravery awards. Thereafter both groups were combined for the purposes of this study.

12. This ratio is in sharp contrast to that of the U.S. Congressional Medal of Honor (CMO) recipients during both the Korean and the Vietnam wars. The figures for these two wars show officer recipients constituting 27.7 percent and 28.1 percent of the total awards, respectively. While the CMO is not an award strictly comparable to those in the Israeli study, it nevertheless reflects the overall award trend in the U.S. military. For further information see Blake, J. A. (1973). The congressional medal of honor in three wars. *Pacific Sociological Review*, 16(2), 166–176.

13. Atzei-Pri, M. (1977). *Response frequencies in officers selection base's files* (Research Report). Classification Branch, IDF, Israel.

14. It is interesting to note that in his recent review of literature pertaining to war heroism, Jeffrey Anderson has delineated six characteristics of the warrior spirit. These are (1) selfless devotion to duty; (2) leadership by personal example; (3) acceptance of "reasonable" risk; (4) decisiveness; (5) effective communication; and (6) team-building. Source: Anderson, J. W. (1984, September). *The warrior spirit* (Working Paper 84–9). Alexandria, VA: U.S. Army Research Institute, p. 1.

15. Of special relevance here is the clear thesis of Sidney Hook, the American philosopher, that heroism requires both great qualities and great circumstances. See Jennings, E. E. (1960). *An anatomy of leadership*. New York: Harper and Brothers; and Hook, S. (1955). *The hero in history*. Boston: Beacon Press.

16. This analysis involved relatively sophisticated statistical methods. For details see the original work of Gal, R. (1983). Courage under stress. In S. Breznitz (Ed.), *Stress in Israel* (pp. 65–91). New York: Van Nostrand Reinhold.

17. From a philosophical point of view, this conclusion is consistent with the Hegelian philosophy regarding the interaction between men and history. In Hegel's view no heroes created history; instead they were evoked by great times and circumstances. In fact, Hegel's argument was that there were no genuine alternatives for the hero. Had a certain individual not come forward as a hero at a given time in history, another would have been called forward instead.

Thus the hero, according to the nineteenth-century German philosopher, is merely a product, or an instrument, of the situation. Hegel, G.W.F. (1861). *Lectures on the philosophy of history* (Translated from the 3rd German Edition by J. Sibree). London: H. G. Bohn.

18. These Israeli figures can be compared with other Western military operations which also occurred in the early 1980s. For instance, after the Falklands War, Great Britain distributed 679 medals among approximately 28,000 of its soldiers, sailors, and airmen who had actually participated in that conflict which lasted seventy-four days at a cost of 255 lives. In the United States, the Army issued 8,663 medals (of all levels) following the Grenada invasion of October 1983. In that operation about 7,000 Army personnel actually took part in the military action which lasted three days at a cost of eighteen lives from all participating services. For their part in the Grenada invasion, the Navy and Marine Corps combined have issued (as of April 1984) only 17 medals, all of them Purple Hearts. Source: Record, J. (1984, April 15). More medals than we had soldiers: Grenada's decoration glut cheapens honor and valor. *The Washington Post*, p. B5.

19. Milshtein, A. (1983, April 6). What was in the past awardable has become part of combat doctrine. *Bamahane*, 30, 6–7.

11

BATTLE STRESS AND COMBAT REACTIONS

Wars are not all glory. They also involve agony, fear and suffering. The Israeli wars are no exception. Israeli soldiers, too, have known, throughout their wars, the full gamut of agony, fear and suffering. Though none of Israel's wars ever came close to the enormous scope and multinational extent of both world wars with their vast devastation and millions of casualties, Israel's repetitious exposure to combat and warlike activities has taken its toll on its soldiers. It is this toll, and the evolution of the awareness of its mental and psychological aspects, which will be discussed in this chapter.

From the Independence War to the Yom Kippur War

In its first few years and first few wars, the IDF neither paid much attention to combat reactions in general nor saw much combat shock in particular. Whether this was due to a lack of awareness of the problem, or because of the swift nature of these first few wars, or because they were perceived as wars of deliverance, the phenomena of battle stress and combat reactions were scarcely recognized. This was in spite of the fact that the rates of casualties in all of Israel's wars were relatively high considering the size of Israel's population at these various times (see Table 11.1).[1]

By comparison, the percentage of American fatalities throughout the Vietnam era did not exceed 0.03 percent of the total population. However, during World War II, American fatalities reached 0.2 percent. The French during World War II lost 1.4 percent of their total population, while the Russians suffered a population loss in excess of 10 percent.[2]

Nonetheless, the fact that Israel suffered these casualties every few years (six wars in three decades) in a relatively small and intimate pop-

Table 11.1
Number and Proportion of Fatalities in Israel's Six Wars

War	Number of casualties	Jewish population at that time	Percentage of fatalities from population
Independence War (1948)	6,000*	672,000	.89
Sinai Campaign (1956)	230**	1,668,000	.01
Six Day War (1967)	810**	2,363,000	.03
War of Attrition (1967-70)	1,370	2,543,000	.05
Yom Kippur War	2,680	2,845,000	.09
Lebanon War	400**	3,283,000	.01

*About 2,000 were killed while not formally on active duty.
**Figures include fatalities in the periods immediately preceding or following these wars.

ulation compounds the impact of these casualty rates. Thus, for example, one of every four persons in Israel has lost at least one relative in one of these wars.[3]

> Israel has a very strict policy regarding the military utilization of sons and daughters of bereaved families. A soldier from a bereaved family (i.e., one in which an immediate family member has been a war casualty) is not permitted to serve in a combat assignment, no matter what his qualifications are. Only with a signed parental waiver will the conscript be allowed a combat role. Indeed, generally there are more who present signed waivers to allow them to fight than there are those taking advantage of this exemption. Likewise, an only child is also exempted from combat assignments unless a parental waiver is presented. Similarly, as in the case of bereaved families, this option out of combat is rarely pursued. In all the combat units in which I served, I was not the sole example of an only child.

While all of these figures may have an impact on the war reactions of the Israeli population in general,[4] the military itself has not been overly affected by psychological ramifications of these casualties. Even during the War of Independence, which remains to this day the costliest of Israel's wars in terms of fatalities, there were very few documented instances of combat breakdown. Only a few cases are known to have been reported. In those cases involving combat stress reactions (as, for example, in the Battle of Latrum where casualties were extremely high), no systematic documentation exists. Certainly the next two wars (the Sinai campaign and the Six Day War) which were brief, victorious and glorious did not leave behind any traces of severe combat stress reactions. The first war to produce extensive psychiatric casualties was the Yom Kippur War.

The Yom Kippur War

The 1973 Yom Kippur War was brief but intense. While the war only lasted approximately four weeks, it nonetheless resulted in heavy casualties. The Israelis were taken by surprise, nearly overrun by the mass of enemy soldiers and equipment, and initially forced to retreat. In its early phases it was in fact fought twenty-four hours a day, often with six to seven enemy pulses each day. Within days the IDF was able to mobilize its reserves, gain tactical initiative, and exploit the adversaries' inflexibility to regain their original positions. However, the IDF, for the first time in its history, suffered a relatively high rate of psychiatric casualties during this war.[5]

Combat stress reactions in battle are generally expressed as a ratio of the psychiatric casualties to the wounded in action. The initial figures concerning psychiatric casualties to wounded in action (WIA) were reported as 14:100 or 12.3 percent of all non-fatal casualties. Much later examination,[6] however, found this figure to be low: the actual ratio was subsequently assessed as 30:100, or 23.1 percent of all non-fatal casualties. The latter figure includes those originally recorded as battle shock casualties, those not formally so recorded but otherwise exhibiting various combat stress reactions, those with delayed reactions, and those who were both wounded and suffering combat stress reactions.[7]

The IDF authorities, concerned by the unexpected number of physical and psychiatric casualties sustained in the 1973 war, conducted an intense review of its "lessons learned," which led to the development of doctrine for treating battle shock casualties. These were subsequently applied during the 1982 War in Lebanon.

Classification and Treatment

Israeli diagnostic procedures regarding combat reactions during the Yom Kippur War were, to say the least, not very accurate. Whether because of lack of previous experience and knowledge, or because of a priori negative attitudes regarding breakdown in combat, the IDF's medical professionals often misdiagnosed these combat reactions.

Some Israeli medical professionals, for whom the 1973 war was their first exposure to such severe combat psychiatric casualties, reacted in what might be considered an unexpected manner. A published report by an Israeli psychiatrist regarding his role in treating these psychiatric casualties exemplifies this point:

"I have never before felt so strongly how debatable it is and how much self-deception is contained in the so-called 'professional' attitude, whereby we attempt only to understand but never to judge.

"To understand this more clearly we have to return to the situation which existed at the beginning of the [Yom Kippur] war. We were all convinced, that in the event of an Arab victory, not only our national integrity, but also the physical existence of everyone of us would be endangered. Starting from this premise . . . it is understandable that the maintenance of a strong army was of vital interest [sic] to all of us.

"When in the middst [sic] of the war, a young and physically healthy man claims, [sic] that he can no longer cope with those difficulties which are endured by everyone else, this attitude is at first sight hard to understand. . . . [Even if] we can understand this . . . can we be expected to feel the same pity for this man, as for all other soldiers? This man is concerned only for himself, in contrast with his comrades, who bear their wounds uncomplainingly . . . and even in the worst situations manage to maintain their dignity and human feeling."[8] (P. 202)

In those instances when a psychiatric casualty was diagnosed, the IDF mental health authorities distinguished between battle shock and battle fatigue. Battle shock, a severe emotional reaction to the stress of battle, usually develops after hours or days of intense combat. In contrast, battle fatigue usually develops after weeks or months of moderate combat. Due to the relatively brief duration of the Yom Kippur War, psychiatric casualties generally were those of battle shock. Incidents of extreme exhaustion, or temporary expressions of fear and depression, were essentially ignored.

Israeli psychiatrists also observed during the Yom Kippur War a new form of combat reaction which they labeled delayed battle shock.[9] Some soldiers who had done well during intense fighting broke down upon receiving their first telephone call from home, or when they arrived at home on their first leave.

Since the 1973 war was the first in which the Israeli military sustained large numbers of psychiatric casualties, the IDF was unprepared in terms of treatment methods and facilities for those casualties. In fact, the IDF's medical and mental health authorities were not even current with the long-existent professional literature dealing with combat stress reactions. The treatment of these psychiatric problems, which was firmly established after World War I, based on the triple principles of proximity, immediacy and expectancy,[10] was not known to, or utilized by, the IDF's medical corps.

Consequently, contrary to all recognized military medical doctrines, during the 1973 war all diagnosed battle shock casualties were evacuated to the rear where they were treated in civilian hospitals.[11] Only a few of these ever returned to their units during the war. Indeed, for many, recovery was slow and their disability prolonged. However, for those who did recover and return to their units, the perceived urgency of the Yom Kippur War played a significant role in their recovery. As observed by an Israeli military psychologist: "During the Yom Kippur war, Israeli soldiers showed a very strong commitment to the army and to their country. In many cases, similar expressions of a strong ego-involvement could be found in soldiers who were in treatment and it seems fair to conclude that this pattern of involvement has played a decisive role in the process of readjustment and reintegration."[12] (P. 528)

Analysis of Combat Stress Factors

A concerted effort was made after the Yom Kippur War to analyze the various antecedent factors which caused the increased psychiatric casualties of the war. Though most of the conclusions were not entirely different from those reached regarding psychiatric casualties in previous world conflicts, there were nonetheless some quite unique to the IDF. These antecedent factors fell into three categories: battlefield and combat-role factors, individual factors, and group factors.

Battlefield and combat-role factors. The intensity of fighting, rather than its duration, directly correlated with the onset of battle shock. Thus, the number of battle shock cases among IDF soldiers was highest during the first extremely intense hours and days of the 1973 war. They accelerated again two weeks later, during the crossing of the Suez Canal, when enemy artillery fire was most concentrated. Indeed, when the IDF mental health investigators[13] retroactively plotted the psychiatric casualties against physical casualties (the latter serving as an indication of intensity of the battle) and across days of combat, the pattern illustrated in Figure 11.1 appeared.[14]

The incidence of battle shock, in addition to varying with battle intensity, also varied with the soldier's combat role. Of all combat units, battle shock was most frequent in armored units, followed by artillery units and infantry units. Apparently the high prevalence in armored units was a result of the Armor troops being engaged in the most intense combat of the war. In addition, reservists were more vulnerable than regular service soldiers, and soldiers from support units were relatively more at risk for psychiatric breakdown than soldiers in combat roles.

Figure 11.1
Percentage of Soldiers Involved in Physical (Wounded) and Psychiatric Casualties by Day of Combat

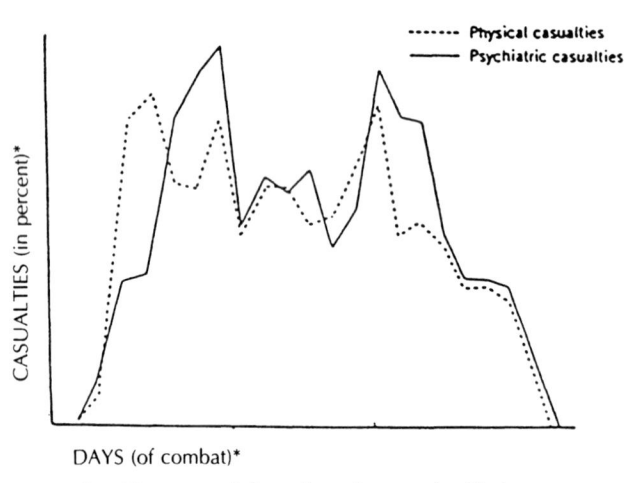

*Specific rates and days of combat are classified.

This distinction between combat and combat-support units is shown in Table 11.2.[15]

As the table demonstrates, combat troops (as represented by those evacuated to one particular medical installation) had the highest frequency of both physical and psychiatric casualties, as one would expect. However, when these casualties are viewed in a relative manner, it is the combat support and combat service support groups who had the highest ratio of psychiatric to physical casualties. Obviously the noncombatants lack the necessary training, cohesion, leadership and expectations which serve to minimize the psychological horror of the battle.

Another aspect of the combat-role factor is that of soldier's rank. Figures from the Yom Kippur War demonstrated that rank was a significant factor in eliciting, or preventing, psychiatric breakdown. This was especially the case with regard to the officer corps. Though IDF officers were extremely overrepresented in the rate of fatalities, because of their frequent exposure to enemy fire, they were clearly underrepresented in the lists of psychiatric casualties. One of the post–1973 reports[16] showed

Table 11.2
Distribution of Psychiatric and Physical (Wounded) Casualties by Military Assignment

Assignment	Percent of Psychiatric Casualties	Percent of Physical Casualties
Combat	69.8	89.4
Combat support	25.5	8.5
Combat service support	4.7	2.0

that while officers comprised 16 percent of all physical casualties, they accounted for only 3 percent of all the psychiatric casualties. In the investigators' words, the IDF officers "were five times less vulnerable to war stress" during the Yom Kippur War than were their subordinates. Thus, battle intensity, primarily, and the soldier's battle role, secondarily, were among the main factors related to battle shock.

Individual factors. A number of individual background variables have been shown to be associated with occurrence of combat stress reactions. An initial examination of a sample of soldiers from the 1973 war suffering from battle shock yielded a clear difference in quality (Kaba) scores between the psychiatric and physical (control) casualty groups (see Table 11.3).[17]

While the relatively greater proportion of high Kaba scores in both the psychiatric and physical groups of casualties is due to their greater representation in combat units, it is quite apparent that they are more susceptible to physical wounds than to psychiatric breakdown; the inverse is true for the lower Kaba categories. It was similarly found in another sample that the soldiers experiencing battle shock had, on the average, a lower level of education (as compared with a comparable group of soldiers without combat psychiatric reactions).

A detailed retrospective examination of forty IDF soldiers who suffered battle shock[18] further revealed the importance of individual background. Each of these forty men received treatment during the acute stage of the syndrome. Thirty-five percent of them had been seriously wounded; and in 70 percent of this wounded group, the physical injury was reported as a direct cause of the battle shock.

More important, 80 percent of the men with battle shock reported personal or family stresses occurring prior to or during the war. Of the total group, 50 percent had pregnant wives or wives who had given

Table 11.3
Distribution of Psychiatric and Physical Casualties by Kaba Scores

KABA Categories*	Percent of Psychiatric Casualties	Percent of Physical Casualties
Low	15.5	8.4
Intermediate	32.8	16.8
High	50.9	75.0

*The Kaba scores of 0.8 percent of the soldiers were unavailable.

birth within the previous year. Twenty-three percent of the cases reported a recent death in the immediate family. Other relevant personal or family stresses included recent marriage, taking on a mortgage, having ill parents, or experiencing a serious personal loss. Based on these findings it was concluded that soldiers who had prior or ongoing stressful home situations were more vulnerable to battle shock.

Surprisingly, however, none of the studies conducted after the Yom Kippur War conclusively revealed a direct relationship between personality disposition and combat psychiatric reactions.[19] The only exception was a report by two psychotherapists from the Mental Health Center of the IDF who, after the war, treated a number of soldiers with chronic post-traumatic symptoms.[20] These clinicians observed a common personality profile which was highly consistent across individual cases. This profile included an extreme need for excellent performance and for winning in competitive situations along with a tendency to assume responsibility at an early stage of their lives. The authors interpreted these tendencies as reflecting an exaggerated facade of the strong-Israeli image, covering serious problems with a masculine identity. When individuals with this facade face feelings of extreme helplessness and lack of control, they tend to collapse.

Group factors. Studies conducted by the IDF after the 1973 war also examined group- or unit-related factors which might have contributed to psychiatric casualties. In one of these studies, 40 percent of the men diagnosed with battle shock reported minimal group cohesion and unit identification and poor identification with their unit. Only 10 percent of

Table 11.4
Unit-Related Factors as Experienced by Two Groups of Combat Soldiers

Factors	Combat Reaction Group	Control Group
1. Perceived unit's morale during combat as low	72%	0%
2. Experienced loneliness	76%	29%
3. Felt no trust toward immediate command	42%	5%
4. Served during this war within the original unit	57%	88%
5. Changed teams in combat	63%	15%
6. Low self esteem about own professional military knowledge	42%	5%

the soldiers in the control group (men not suffering battle shock) reported the same.[21]

Another IDF study yielded similar findings.[22] This study compared a sample of seventy-four reserve combat soldiers suffering from acute or delayed combat reactions with a control group of one hundred combat soldiers, randomly selected from a reserve paratrooper unit. The two groups differed markedly on a list of variables pertaining to their perceived unit morale and their own experience with their units.

As can be seen from Table 11.4, many of the men suffering from battle shock did not serve with their usual reserve unit or had poor relationships with their peers and commanders.[23] They also reported low unit morale and low self-esteem as combatants. In contrast, a great majority of the soldiers who were not psychiatrically impaired served with their usual unit and team, had good relationships with their peers, trusted their commanders, and had high self-esteem.

Thus soldiers are most vulnerable to either the immediate or delayed onset of battle shock when they have experienced intense fighting, have low morale, have personal or family stress or are physically or psychologically detached from their unit.

Most important, the IDF's medical and psychological services heeded the "lessons learned" from the Yom Kippur War concerning the appropriate treatment to be given to psychiatric casualties. From these "lessons learned" the IDF prepared its contingencies for its next war.

In Between Wars

The vast number of combat stress reactions exhibited during the Yom Kippur War affected more than the medical services of the IDF. The IDF manpower authorities, their behavioral scientists and, above all, commanders began to pay more attention to this previously neglected area, focusing mainly on prevention. Numerous reports (all highly classified) by the IDF's Unit of Military Psychology linked the relationships between morale, cohesion and leadership factors with the perceived successes and failures of units functioning in the war. The importance of morale surveys, field psychologists in the units,[24] immediate feedback to commanders and brief seminars regarding human aspects of combat was rapidly acknowledged throughout the combat units of the IDF.[25]

The IDF's behavioral science authorities adopted the Organizational Development (OD) Model which had been applied by industrial psychologists for quite some time. They have transformed it into an Emergency Organizational Development Model (EOD) which is better suited to military needs.[26] Consequently, an integrated system of field psychologists had been implemented for all line divisions (regular and reserve) of the IDF. Their function was to consult with commanders on issues of morale, motivation and cohesion; to conduct surveys in these areas; to give the commanders survey feedback regarding their troops; and to conduct periodic short seminars on these issues. Within a relatively short time the field psychologists became among the most important sources of information and advice for line unit commanders.[27]

To outside observers, the high status and regard accorded to field psychologists in their respective units seems rather astonishing. The seriousness with which commanders view their unit morale surveys is also surprising. The following description is taken from a *Visit Report* of a Canadian military psychologist to the Israeli military in November of 1982.

"I was somewhat surprised to hear that the results are generally eagerly awaited by commanders at all levels. This is probably because a specific commander always sees his results first, and while results are communicated in aggregate form to successive levels of command, each commander's frame of reference is based on an average calculated over the organization at his level.... Further, since the surveys are conducted regularly, a commander can trace the results of any leadership initiatives that he may have taken.... The results of these surveys are prepared for presentation to the various levels of command in graphical form. The information is considered a very important indicator of operational effectiveness, and a source for problem identification and resolution."[28] (P. 10)

This integrated system has achieved its high status as a result of the recognition that the only available preventive measures against excessive psychiatric casualties involve enhancing unit morale, interpersonal relationships and effective leadership. Thus this network of field psychologists has been increasingly active in the peacetime period following the 1973 war and would be put to the test in the 1982 War in Lebanon.[29]

The mental health services of the IDF also reorganized in response to the lessons learned from the Yom Kippur War. Major changes were in two directions. In the first place their professional model shifted from an individual-medical to a unit-intervention emphasis.[30] In addition, these mental health professionals also reorganized their treatment system for psychiatric casualties based on both the Yom Kippur War's lessons and those of other Western militaries.

These reorganizations resulted in the formation of professional psychiatric teams, each assigned to a medical battalion at the division level. During peacetime this team's mission was to educate commanders regarding the occurrence of, and symptoms associated with, battle shock. They were also prepared to expect the majority of these casualties to return to their units after a brief period of treatment. During wartime this team was to provide the first echelon of treatment for battle shock.[31] The team would treat these battle shock casualties for twenty-four to seventy-two hours with the expectation of rapid return to their units. A second echelon of treatment for the more severe and unresponsive cases was planned to be located in rear areas, within military camps, away from civilian hospitals. The guidance policy for these centers emphasized maintaining a military atmosphere. Activities were to include abreactive therapy (both individual and group) and military drills, along with sports activities. The expected stay was for a maximum of two weeks. These centers were to encourage a strong expectation of return to duty on the part of the treated soldiers.

All of these preparations, reorganizations and interventions took place in the years following the Yom Kippur War. In June 1982, when the IDF units moved into Lebanon, this entire infrastructure was put into operation to confront the reality of combat stress reaction.

The Lebanon War

The 1982 War in Lebanon differed in many respects from the 1973 Yom Kippur War.[32] Unlike the previous war, the Israelis determined the time and the manner of the 1982 war. Israeli preparation was very thorough. The war had only one front and did not engage the entire IDF. Reserve personnel in both the medical and behavioral science corps had received relevant training according to IDF updated doctrines prior to the war and were well integrated into the fighting units. The Israeli forces in general had long anticipated this confrontation.

Despite this excellent preparation by the IDF, the war was unexpectedly difficult and costly. The Palestine Liberation Organization (PLO) units, fighting in the built-up urban areas along the coastal plain, managed to evade the IDF forward advance, conducted scattered suicidal defense operations along the coast, and were able to retreat with the bulk of their personnel into Beirut. Likewise, Syrian armored forces in the Bekka, despite sustaining heavy casualties themselves, also slowed the parallel IDF advance inland and caused many Israeli casualties.

During the intense period of fighting in Lebanon (June to August 1982), the IDF suffered approximately 2,600 wounded and 400 killed. Of the total number of wounded, 600 were reported to be psychiatric casualties.[33] The majority of these casualties were diagnosed with "pure" battle shock. The remainder were either mixed syndromes (combat stress combined with underlying personality disorder), delayed psychiatric casualties, or combat stress reactions among the wounded.

Derived from these figures, the ratio of psychiatric casualties to wounded for the IDF in Lebanon was 23:100 (in actual numbers 600:2,600, or 18.7 percent of all non-fatal casualties). Thus psychiatric casualties were proportionately lower during the 1982 war than during the 1973 Yom Kippur War.

Yet, there was the impression, even among the IDF's own medical authorities, that these rates were largely exaggerated and that during the Lebanon War there was a tendency to overdiagnose cases of combat stress reaction. Though no empirical evidence exists to support this, it may well be that cases which earlier might have been considered to be combat exhaustion, fatigue, or normal anxiety reactions were now instead diagnosed as psychiatric casualties.[34] One possible reason for this phenomenon could be found in the extensive preparations the IDF had made in anticipation of great numbers of these casualties. It may also be a result of the apparent "stamp of approval" given to combat stress reactions by the IDF's hierarchy throughout its extensive education of the command structure. There are those, however, who consider these unexpectedly high figures of psychiatric casualties as a warning signal indicating a certain weakening in the mental immunity to stress of the Israeli soldier.[35]

Symptoms and Diagnosis

The clinical symptoms evidenced by Israeli psychiatric casualties in Lebanon were similar to those reported by the Western forces in World War I, World War II, and the Korean War, and by Israeli forces during the 1973 war. Battle shock cases were characterized by anxiety and incapacitating fear, depression and sleep disturbances. In most cases, breakdown was associated with intense fighting and sleep deprivation. Tactical errors such as being strafed by friendly fire or unexpectedly ambushed further increased the incidence of battle shock. Events preceding the immediate onset of psychiatric breakdown were fierce combat, one's near miss with death, or witnessing the death or injury of friends or one's own commander.

As in the 1973 Yom Kippur War, cases of delayed psychiatric breakdown also occurred in men who had been demobilized or who were home on leave.[36] These delayed psychiatric reactions were characterized by deep depression, repetitive images of combat, loss of appetite and sleeplessness. Soldiers suffering from these delayed reactions were referred for treatment to the military Mental Health Clinic in central Israel. Retrospectively, however, IDF psychiatrists concluded that some of these soldiers would have been spared their delayed psychiatric breakdown had they remained with their units in Lebanon. In the view of these psychiatrists, going home a short time after combat engagement weakened soldiers' supportive ties with their units and hence reduced their ability to cope with their recent combat experiences.

Treatment

Despite all of the plans for forward treatment, not all psychiatric casualties in the Lebanon War were treated close to the front. Some were evacuated to rear civilian treatment centers because of the pressure battalion surgeons exerted for rapid rearward evacuation. It also reflected the tactical and geographical conditions in Lebanon where ground evacuation to the rear was virtually impossible. Thus evacuation from the battlefield for both physical and psychiatric casualties was frequently by helicopters which flew them directly back to civilian hospitals in Israel. Hence, despite prewar planning, only approximately half of these psychiatric casualties reached the Advanced Medical Battalion (AMB) while the other half were transported to civilian hospitals in Israel.

Many from this latter group were subsequently transferred to the second echelon treatment facility which was put into operation on the sixth day of the war. This facility was located in a military base in the northern part of Israel, about fifteen miles from the Lebanese border.

This special military installation received soldiers suffering combat shock from both the AMBs and civilian hospitals in the rear. Here treatment was centered around three main principles. First, a total military atmosphere was maintained in terms of living conditions, uniforms, discipline, etc. Second, these psychiatrically impaired soldiers were kept constantly busy, whether with physical or therapeutic activities. And finally, most of the therapeutic procedures were conducted in small group settings.[37]

> The IDF's preplanned policy of the second echelon treatment facility was to keep the psychiatrically impaired soldiers within a strict military setting, with minimal contact with their families, so as not to further complicate the situation. As described by two of this installation's senior psychiatrists, these plans were merely hypothetical:
> "Life, however, was much stronger and more flexible and realistic than we were. Israel is a small country and the 'Jewish mothers' of our soldiers soon found out the location of our installation and 'invaded' us in large numbers, at all hours. We soon realized that there was no way to stop these visits and had to change our policy. 'If you can't beat them, join them.' We arranged talks with family members and explained the problems of our patients. Contact between therapists and family was found to be positive and constructive. Use was made of families which was not regarded as an obstacle to cure, but as an additional therapeutic resource, which could assist in recovery and rehabilitation. We even held group meetings of soldiers and their wives, in which many important and intimate matters were openly discussed."[38] (P.199)

The doctrine of forward treatment, whenever it was applied by the IDF, proved to be quite effective. In fact, a few aggressive teams returned 95 percent of their battle shock cases to duty with their units.[39] Overall, the return-to-unit rate was between 60 and 70 percent, with the majority being sent back to their units within seventy-two hours.

In the AMBs the division psychiatric teams were frequently reinforced with psychologists from the division field psychologist teams. Treatment was according to the traditional principles of military psychiatry (i.e., rest, physical replenishments and brief, but supportive, psychotherapy). However, various teams developed additional techniques which molded the Israeli version. Thus, for example, in a number of cases a soldier suffering from combat shock was, as part of his treatment, assigned various specific military chores such as cleaning weapons or even instructing newly arrived soldiers on weapons usage. In other cases the psychiatric team arranged for the unit commander and peers from the treated soldier's unit to visit the soldier. Occasionally the soldier himself was taken to visit his unit. By doing this, mutual confidence between the soldier and his unit was restored. When the soldier had recovered from his psychiatric breakdown, the team would arrange for peers from his unit to pick him up. Thus the mental health teams were able to take advantage of their proximity to the front and the soldier's unit, allowing them to maximize the expectation that he would return to that unit. It was further observed[40] that these units were happy to have the impaired soldier return, thus confirming that group members prefer to have someone they know well (despite a breakdown episode) to someone they do not know at all.

Fear and anxiety were occasionally experienced by many of these mental health professionals themselves, either because of their proximity to the front or because of their continual exposure to terrified psychiatric casualties. The fears of these mental health professionals were dealt with in daily staff meetings in which cases were discussed, mutual support was provided, and emotional conflicts were worked through.

Of the 600 soldiers evacuated as psychiatric casualties, 60 required further institutional treatment after two to three weeks of apparently unsuccessful first or second echelon psychiatric care.[41] These soldiers were sent to the Combat Fitness Retraining Unit (CFRU) which was located in central Israel on the grounds of a civilian sports institute. The 60 psychiatric casualties came predominantly from combat units with equal representation from both regular and reserve components. The staff included psychiatrists, psychologists, social workers and sports coaches. The atmosphere could be characterized as quasi-military in that soldiers wore their uniforms and essentially maintained a daily military schedule. The guiding idea of the CFRU was labeled by its staff as "walking and talking." It consisted of individual and group psychotherapy combined with abundant physical activities (e.g., physical training, military training, etc.). The average treatment stay in the CFRU was twenty-six days, and the recovery rate for the regular service soldiers (in terms of return to unit) was 43 percent; the rate for reservists was 38 percent.

The soldiers treated in the CFRU were thoroughly tested using various personality instruments. From test results, 90 percent of the 60 soldiers were diagnosed as suffering from some form of character disorder.[42] In contrast, the mental health officers in the front echelons detected character disorders in only a small proportion of their battle shock casualties.

These results confirm the conclusion from other wars and armies that personality is weakly associated with psychiatric breakdown in combat but may be substantially related to the prognosis once breakdown has occurred.

Analysis of Combat Stress Factors

Data regarding background variables related to psychiatric casualties were quite similar to that acquired from the 1973 war. For instance, the fiercer the battle, the more psychiatric casualties there were.[43] Differences in vulnerability to psychiatric breakdowns were again found to be related to age differences. Soldiers aged eighteen to twenty-one (i.e., those in their compulsory service period) appeared the least vulnerable, while soldiers aged twenty-six to thirty appeared the most vulnerable. Other factors associated with psychiatric breakdown were a low level of education, motivation and intelligence. Being a reservist, having low enlisted rank, and belonging to a support unit were also risk factors for psychiatric breakdown.[44] Some of these factors are interrelated: in the IDF, low levels of education, motivation and intelligence usually mean an assignment to a support unit.

Finally, the IDF investigators have accumulated adequate data to substantiate the long-held belief that unit morale and confidence in commanders could be major factors not only in enhancing combat effectiveness but also in better enabling soldiers to cope with the horrors of war, thus minimizing psychiatric casualties.[45]

The Impact of Wars

The overall assessment of the Israeli soldier's reaction to the stresses of combat yields a rather ambiguous picture. With regard to immediate combat stress reactions in the form of psychiatric casualties, the Israeli soldier apparently does not markedly differ from his Western counterparts. The rates of psychiatric casualties in both the Yom Kippur and Lebanon wars were found to be within the familiar range of 10:100 to 30:100, a rate which had, in general, been found in many combat theatres throughout Western military history. However, as far as long-term, ongoing effects of combat stress reactions are concerned, there is not enough data to adequately evaluate this effect. Israel has not enjoyed a long enough breathing spell to enable a thorough examination of that nature.

The Israeli soldier, however, has several advantages as compared to most of his Western counterparts. Israeli wars have always been relatively brief, usually a matter of a few days or weeks. That is in stark contrast to the long years which characterized, for example, World War I and II. The Israeli soldier, thus, has been spared the devastating effects of combat exhaustion, which was one of the major causes of breakdown in both world wars.

Second, the Israeli soldier also had the advantage of clearly knowing what he was fighting for. That is not always the case for many militaries engaged in combat. And even though during the Second World War the allied troops also knew what they were fighting for, the most frequent response of the American G.I.s to the question, "What keeps you going?" was "To get the job over with and go home."[46] In most cases an Israeli soldier's response to an identical question would be more concrete, involving a sense of defending his family and country. From a psychological point of view, such a concrete perception is a distinct advantage.

Finally, the combination of Israel's small size and battlefield proximity has always enabled its soldiers to keep in frequent contact with their families, sometimes even at the midst of combat activities—a luxury which is seldom possible for soldiers fighting far from their homes.

> During a lull in combat in the Lebanon War, a diligent communications officer in one of the armored battalions which had just disengaged from heavy fighting in the Bekka Valley managed to set up an improvised communication network which enabled his troops to talk directly to their families at home. It was not long before there was a long line of troops, each waiting for his two-minute turn to call home. In addition to the ordinary conversations—"hello," "I'm all right" and "How is cousin Moshe doing on his front?"—some also used this direct contact for special requests. One soldier who belonged to the Yeshiva students company anxiously told his mother in Jerusalem that his tank had been hit by enemy fire and his own rucksack, and in it the "tefillin" (Jewish phylacteries, used by Orthodox Jews during morning prayers), had been destroyed. "Please quickly send me new tefillin," he asked his mother on the radio. And most probably it arrived in Lebanon within a day or two.

Indeed, the effects of war have not always been seen by the Israeli soldier as purely negative. Thirty-four veterans of the Yom Kippur War were randomly interviewed by a clinical psychologist about two years after the war. When asked how they would evaluate the effect of the war on themselves (in overall positive or negative terms), 51 percent of the sampled group reported the war had "mainly positive, though also some negative" effects on them. Another 9.7 percent reported "positive effects" only. In contrast, 32.2 percent of the same group had "mainly negative, though also some positive" effects, while only 3.2 percent reported "negative only." The main positive effect reported by these veterans fell within the scope of the individual's "existential" experience. It involved reevaluation of one's personal values and priorities in life and frequently resulted in a greater maturity as evidenced by a greater appreciation of life.[47]

Other reactions among IDF veterans were more negative, though not necessarily in direct response to their combat experience. In 1984, for example, an interview with a senior Israeli civilian psychiatrist was published in which he reported a recent increase in the number of young men released from military service who were now visiting psychiatric clinics because of emotional difficulties. While most of these difficulties could be traced to their military service, they were not necessarily all related to combat experiences. This was, in the psychiatrist's opinion, a new phenomenon.[48]

A new trendy behavior of young Israelis after completion of compulsory service is that of heading out alone for wide travels around the world. Typically they will choose hazardous travels to the jungles of South America, India or the Far East, stretching their journeys to a year or more, sometimes completely dropping out of sight. When asked, they will say that they need something different after three or more draining years of service. Surprisingly, however, that something else is really quite similar, in terms of risks, difficult conditions and stresses involved, to what they have just left behind.

While many of these adventurous youth return home to Israel at the end of their journeys, many IDF veterans, sometime after completion of compulsory service, decide to leave Israel and take up residence in another country—an act which is viewed negatively in Israel. Among the more common reasons given by these youth is that of the stress from military service and their despondency regarding the certain prospect of their continual reserve service.

Whether or not IDF veterans apply more frequently to psychiatric clinics than other portions of the population, or embark on more adventurous journeys around the world than youth from other countries, or even consider permanent emigration from Israel to escape the stresses of military life remains ambiguous. But what is clear is that whenever a war breaks out in Israel, these veterans (who are now reserve members of IDF fighting units) can be counted on to promptly respond to the needs of their country. With no formal requirement and without waiting for their call-ups, thousands of these men take the first available plane and immediately report to their units. Being a veteran of the IDF turns one into a permanent "minuteman."

Conclusion

It is difficult to differentiate between the specific stress factors affecting Israeli soldiers (regulars and reservists alike) and those affecting the citizens of Israel in general. All citizens of Israel suffer from these stress factors which include the security, economic and social situations characterizing everyday life in Israel.[49] In fact sometimes it seems as though the mandatory military service required of Israeli youth gives them a moratorium before entering the hectic life which is Israel today.

Yet to be assessed is the cumulative effect of years and years of bearing the continual security responsibility for Israel, not to mention the repeated wars and the endless lists of casualties. In the long run, the aggregate impact of all this stress may well be devastating to Israeli society in general and Israeli youth in particular.

Notes

1. Zusmann, P. (1984). Why is the defence burden so heavy in Israel? In Z. Offer & A. Kober (Eds.), *The price of power* (pp. 17–25). Tel-Aviv: Ministry of Defence Publications.
2. Ibid., p. 18.
3. Ibid., p. 19.
4. See, for example: Breznitz, S. (Ed.). (1983). *Stress in Israel*, New York: Van Nostrand Reinhold; and Offer & Kober, *The price of power*.
5. The following review, especially with regard to the 1973 and 1982 psychiatric casualty figures, is based primarily on Belenky, G. L., Tyner, C. F., & Sodetz, F. J. (1983, August). *Israeli battle shock casualties: 1973 and 1982* (WRAIR Report NP 83-4). Washington, DC: Walter Reed Army Institute of Research.
6. In contrast to 1973, the mental health authorities of the IDF were better prepared for psychiatric casualties in the 1982 War in Lebanon. It was partially due to retroactive application of 1982 criteria to the 1973 cases that resulted in these new ratios.
7. Comparable figures are available for the U.S. Army in its major wars. While Vietnam figures were remarkably low (around 3 to 4 percent of all medical evacuations were designated psychiatric casualties), the comparable figure for the Korean War was 6 percent, and for World War II the average figure was 23 percent. Johnson, A. W. (1969, December). Combat psychiatry. Part II. The U.S. Army in Vietnam. *Medical Bulletin U.S. Army Europe*, 25(11), 335–339. In some instances, however, when battles were extremely fierce and intensive, these percentages may reach 40 percent of medical evacuations (e.g., on the Guadalcanal battlefield). See Rosner, A. A. (1944). Neuropsychiatric casualties from Guadalcanal. *American Journal of Medical Science*, 207, 770–776.
8. Kalman, G. (1977). On combat neuroses. *International Journal Social Psychiatry* (England), 23(3), 195–203.
9. Belenky et al., *Israeli battle shock casualties*.
10. Salmon, T. W. (1919). The war neuroses and their lesson. *New York Journal of Medicine*, 109, 993–994.
11. There are no military hospitals in Israel. All civilian hospitals are designated to treat IDF casualties during war. During peacetime several hospitals provide in-patient medical treatment for IDF personnel. These hospitals also have part of their staff who are uniformed medical professionals.
12. Sohlberg, S. C. (1976). Stress experiences and combat fatigue during the Yom Kippur War—1973. *Psychological Reports*, 38, 523–529.

13. Levav, I., Greenfeld, H., & Baruch, E. (1979, May). Psychiatric combat reactions during the Yom Kippur War. *Am. J. Psychiatry, 136*(5), 637–641.
14. Ibid., p. 639.
15. Ibid.
16. Ibid.
17. Ibid.
18. Noy, S. (1978, June). *Stress and personality as factors in the causality and prognosis of combat reaction.* Paper presented at the Second International Conference on Psychological Stress and Adjustment in Time of War and Peace, Jerusalem, Israel.
19. Review of the military psychiatric literature reveals, in fact, that this is not so "surprising": non-Israeli studies also failed to show distinct personality dispositions as predictors of combat breakdown. See for example: Glass, A. J. (Ed.). (1973), Lessons learned. In *Neuropsychiatry in World War II, volume II Overseas theaters.* Washington, DC: U.S. Government Printing Office.

One study comparing Israeli combat psychiatric casualties with combat physical casualties using the MMPI (the Minnesota Multiphasic Personality Inventory—a diagnostic tool frequently used to assess psychiatric impairment) yielded significant differences on three of the thirteen MMPI scales. However, these results are questionable because of the extremely small sample size and the severity of psychiatric impairment involved. See Merbaum, M., & Hefez, A. (1976). Some personality characteristics of soldiers exposed to extreme war stress. *Journal of Consulting and Clinical Psychology, 44*(1), 1–6.

20. Alon, N., & Omer, H. Treatment of the chronic post-traumatic syndrome. Unpublished manuscript. Cited by Lieblich, A. (1983). Between strength and toughness. In S. Breznitz (Ed.), *Stress in Israel* (pp. 39–64). New York: Van Nostrand Reinhold.
21. Noy, *Stress and personality*.
22. Steiner, M., & Neumann, M. (1978). Traumatic neurosis and social support in the Yom Kippur War returnees. *Military Medicine, 143*(12), 866–868.
23. Ibid., p. 867.
24. The seeds of the field psychologist system were, in fact, in the IDF prior to the Yom Kippur War. See Lester, J. T. (1973, June 26). *Israeli military psychology* (ONR Report #R–13–73). London: Office of Naval Research, U.S. Navy, Branch Office.
25. An article written by a group of IDF psychologists reviewed the experience of the military psychologist during the Yom Kippur War and the organizational model which evolved from that experience. See Greenbaum, C. W., Rogovsky, I., & Shalit, B. (1977). The military psychologists during wartime: A model based on action research and crisis intervention. *Journal of Applied Behavioral Science, 13*(1), 7–21.
26. Babad, E. Y., & Salomon, G. (1978, September). Professional dilemmas of the psychologist in an organizational emergency. *American Psychologist, 33*(9), 840–846.
27. Gabriel, R. A. (1982, December). Stress in battle: Coping on the spot. *Army, 32*(12), 36–42. See also a response to Gabriel: Marlowe, D., & Ingraham, L. H. (1983, July). Emphasizing cohesion, morale can help prevent battle stress. *Army, 33*(7), 16–17.

28. Rampton, G. M. (1983). Visit to Israel. *Visit Report*. National Defence Headquarters, Canada.
29. A recent paper by the author includes a description of the various functions of the field psychologists in IDF line units. See Gal, R. (in press). Unit morale: From a theoretical puzzle to an empirical illustration—an Israeli example. *Journal of Military Psychology*.
30. Weisman, G. (1974, June). A psycho-social model for limiting mental reaction during stress. *The Israel Annals of Psychiatry and Related Disciplines, 12*(2), 161.
31. This team could be reinforced as needed by the division team of field psychologists. The latter, even though their primary mission was consultation at the unit level, were also trained to assist in individual neuropsychiatric treatment in emergencies.
32. Detailed descriptions of the 1982 War in Lebanon can be found in the following three books: Schiff, Z., & Ya'ari, E. (1984). *Israel's Lebanon war* (Translated from the Hebrew by Ina Friedman). N.Y.: Simon and Schuster; Gabriel, R. A. (1984). *Operation peace for Galilee: The Israeli-PLO war in Lebanon*. New York: Hill and Wang; and Dupuy, T. N., & Martell, P. (1985). *Flawed victory—The 1982 war in Lebanon*. Fairfax, VA: HERO Books.
33. Shipler, D. (1983, January 8). The other Israeli casualties: The mentally scarred. *New York Times*, p. 2. These figures were subsequently confirmed by various IDF sources. A brief summary of the Israeli experience in Lebanon with regard to battle stress reactions was also published by the U.S. Medical Command in Europe whose representatives were invited to Israel to share the lessons learned in the 1982 war. See Rock, S. K., & Schneider, R. J. (1984). Battle stress reactions and the Israeli experience in Lebanon: A brief summary. *Medical Bulletin, 41*(1), 9–11.
34. This was also suggested by Belenky et al., *Israeli battle shock casualties*, p. 22.
35. In an interview in an Israeli magazine, I have already expressed this concern. I was not, however, alone in this assessment. See Oren, A. (1983, May 11). We may have spoiled our soldiers too much. *Coterett Rasheet, 23*, 20–21, 39.
36. It is customary in the IDF, if at all possible, to rapidly demobilize (in the case of reserve units) or at least to give forty-eight hours of home leave (in reserve or regular units) to troops recently engaged in severe actions.
37. A detailed description of this treatment facility was reported in Neumann, M., & Levy, A. (1984, April). A specific military installation for treatment of combat reactions during the war in Lebanon. *Military Medicine, 149*, 196–199.
38. Ibid., p. 199.
39. Enoch, D., Bar-On, R., Barg, Y., Durst, N., Haran, G., Hovel, S., Israel, A., Reiter, M., Stern, M., & Toubiana, Y. (1983, January). *An indigenous military community as a psychotherapeutic agent: Specific application of forward treatment in combat*. Paper presented at the Third International Conference on Psychological Stress and Adjustment in Time of War and Peace, Tel-Aviv.
40. Ibid.
41. Margalit, C., Segal, R., Nardi, C., Wozner, Y., & Goren, Y. (1983, January). *Combat fitness retraining unit (CFRU) for treatment and rehabilitation of combat reactions with poor prognosis in the June 1982 conflict*. Paper presented at the Third

International Conference on Psychological Stress and Adjustment in Time of War and Peace, Tel-Aviv.

42. Segal, R., Margalit, C., Reish, M., Zilberman, S., & Friedman, Y. (1983, January). *The contribution of combat physical fitness in a rear unit (CFRU) for the treatment of combat reactions with poor prognosis.* Paper presented at the Third International Conference on Psychological Stress and Adjustment in Time of War and Peace, Tel-Aviv.

43. Noy, S., Nardi, C., & Solomon, Z. (1983, January). *Battle characteristics and the prevalence of combat psychiatric casualties.* Paper presented at the Third International Conference on Psychological Stress and Adjustment in Time of War and Peace, Tel-Aviv.

44. Solomon, Z., & Noy, S. (1983, January). *Who is at high risk for combat reaction?* Paper presented at the Third International Conference on Psychological Stress and Adjustment in Time of War and Peace, Tel-Aviv.

45. See Belenky et al., *Israeli battle shock casualties*, pp. 20–22.

46. Stouffer, S. A., DeVinney, L. C., Star, S. A., & Williams, R. M. (1949). *The American soldier, volume II.* Princeton, NJ: Princeton University Press.

47. Yarom, N. (1983). Facing death in war—an existential crisis. In S. Breznitz (Ed.), *Stress in Israel* (pp. 3–38). New York: Van Nostrand Reinhold.

48. Galilli, L. (1984, March 21). IDF veterans complain of emotional difficulties regarding their service. *Ha'aretz.*

49. See for example, Breznitz, *Stress in Israel*, particularly R. Moses, Emotional response to stress in Israel: A psychoanalytic perspective (pp. 114–137); Offer, Z., & Kober, A. (Eds.), *The price of power*; and finally (though somewhat less empirical), Elon, A. (1983). *The Israelis: Founders and Sons.* New York: Pelican Books.

12

MILITARY NORMS AND ETHICS

Militaries are characterized not only by their organizational structure, their personnel and materiel, or by their missions but also by a set of both written and unwritten regulations and values which together comprise the norms and ethics of the military. Generally these norms and ethics are a reflection of those found in society as a whole. Sometimes, though, they are quite distinct. Normally they develop within the military over the years and the generations. In the Israeli Defence Forces the norms and ethics are only partially a reflection of the larger Israeli society; obviously, they do not stem from a long military tradition nourished by extensive historical roots.

In the previous chapters some of the norms and ethics regarding the fighting spirit of the IDF have been discussed. This chapter will bring these into greater focus by concentrating on the following three subject areas: normative discipline, soldiers' camaraderie, and the concept of purity of arms. The means by which these norms and ethics have been developed and propagated among Israeli soldiers will also be discussed.

Normative Discipline

As might be expected of a military that was literally fighting for its survival before it was officially formed, the fate of discipline in the IDF was identical to the fate of ceremonies and rituals: external displays were pushed aside and paid scant attention, with effort instead concentrated on their true essence. The required behavior of the Israeli soldier is governed by operational discipline rather than ceremonial discipline. Reliable reports, clean weapons and prompt performance are perceived as being much more important than dust free windowsills, perfectly creased uniforms, or letter perfect military correspondence. In fact, fancy uniforms are never seen in the IDF (they are only ordered for military attachés serving abroad). In many of the elite units, military rituals such as saluting or standing at attention are looked upon with great scorn. All of this does not mean that military discipline does not exist in IDF units. Rather, discipline is centered around the critical areas of military performance and combat operations.

The traditional involvement of the IDF in various activities which are not strictly military (education, settlements, agriculture, working with juvenile delinquents, etc.) further increases the general impression that much of the work of the IDF soldier does not fall within typical military behavior. Nahal soldiers, for instance, hardly resemble soldiers during the "agricultural" phase of their duties; in the educational centers the atmosphere is closer to that of a school or community center rather than a military camp; and with regard to their work with juvenile delinquents, strict military discipline is very seldom the policy of choice.

This lack of rigid and formal discipline stems from the flexible and adaptable nature of the IDF. In the same way that the transition back and forth between civilian and soldier (for both reservists and regulars) is so frequent and normative in Israel, so it is that when he is in uniform, the Israeli soldier shifts rapidly from strict "soldierly" behavior to youthful, spontaneous behavior, then back again to military propriety, sometimes within moments. His behavior, thus, fluctuates according to the circumstances and nature of his assigned mission.

In April 1982 (just two months before the incursion of the Israeli forces into Lebanon) a large cross section of the IDF was assigned an extremely unmilitary task—the evacuation of the city of Yamit. This recently erected town in the northern Sinai was scheduled to be evacuated according to the Camp David Agreement, but its dedicated Israeli settlers, like a great majority of the Israeli public, vigorously rejected this decision of the Israeli government. The difficult task of forcefully evacuating these objecting citizens was given to the IDF.

In my position as Chief Psychologist of the IDF, I was in Yamit during the week-long evacuation process. Never in all my years have I seen a military fulfilling its mission in a way that was so gentle and compassionate and unmilitary. Orders were given and a minute later cancelled, modified, or delayed out of concern for the civilian population. Every order was followed with instructions to "do it carefully, gently, and use your common sense." Soldiers carried children and women in their arms, patiently explaining to them why they had to carry out the evacuation order. Occasionally one would see a soldier weeping alongside a street, then regaining his composure and returning to his duties.

The military discipline exhibited by these soldiers in Yamit was the

> ultimate in discipline in terms of the outcome rather than of their appearance.

The Israeli soldier's aversion to ceremonies and pomp is too deep to change. Indeed, many will cite historical reasons for this. Throughout the years of the Diaspora, Jews were alien to the idea of military service in the countries where they lived. Military rituals always seemed to them to be strange and rather ridiculous. It was part of what Jews used to label in Yiddish as "Goim-nachess" which translates to "silly Gentile games." In fact, when one of the early Chiefs of Staff tried to issue fancy "saucer" hats to his IDF officers, his attempts failed. Very few selected that option, and eventually these hats were removed from issue.

The predominance of the reserve corps within the IDF also affects the "civilianization" of military discipline. Reservists who are called for active duty are not expected to report in "spit and polished" condition. Their uniforms, too, are not exactly the best example of what one sees on official military posters. Relationships between troops and their leaders in these reserve units (particularly in the combat units) are extremely informal—certainly not ceremonial. Further, the frequent intermixing of reserve units with regular units results in a partial transfer of these characteristics into the regular units themselves.

There are still other reasons for the clear dominance of operational discipline over ceremonial discipline. One of these is the repeated exposure of IDF units to combat operations. Such a shift from ritual to operational discipline has always characterized militaries during times of war.[1] Furthermore, the IDF lacks the long standing traditions which usually serve as the wellspring of military ceremonies. In its three and a half decades the IDF has not had the luxury of any prolonged periods of peace which are needed for the evolution of such formal trappings. In contrast, the IDF has the short tradition of the Palmach and underground organizations wherein the importance of effective performance and mission completion was always strongly emphasized.

> Even the Yom Kippur War, in which many misdeeds were referred to a lack of discipline and recklessness (the Agranat Commission devoted an entire chapter in its report to the subject of military discipline), could not change the basic approach characterized by the IDF and its personnel. One expression of that was given by Lt. General Mordechai ("Motta") Gur, the Chief of Staff who was assigned after the Yom Kippur War to rehabilitate the military:
>
> "The current IDF did not develop in a vacuum. Its character was determined predominantly by veteran 'Palmach' commanders, who strongly emphasized operational discipline. This 'Palmach' tradition

has prevailed over other schools of thought, apparently because it best suited our nature.... If we decide now to focus more on formal discipline we may risk a great and successful tradition. In the [Yom Kippur] war we saw heroism, devotion, and perseverance in a form that has seldom been seen in other armies where formal discipline is predominant. In this war we discovered that the IDF preserves personal basic trust, strong motivation and deep personal commitment which we ought to be careful not to lose."[2]

Obviously what has enabled this type of discipline to become dominant in the IDF was the overall attitude of high motivation and readiness to serve. However, in a compulsory service composed of draftees who represent essentially the entire eligible population there will always be those who lack this motivation and readiness. For these youths, military discipline poses an adjustment problem. Many of them struggle with the confines of military life. The majority of military offenders confined to the IDF's military prisons are conscripts who were absent without official leave (AWOL) or demonstrated other forms of difficulty in adjusting to military life. Most of these maladjusted conscripts (about 70 percent) come from the bottom Kaba category (about 20 percent of the entire conscript corps) and are normally assigned to service support units.

For the mainstream IDF, however, basic training, high motivation and a strong sense of commitment serve as a substitute for strict formal discipline and blind obedience. Such a substitution does not necessarily make life easier for the Israeli soldier. On occasion it may even be to the contrary. When military compliance is based on obedience, it is straightforward and spares the soldiers any doubts or confusion. But it is the compliance generated by personal commitment that at times elicits questions and reservations. The notion of "just following orders" strikes a stunning echoed chord in the minds of many Israelis. As a rule they would always rather struggle with their questions and reservations than compliantly follow any decision.

It becomes particularly the case when questions are raised concerning the legitimacy of a military action. Such was the case during the 1982 incursion into Lebanon. In at least one reported case, an Israeli senior officer expressed an overt act of protest against contingent military plans which he did not feel were legitimate. This officer, Colonel Eli Geva, was relieved of his command and released from military service, thus paying with his career for what he considered was his right, if not his duty, to protest. Several other officers also joined that protest. The military authorities, like the political leaders, could not afford to ignore or tolerate these voices of protest.[3]

Military discipline and military ethics are thus very closely interrelated. This relationship, however, is especially crucial when the military discipline is more internal than external, more mission-oriented than maintenance-oriented, and stems more from commitment than from mere obedience.

Soldiers' Camaraderie

Camaraderie, bonding, brotherhood, cohesion—these are all universal concepts among soldiers. The Israeli military is no different. However, in the IDF these concepts have been translated into a code of behavior, a sacred norm. Scrupulous observations made of the Israeli military have concluded that this camaraderie—along with unit cohesion and effective leadership—is the most important source of combat motivation for the Israeli soldier.[4] Usually called "achavatt lochameem" in Hebrew (literally translated as "combatants' brotherhood"), this concept has also been labeled by a prominent Israeli poet (Haim Guri) as "re'utt" (literally "companionship" or "love, sanctified by blood").

This sense of mutual responsibility always reaches its apex during wartime. It was empirically demonstrated, for example, in a study conducted by the IDF's Unit of Military Psychology immediately after the 1973 war regarding the combat reactions of the Israeli soldier.[5] Specifically, an item concerning the occurrence of mutual support and responsibility ("In those instances where you have actively engaged in combat, were there any cases in which soldiers did not provide mutual support?") yielded virtually 100 percent endorsement ("there were none") among the surveyed soldiers.

Furthermore, providing social support is a behavior pattern considered to be one of the most important elements of good soldiery in the IDF. In another study conducted after the Yom Kippur War, the investigator[6] was seeking the determinants of effective combat performance among combat soldiers (Infantry soldiers from the Golani brigade). Using peer rating methods, the personal characteristic which was most strongly associated with combat performance was "providing social support." In an attempt to explain this finding the author suggested

that in the tightly-knit small combat units studied here, a soldier's physical survival and vulnerability to psychological attrition, as well as the successful accomplishment of the unit's mission, depend to a large measure upon the extent to which cooperative and mutually supportive interpersonal relationships prevail in the small unit.[7]

Mutual social support, then, is an important attribute of the fighting spirit of the IDF, even though it may carry, like the follow me leadership model, a high price. It has been exhibited in the gallant behavior of individuals in combat who have risked their lives to rescue their buddies, sometimes at the cost of their own lives. Approximately two-thirds of the awarded heroic acts performed in the Yom Kippur War involved rescuing the wounded; about one-third of these cases ended up in the death of the rescuer.[8]

The concept of "achavatt lochameem" is such an ingrained norm in the IDF that it applies not only to situations involving providing social support and rescuing of the wounded, but also to the enormous effort expended to retrieve the bodies of the dead. Whether this stems from the Jewish religion which requires the proper burial of the individual, including his body parts, or whether this is just an extension of mutual responsibility and support among combatants, it is certainly a norm which affects the morale of the Israeli soldier. Barbara Tuchman, in her essay, "Israel's Swift Sword," succinctly describes this norm.

> No aspect of the IDF is more striking than its concern for casualties. Every man wounded or dead is brought back regardless of cost, even that of mounting an offensive to recover the missing. In most cases the wounded were in hospitals within an hour, transported directly from the place they fell by helicopter, and the knowledge of this was a strong morale factor."[9] (P. 186)

The willingness to sacrifice oneself to retrieve wounded or killed friends became a common occurrence during the desperate battles of the Yom Kippur War when, in most cases, the IDF forces were numerically outnumbered and the number of casualties was unaccustomedly high. Many units were almost completely exhausted in their endless attempts to rescue their casualties.

> One of the epic stories concerning rescuing casualties involves the actions of a paratrooper battalion commanded by Lieutenant Colonel Nathan in the "Chinese Farm" in the Sinai Desert. This paratrooper battalion was involved in the overall effort to cross the Egyptian controlled Suez Canal.
>
> "As Nathan's forces advanced, it was not clear to him that he was leading his paratroopers against a major, concentrated Egyptian force of at least divisional strength. . . . Nathan's advanced half-tracks, under command of Gideon Halevi, stopped. Halevi reported that he could not move and had incurred severe casualties. As the remaining half-tracks in his [Nathan's] force maneuvered to help Halevi, they too were hit. . . . The unit was now caught in the open under murderous fire, unable to move in any direction and unable to relieve the forward

elements which had been cut off. The men lay on the ground digging into the sand with their fingernails in an endeavour to find shelter. As soldiers were hit, others rushed forward to carry them out of danger and were mowed down themselves. By a miracle Nathan and some of his vehicles managed to withdraw from the fire-stricken area, but to his horror he saw that only remnants were left of his force.

"A company of tanks joined Nathan and moved forward in an attempt to rescue the trapped force.... They rushed forward in a suicidal effort to reach the paratroopers, firing everything they had into the ditches and at the Egyptian positions—but in vain; a hail of Sagger and Shmel missiles pursued the tanks wherever they moved.... As time went on, it dawned on Nathan that hopes of rescuing the trapped men were dwindling. All attempts to reach the surrounded advance forces failed.

"Halevi, it transpired, had sustained a number of casualties and he and his men had refused to abandon the wounded. He tried to leapfrog his unit out of the battle area with the wounded, covered by two sections of heavy machine guns, but as they moved slowly and painfully towards their own lines Egyptian armoured forces closed on them and blocked their route of withdrawal. In the battle which ensued, the entire Israeli force was wiped out. As Nathan reorganized his force (which had sustained twenty-four killed and eighteen wounded) his closest friend called him aside and revealed to him that one of the dead in the battle had been his brother."[10] (Pp. 215–216)

This observed willingness to sacrifice evolves within units through unit cohesion and the long-standing bonds between the men, who often have gone through several wars together. However, this willingness exists across units as well. The sense of "achavatt lochameem" provides a bridge across units beyond the mutual responsibility based on familiarity and belonging to the same group. In the IDF it has a meaning which transcends the personal acquaintance and the "regimental" boundaries.

An example taken from the Golan Heights frontier of the Yom Kippur War further demonstrates the phenomenon of "achavatt lochameem" across units. The Armor units which lead the Israeli counterattack toward Damascus were reorganized remnants of the same units which had two days earlier halted the massive Syrian attack. One of these Israeli units was an armored division commanded by Major General Dan Laner.

"Part of Laner's force was now cut off, unable to evacuate its wounded or to receive supplies. All night long the area was a virtual death trap for Israeli tanks, swarming as it was with Syrian infantry with bazookas. The forces Ori had left behind to cover his advance began to move in. The commander of the first group was killed; the commander of the second wounded.

"At this point the division sent in a parachute battalion, which was heavily engaged all night mopping up the Syrian forces and evacuating the Israeli wounded. When the paratroopers saw the condition of the tank crews, they were horrified. They begged them to rest and without a word began to load the tanks with fuel and ammunition, to prepare tea and food for the crews and to do everything they could to relieve them."[11]

The tank crews who risked their lives to rescue the trapped paratroopers in the "Chinese Farm" did not personally know these men, nor did the paratroopers who helped the armored troops in the Golan Heights even belong to the same parent unit. Here, indeed, one has to look for an explanation that transcends personal bonds. This sense of combatants' fraternity has become so internalized in the IDF that every combatant feels obliged under any circumstances in which he may find himself to act upon this norm.

This personal commitment to one another has been given institutional recognition by the IDF's policy concerning prisoner exchanges. Following each of its wars, Israeli authorities have conducted tireless negotiations to secure the return of Israeli captured and killed as quickly as possible. For this, Israel has always been willing to pay almost any price. Thus, for example, after the Six Day War, Israel exchanged 591 captured Syrians for 1 Israeli pilot along with the bodies of 2 Israeli soldiers. Following the Yom Kippur War, the exchange, the result of complex negotiations, involved approximately 8,400 Egyptians for 232 Israelis, and 392 Syrians for 65 Israelis. And in May 1985, 1,150 PLO members, most of whom had been detained in Israel for terrorist acts, were exchanged for 3 Israeli soldiers captured in Lebanon.

Another expression of the IDF's institutional recognition of this "love sanctified by blood" is evidenced in the newly designed Merkava (Chariot) tank. The Israeli armored corps, which suffered almost two-thirds of the total casualties of the Yom Kippur War sought a new vehicle which could maximize crew protection. The revolutionary design of the Merkava tank not only includes increased frontal protection but also includes the addition of a special rear compartment to transport casualties.[12]

The Israeli soldier thus knows quite well that he will never be abandoned on the battlefield. If he is wounded, he knows his friends will rescue him, no matter what the circumstances may be. If he is captured, he knows he will promptly be exchanged no matter the price. Should he die, he knows his body will be returned home, again, no matter the circumstances or price. This knowledge, with the confidence it brings, is the essence of the achavatt lochameem concept so central in the code of ethics of the Israeli soldier.

The Purity of Arms

The concept of "tohar haneshek" (purity of arms) was inherited from the years preceding the formation of the IDF. On the one hand, it was an inevitable product of the self-restrained policy that the Haganah adopted during the 1930s as a response to the Arab riots and guerrilla attacks on the Jewish community. Stemming from socialistic-humanistic ideology as well as from political wisdom, the Haganah members refrained from armed reprisals against "innocent Arabs" (as they were referred to) and kept their weapons "pure" by preserving them only for clear self defense.

The other source, however, is deeper and more remote. Tohar haneshek means not only a restricted and cautious use of arms. It also means preserving humanistic norms in combat, refraining from unnecessary bloodshed, and avoiding, at all cost, harming civilians in general and women and children in particular.[13] It further means avoiding damage to sacred buildings, treating POWs in a humane way, and totally refraining from looting, raping, and other atrocities. Hence, the Israelis have strongly adhered to Western democratic-humanistic ethics, which are not all that common in the Middle East.

An attempt to analyze the reasons for the existence of the concept of purity of arms within the IDF was made by Colonel (Res.') Meir Pa'il, an important voice regarding the Israeli military thinking and an educator of several generations of IDF officers. In addition to the usual moral justifications generally cited, Pa'il suggests that for the sake of possible future relationships with its Arab neighbors, Israel should pursue this policy of purity of arms to its utmost.[14]

Tohar haneshek, however, is a difficult ideal to preserve. This is especially true when the wars keep occurring, and it seems that there will be no end to them and particularly when your enemy follows a different set of rules. Under such circumstances it is no wonder that the Israeli soldier sometimes departs from his own rules. Back in October 1953, the IDF 101st commando unit led by then Major Ariel Sharon executed a brutal raid on the village of Kibiya in which more than forty civilians were killed. Later on during the Six Day War, there were several occasions where soldiers departed from the rules regarding looting and treatment of POWs. More recently, following the Litani operation in 1980, a paratrooper lieutenant was court martialled for the murders of several POWs. Throughout the years of the West Bank occupation, there were a number of cases involving cruelly assaulting or mistreating civilian Arabs, including one which led to a court martial. Finally, most recently there were the traumatic events in the Sabra and Shatilla refugee camps during the Israeli occupation of Lebanon.[15]

While in this most recent case it was absolutely clear from the beginning that Israeli troops were not directly involved in the atrocities, just the possibility of indirect responsibility was enough to call for the establishment of an investigative commission. The strong Israeli public outcry in reaction to those events best reflects the sensitivities of the Israeli populace concerning the moral aspects of conducting wars. Particularly in the Lebanon War, where battles against the PLO were fought in heavily populated civilian areas, the Israeli concept of tohar haneshek was brought to a new apex.

Throughout the War in Lebanon, the IDF maintained strict instructions concerning the avoidance of any harm to innocent civilians. A senior combat officer referred to this in a monologue which was published in an Israeli newspaper.

"I can unequivocally [state] that we had a large number of casualties caused directly by the instruction of not harming civilians, women and children. Usually when you conduct a battle, you first neutralize the target with artillery fire in order to minimize your casualties. Here in Lebanon we were prohibited from doing that out of concern of hitting civilians. . . . Every target was carefully checked before assaulting it. We dropped pamphlets, announced it on loudspeakers. We certainly could have advanced more quickly, captured more terrorists, and most importantly saved lots of our own lives [had we not exercised these cautions]. The terrorists knew all of this and deliberately mingled with civilians; and we—there was nothing we could do because of the strict instructions . . . that we should not open fire unless we were positively certain that terrorists were there. . . . Where is this red line by which a commander must decide what is more important—to protect the lives of his own troops or to consider first the lives of other civilians, some of whom support the terrorists? It seems to me that the Israeli commanders have gone far beyond that red line in favor of protecting civilians lives even when it came at the cost of their own soldiers lives."[16]

All the reports concerning the Lebanon War[17] repeatedly describe the enormous effort expended by the IDF to minimize harm to innocent civilians. The infantry, the artillery crews and the pilots all were reminded again before each operation of the need to avoid any target which might involve civilians. It can never be known how many Israeli casualties were suffered because of this policy. Nonetheless, those instructions were strictly followed by the Israeli soldiers, even under the most difficult of circumstances. As put by an anonymous Israeli combat soldier, "You carry your moral burden with you wherever you go.... You don't stop being a human being because you are fighting for your life.... That is the dilemma of the Israeli soldier."[18]

On February 8, 1983, about five months after the Sabra and Shatilla massacres, the Kahan Commission published its final report. In its closing remarks the committee of two Supreme Court justices and a retired major general devoted considerable discussion to the extremely high moral level which had characterized the IDF in the Lebanon War.

During the months of the war, IDF soldiers witnessed many sights of killing, destruction, and ruin. From their reactions (about which we have heard) to acts of brutality against civilians, it would appear that despite the terrible sights and experiences of the war and despite the soldier's obligation to behave as a fighter with a certain degree of callousness, IDF soldiers did not lose their sensitivity to atrocities.... It seems to us that the IDF should continue to foster the [consciousness of] basic moral obligations which must be kept even in war conditions, without prejudicing the IDF's combat ability. The circumstances of combat require the combatants to be tough.... But the end never justifies the means, and basic ethical and human values must be maintained in the use of arms.[19]

Modes of Socialization

The military profession is obviously different from most, if not all, other professions found in civil society.[20] Normally the code of ethics of the military is not only different from that of any other profession, but also frequently varies in its essence and spirit from the commonly shared values of its own larger society.[21] Such was the case with mercenary armies, but it apparently also applies to many professional militaries with long and glorious traditions which do not always parallel those of the surrounding society.

The Israeli military, being a true civil military, is different. Its norms and ethics come from its people and return to them. The sources from which they derive are the historical, cultural and societal essence of the people of Israel. Yet while in some aspects the Israeli soldier builds his military identity upon the ancient Jewish history and biblical references, in other aspects he continuously transforms this identity and thus becomes a dynamic reflection of the still-evolving Israeli society.

The Old Testament, in any case, is one of the major sources of the IDF's norms and ethics. On various occasions, and with regard to various subjects concerning ethical issues, the Israeli soldier often turns to the Bible for reference. The Kahan Commisssion report is a good example of this. The commission members, none of whom were Orthodox, nonetheless frequently cited the Old Testament as a reference for the moral perception of the IDF's fighting spirit and as a rationale for the issue of "non direct responsibility" which evidently characterized the IDF's involvement in the Sabra and Shatilla events.

A basis for such responsibility may be found in the outlook of our ancestors, which was expressed in things that were said about the moral significance of the biblical verses concerning the 'beheaded heifer'.... It is said in Deuteronomy (21:6–7) that the elders of the city who were near the slain victim who has been found (and it is not known who struck him down) 'will wash their hands over the beheaded heifer in the valley and reply: our hands did not shed this blood and our eyes did not see.'[22]

The commission members referred to some other historical aspects of Jewish history which also have relevance for this case.

It should also not be forgotten that the Jews in various lands of exile, and also in the Land of Israel when it was under foreign rule, suffered greatly from pogroms perpetrated by various hooligans.... The Jewish public's stand has always been that the responsibility for such deeds falls not only on those who rioted and committed the atrocities, but also on those who were responsible for safety and public order, who could have prevented the disturbances and did not fulfill their obligations in this respect.[23]

Other examples of biblical references to ethical issues can be found. In the newsletter distributed among Israeli soldiers in Lebanon on the fifth day of the war (published by the IDF's Education corps) and titled "The Face of the Israeli Soldier," a strong warning was issued prohibiting looting, harming innocent civilians (especially women) and damaging holy places. They were instructed, in general, to maintain moral norms of behavior. Here again, as a rationale for this warning, the newsletter quoted a long and relevant paragraph from Joshua, chapter 7.[24]

In various IDF leadership courses, discussions and examples are used of biblical figures such as Moses, Joshua, Gideon, David, and numerous others. Likewise, in military barracks one often finds posters and slogans of Old Testament verses dealing with war morals, leadership characteristics and principles of military ethics.

The instillment of military norms and values into the Israeli soldier does not take the form of strict military indoctrination. The IDF does not attempt to separate its members, neither career nor conscript, from the rest of Israeli society. Rather it simply requires higher standards from them. Nor does the military socialization process begin at induction. It starts much earlier in the home, in schools and in youth movements. Similarly, this socialization does not end with separation from active duty, but essentially continues throughout the life of any Israeli adult.

While in the service, the Israeli soldiers undergo ethical indoctrination through exposure to various segments of Israeli society. As part of their regular training, these soldiers visit different types of Israeli settlements: kibbutz, moshav, development towns, etc. They also go to Yeshivas (Orthodox schools), museums, and historical sites. One important tour is that of the Yad-Vashem, a monument to the victims of the Holocaust. A part of every IDF course involves discussions of the IDF's combat heritage, not necessarily from a tactical point of view, but instead predominantly analyzing the ethical and moral aspects of these significant events. From all of these activities, the Israeli soldiers absorb the spiritual and cultural essence which better prepares them to be effective, yet moral, soldiers.

Conclusion

This extra emphasis on moral values—achavatt lochameem, re'utt, tohar haneshek and the like—is not only a reflection of high moral standards, a history of personal suffering, or humanistic beliefs. The strict adherence to these ethical norms also has a function (called a "latent" function by sociologists): self-preservation. Against all of these repeated wars, the exposure of youngsters to the horrors of combat, and this continual need to deal with the suppression of other populations, there is the concern that under these circumstances Israelis will lose sight of their ethical values. This concern was best expressed by the Israeli mother of a kibbutznik soldier, who herself had been a victim of Nazi atrocities: "How many wars will our boys fight before they will become animals?"[25]

It is out of this concern for the spirit and moral values of the Israeli soldier that the IDF so conscientiously reminds itself of these humanistic slogans. Like any other victorious force, the danger facing the IDF is not in its level of morale but rather in its moral level.

Notes

1. See Kellett, A. (1982). *Combat motivation*. Boston: Kluwer Nijhoff Publishing.
2. An interview with Lt. Gen. Mordechai Gur. (1975, March 12). *Bamahane*.
3. A more detailed analysis of the Eli Geva case and its implications for the military profession can be found in Gal, R. (in press). Commitment and obedience in the military: An Israeli case study. *Armed Forces and Society*.
4. Rennie, C. G. (1984, October). *Military motivation and the regimental system in the Israeli army* (Project Report No. PR 258). Ottawa, Canada: Operational Research and Analysis Establishment, Department of National Defence. See also

Henderson, W. D. (1985). *Cohesion: The human element in combat*. Washington, DC: National Defense University Press.

5. Zvulun, E. (1974, April). *The reactions of the Israeli soldier during the Yom Kippur War* (Research Report). Unit of Military Psychology, IDF, Israel.

6. Shirom, A. (1976, September). On some correlates of combat performance. *Administrative Combat Quarterly, 21*, 419–432.

7. Ibid., p. 430.

8. Gal, R. (1983). Courage under stress. In S. Breznitz (Ed.), *Stress in Israel*. New York: Van Nostrand Reinhold.

9. Tuchman, B. W. (1981). Israel's swift sword. In *Practicing history: Selected essays* (pp. 173–187). New York: Ballantine Books.

10. Herzog, C. (1975). *The war of atonement: October 1973*. Boston: Little, Brown and Company.

11. Ibid., pp. 134–135.

12. Hellman, P. (1985, March). Israel's chariot of fire. *The Atlantic Monthly*, pp. 81–95.

13. In none of its wars, and in contrast to its enemies, has Israel ever utilized strategical bombardment of civilian targets or heavily populated areas. When necessity dictated, the IDF sent jet fighters to fly over Arab capital cities, creating sonic booms, thus sending a clear warning as to what the IDF was capable of doing but never did.

14. Pa'il, M. (1970, August). Combat discipline or purity of arms. *Ma'archot, 209*, 1–11.

15. On September 18, 1982, after the evacuation of the PLO troops from Beirut, the Lebanese Christian Phalange undertook, with the approval of the Israeli military authorities, the task of "cleaning" these Palestinian refugee camps from the remaining PLO members. Driven by a desire for revenge on their Moslem rivals, the Phalangists killed, indiscriminately, several hundred unarmed dwellers of these camps, including many women and children.

16. Amikam, Y. (1983, February). They have turned the army into a punching bag. *Yedi'ot Ahronott*, p. 10.

17. See for example: Dupuy, T. N., & Martell, P. (1985). *Flawed victory: The 1982 war in Lebanon*. Fairfax, VA: HERO Books; Gabriel, R. A. (1984). *Operation peace for Galilee: The Israeli-PLO war in Lebanon*. New York: Hill and Wang; Schiff, Z., & Ya'ari, E. (1984). *Israel's Lebanon war*. New York: Simon and Schuster.

18. Gavron, D. (1984). *Israel after Begin*. Boston: Houghton Mifflin Company, p. 22.

19. Kahan, Y., Barak, A., & Efrat, Y. (1983). *Final Report of the Commission of Inquiry into the Events at the Refugee Camps in Beirut*. Jerusalem, Government Publication Office, p. 49.

20. See for example: Hackett, J. (1962). *The profession of arms*. London: Times Publishing Company; Janowitz, M. (1960). *The professional soldier: A social and political portrait*. Glencoe, IL: Free Press.

21. Gabriel, R. (1982). *To serve with honor*. Westport, CT: Greenwood Press; Huntington, S. P. (1959). *The soldier and the state*. Cambridge, MA: Harvard University Press.

22. Kahan, Barak, and Efrat, *Final Report of the Commission of Inquiry*, p. 26.

23. Ibid.

24. *A newsletter to the soldier in Lebanon.* (1982, June 11). Education Corps, Doctrine and Training Branch, IDF, Tel Aviv.

25. Elon, A. (1983). *The Israelis: Founders and sons.* New York: Pelican Books, p. 231.

13

FAULT LINES

From a historical perspective the Israeli Defence Forces is a young military in a young country. With its three and a half decades, it is still evolving its traditions, developing its norms and crystallizing its identity. In spite of its highly respected image, the IDF has experienced many ups and downs throughout its years. Some of these fluctuations were quite extreme. The 1950s, for example, saw an IDF which was relatively weak, unadventurous and failure-prone. After the Six Day War, in contrast, there was an upsurge in the IDF's image which placed the Israeli soldier in something approaching a Superman image. Shortly thereafter, during the grinding War of Attrition, there was again a deterioration in the IDF soldiers' self-image. These fluctuations continue to this day. Many see the IDF of the mid–1980s in the post Lebanon era as facing an impending crisis and being at one of the lower points in its history.[1]

It is difficult to assess the extent to which this is really true. To do that, one would need a more remote perspective in time. While this book has provided a descriptive portrait of today's Israeli soldier, a preferable approach to discussing the severity of this impending crisis might have been a historical one which could potentially delineate a more accurate picture. Indeed, from such a historical perspective some of the IDF's past low spots have been deemed to be not particularly significant.

Thus, rather than making inferences about a critical downward trend, one should first carefully examine the fluctuations over time; instead of declaring impending crises, it is more justified to talk about afflicted areas, or fault lines, along which ruptures may someday occur.

This chapter will focus on four such areas which pose a threat to the very foundation of the Israeli military during the decade of the 1980s and thus might alter the revered image of the Israeli soldier. These involve the areas of motivation problems, moral-ethical concerns, military competency, and quality of personnel.

Motivation Problems

The Israeli Defence Forces emerged in the midst of the War of Independence. During these early years of the State of Israel, the IDF soldier knew exactly why he was serving and what he was fighting for. Military service was an obvious need resulting from the surrounding threats. The IDF was viewed as the only force which could provide the security, in fact the very existence, of the newborn state. Hence the military service enjoyed full consensus throughout the Israeli population. Patriotism and military service were virtually synonymous.

In the last decade and a half, however, a serious erosion has begun to affect this relationship. Years of being an occupying force, the polarization of Israeli society into hawks and doves, an undermining of the national consensus which viewed the military force as the only guarantee of Israeli society, and finally the Lebanon misadventure have all combined to make the Israeli soldier of the mid-1980s highly vulnerable.

To put it simply, the IDF's contemporary soldiers find themselves more and more engaged in activities which they have difficulty supporting. There is hardly a soldier who has not had to take his turn serving in the occupied territories—the West Bank or the Gaza strip. This service resembles a police action more than a military mission. On occasion, when the occupied Palestinian population's demonstrations become vehement and violent, this duty turns into one of the worst. The Israeli soldiers, regulars and reservists alike, have a strong distaste for these duties, and though they comply with the orders (with reluctance), their motivation and morale are nonetheless affected. Serving in these occupied territories occasionally creates deep conflicts for the Israeli soldier. This, for example, was the case when soldiers in the occupied territory on the Golan Heights were required to confiscate the identification cards of the Druze villagers—a community normally supportive of Israel; or when they are ordered to blow up the homes of alleged PLO collaborators.

In early 1979, long before the Lebanon War, 350 reserve officers and enlisted men, the majority of them members of combat units, sent an open letter to Menachem Begin, then Prime Minister. In this letter of protest they warned against the increasing difficulties they were having identifying with the Israeli government's policy regarding the occupied territories: "A government policy that leads to continued rule over one million Arabs is liable to change the Jewish democratic nature of the state, . . . and would make it difficult for us to identify with the basic direction of the State of Israel."[2]

The publication of this letter, combined with the prevailing mood in Israel, prompted the formation of a spontaneous protest movement called "Peace Now," which became a significant influence in the Israeli political arena. Members of this movement, which supports the withdrawal of all Israeli forces from the occupied territories and actively searches for alternative routes to solve the Palestinian problem, are generally young Sabras (Israeli-born citizens) and mostly veterans of military service.

> One of the senior leaders of the Peace Now movement is Brigadier General (Res.) Mordechai Bar-On, a former chief education officer of the IDF. When asked about his personal motivation to join Peace Now, the general said that when security was the central problem of the country, he chose to make the Army his career. After the Camp David accords, however, when "there is a chance for a genuine peace and *peace* is the best possible guarantee for our survival," his contribution, he felt, could be the greatest within the Peace Now movement. He said it is not surprising that the Israeli peace movement is spearheaded by former members of the IDF combat units. "After all, they know better than anyone what war is all about."[3]

Another activity in which IDF soldiers are occasionally obliged to participate, despite their own political views, is that of implementing the government decisions regarding the evacuation of Jewish settlements within the occupied territories. The most strenuous incident of this involved the evacuation of the Israeli settlements in the northern Sinai, culminating with the evacuation and razing of the town of Yamit, before returning the area to Egypt as part of the Camp David accords. In Yamit, one could see Israeli soldiers literally in tears as they carried out their orders. There was not a single case of clear disobedience, but these soldiers performed their tasks with heavy hearts, with ambivalent motivation, and with low morale. While the violence in Yamit was confined to rock throwing, burning tires and fistfights between right-wing resistors of the evacuation and IDF soldiers, it was only a step or two away from bloodshed. There are those in Israel who predict that future evacuations performed again by IDF soldiers will be more violent and may indeed lead to civil war. Beyond the political impact of such a national split, it is appalling to think of the possibility of one Israeli soldier taking aim against his comrades.

However, it was the recent incursion into, and subsequent occupation of, Lebanon which confronted the Israeli soldier with his worst ideological conflict. This was the first war that was met with protests and demonstrations by the Israeli public, which unavoidably penetrated military lines. True, on the eve of the Lebanon War, no one considered refusing military service. Throughout its many years and wars, Israel had never dealt with large numbers of conscientious objectors.[4] The recognition of national security needs always outweighed any political or conscientious ambivalencies. Even the Peace Now movement did not dare to attempt to influence the military, nor did they ever suggest to their members at the outbreak of the Lebanon War that they should refuse duty there.

> "This is an Israeli movement," said Avshalom Vilan, one of the Peace Now leaders in an interview with Gavron.[5] "You can't compare it to the American peace movement [during Vietnam] where they burned draft cards. Israel is a small country and it has to defend itself. When we are mobilized, we go and fight; when we are demobilized, we do everything we can to oppose the war by political means."
>
> Vilan is a combatant in one of the elite units of the IDF and a member of Kibbutz Negba. He fought in 1973 in the northern Suez front and when called with his unit to Lebanon once again fought valiantly.

Yet, concurrent with the escalation of the Lebanon misadventure, new, though rather small, anti-war groups emerged. The "Yesh-Gvul" ("There's a Limit") and the "Soldiers Against Silence" groups (essentially composed of reserve military personnel) have expressed a clear objection against the IDF's occupation of Lebanon even going so far as to call on their members to refuse service there. Indeed, starting with a few scattered refusals by reservists to serve in Lebanon, the incidence of these refusals has become more frequent. By February 1985, when the IDF began its withdrawal from Lebanon, these cases totaled approximately 150 reserve troops.

While this number is rather negligible given the huge size of the IDF's reserve corps, it is still a cause for concern because of the underlying motives involved.[6] And although this resistance has virtually disappeared with the beginning of the withdrawal from Lebanon, it nonetheless established a dangerous precedent with regard to one of the most "sacred cows" in Israel.

The young conscripts, likewise, are not immune to these societal reservations.[7] These draftees have traditionally been considered to be invulnerable to questions of legitimacy. In fact, even empirical studies based on morale surveys have shown that during the initial phase of the Lebanon occupation, issues regarding the legitimacy of this occupation, though preoccupying the conscripts, had not spilled over into their unit morale level. In the short term, apparently, the morale of any military unit is not determined by external political factors but rather by what is happening within the unit, between its members and commander.[8] The real psychological danger, however, is in the long run. Unit cohesion and morale may not be able to ward off a situation where military goals are not perceived as sacred and beyond question by the conscripts who must implement them. This was reflected, for example, in a description by a reserve battalion commander during the first year of the IDF's presence in Lebanon: "In my battalion there are no signs of demoralization. . . . But one has to absolutely distinguish between this and the severe alienation from the missions and goals of staying in Lebanon. This can not be compensated by high morale. This alienation is perhaps the worst damage presently caused to the military."[9]

> In the latter stages of the IDF's occupation of Lebanon, there were indications that unit morale was in fact beginning to be adversely affected by the societal debate regarding Israel's involvement in Lebanon. In a series of interviews with commanding officers serving in Lebanon, a military correspondent observed such concerns. One of these young commanders complained, "We try hard to instill in our soldiers motivation, pride, proficiency. But when they go home on leave everything turns around. Instead of reassurance they get a slap in the face. And these soldiers who work so hard become depressed. . . . Eighty percent of our problems with the troops would disappear had there not been a public debate in the rear. . . . Sometimes I wonder: where do these soldiers continue to get their strength and their motivation to accomplish everything in the best manner?"[10] (P. 10)

The apparent long-term impact of the public debate regarding Lebanon has already begun affecting not only the troops but also their leaders. This adverse impact on morale and motivation has become evident not only during periods of compulsory service but also in terms of long-range decisions regarding signing into the permanent service corps[11] or volunteering for officer training.[12]

Moral-Ethical Concerns

The "Ein breira" (no alternative) ideology, which was the underlying motive of the IDF throughout the years, not only provided a major source of high motivation and dedication; it also always served as a moralistic basis for the decisiveness of the Israeli soldier's fighting spirit. As long as the Israeli Defence Forces was literally perceived as a defensive force, the Israeli soldier had no qualms about sacrificing himself to protect his country. In the years following the Six Day War, however, Israeli society witnessed the development of a new image. The IDF became a more adventurous, offensive military force. Israeli society became intoxicated with the power of the IDF, believing that there was nothing which could withstand that force and that every problem could be solved by military power. The outcome of the Yom Kippur War in 1973 did not diminish this belief. And the Lebanon War of 1982 was the latest expression of it.

The Lebanon War brought the IDF for the first time in its history to the outskirts of an Arab capital, forcing the Israelis to fight their way through heavily populated areas. This experience illuminated many ethical concerns regarding the limits of moral legitimation dictating the behavior of the IDF's soldiers. The tohar haneshek concept (purity of arms) was put to its most extreme test in this war. Not once did the absoluteness of this concept compete with the probability of high Israeli casualties. Even though in most cases the Israeli troops stuck to the dictates of the tohar haneshek concept, it was obviously impossible in a war of this nature to avoid all exceptions.

After the Lebanon War an Israeli combat pilot, who had participated in the aerial bombardment of Lebanese cities, wrote a short article expressing his own personal feelings.

"In this operation a new generation of pilots emerged who set their peep-sight on a city with the same ease that their predecessors did on airfields. . . . True, one may say 'this has been done before.' We were not the first to bomb cities, we have not invented the anonymous and technical evil; but this time it's our problem. If we continue [to fool ourselves] the concepts of conscience and moral justice will remain buried in our dictionaries."[13] (P. 14)

But it was mainly during the protracted occupation of Lebanon between 1982 and 1985, when the IDF was transformed from a force known for its mobility and combat decisiveness into a largely static military engaged in quasi-police functions, that most of the damage to its spirit was done. Here again, as in the case of the ongoing military control in the West Bank and Gaza strip areas, IDF soldiers were forced into continual friction with the local population, with all the degrading effects that such exposures are bound to have.

Thus, the recent years have seen the IDF soldier struggling with growing numbers of missions which are morally questionable and ethically inconceivable. Whether it has to do with fellow Israelis (such as in the Yamit evacuation) or policelike missions in the occupied territories, many Israeli soldiers now find themselves reacting with confusion, doubts and, on occasion, even disapproval. Long years of control and occupation are bound to erode not only their motivation and morale but also their traditional sense of ethics and morality.

Sometime after the Six Day War an open letter was published in the *New Statesman*. Richard Crossman, a British labor leader and a known friend of Israel, wrote to Abba Eban, then Israel's foreign minister: "The Arabs can survive a decade of Jewish military domination. The Israel you and I believe in can't."[14] Thirteen years later, in early 1983, an Israeli officer and six soldiers were court-martialled for mistreatment of Arab civilians in the West Bank.

The rarity of such an extreme deed should not lessen its importance. Rather it may be viewed as a tremor along the faultline, a warning of the impending arrival of the quake.

Military Competency

Among other things, the IDF has traditionally been famous for its tactical thinking, innovative strategies and unconventional operations—in short, its outstanding military competency. A growing number of military experts, however, suggest that the IDF may be losing this uniqueness. True, unconventional achievements have not been lacking in recent times: in the Yom Kippur War the Israelis managed to quickly turn a massive Arab surprise attack into a resounding Israeli victory by bringing the war, on two different frontiers, into their enemies' territories; and special operations such as the raid on the Entebbe airport and the destruction of a nuclear reactor in Iraq are also distinct reminders of Israeli daring and originality. However, especially since the recent incursion into Lebanon, recollections of these past events have given way to critical perceptions regarding the IDF's current competency.

Various sources[15] have pointed out serious defects in the IDF's tactical thinking, planning and execution in Lebanon. Several major areas of criticism were involved. First, it was argued that the IDF was too heavily dependent on armored forces and also used tactics which were perfected in its previous wars. These tactics, however, did not work well in Lebanon given the nature of the enemy, the terrain and types of combat involved.[16] By using these tactics, a disturbing picture emerged of "the tendency of the IDF units and their commanders to be harnessed to conventional military thinking."[17]

It has been further argued that the entire planning of the Lebanon operation was non-innovative. This operation involved deploying massive forces in a relatively small and difficult area in which to maneuver, instead of employing creative approaches to overcome these tactical limitations.[18] In terms of efficient utilization of military units, serious criticisms were also voiced. These in particular centered around the IDF's frequent practice of only pursuing the enemy during daylight hours, ceasing operations at nightfall and thus allowing the enemy to regroup and resupply.[19] Finally, the frequent coordination foul-ups between units were cited as indicative of defective operational performance. Schiff and Ya'ari, for example, describe several instances in which this poor coordination ended with tragic results.[20]

All of these criticisms cannot be viewed simply from the perspective of this particular operation in Lebanon. Indeed, every war has its foul-ups. The frequency and costliness of foul-ups as delineated above might be more indicative of an underlying faultline within the IDF. Furthermore, they are especially viewed as serious in light of the IDF's previous image of super-competency.

It is also true that the Lebanon War, like any war, has generated numerous critical reviews of dubious value both in Israel and abroad.[21] At the same time, some of the strongest criticism came directly from Israeli or pro-Israeli experts whose views are regarded as highly reliable.[22] Indeed, it was a senior officer in the Israeli Army who made the statement (which subsequently became popular in Israel in mid-1985) that "after we get the IDF out of Lebanon, our main challenge will be to get Lebanon out of the IDF."

> The most painful critical views regarding the IDF's competency were expressed by the IDF combat soldiers and officers themselves. On different occasions, including media interviews and open letters to Israel's Prime Minister and defense minister, these elite combatants have communicated their anxieties regarding the fate of the fighting spirit of the IDF.
>
> "The damage to the IDF's spirit and strength is unprecedented" wrote twenty-seven soldiers and officers from a combat unit.
>
> "It seems to us that the most serious damage in the long run is to the regular forces who don't know any other IDF than the Lebanon's IDF," wrote another group of combat soldiers. "The loss of initiative eventually increases fear and lack of confidence and as a result the army tends to barricade itself in posts and strongholds." (P. 12)
>
> Furthermore, a reserve officer from this group went on to explain: "For them [the new conscripts] the IDF is an army that doesn't operate at night, an army which stops operating at dusk. . . . an army that only moves in groups or convoys—and this is an army which used to consider high mobility as one of its prime principles."[23] (P. 12)

Critical comments, however, are not entirely new phenomena in the IDF. While they became more frequent in the period following the Lebanon invasion, similar criticisms had been expressed, for instance, during the Yom Kippur War era. In 1974 a retired combat officer and veteran of several wars and combat operations published a series of articles entitled *Truth in the Shadow of War*. Colonel Yaacov Hasdai warned against what he labeled "deterioration in the level of military thinking." In Hasdai's words, "Once, the IDF's greatness consisted in its ability to come up with original answers that reflected creative military thinking and an atmosphere that encouraged creative people. In time, however, conformity became the rule, and commanders showing imagination and originality came to be considered a nuisance."[24] (P. 16)

Others[25] as early as the mid-1970s have also addressed the danger of increasing mediocrity within the officer corps of the IDF. These warnings then regarding "cracks in the foundation" have been raised a number of times over the years.

The IDF is not oblivious to these concerns. Awareness of these cracks exists, and their presence worries many senior IDF commanders, the General Staff and Israel's defense ministers. Future years will show how well the IDF is learning its lessons, correcting its weaknesses, and returning to its prior image of outstanding military competency.

Quality of Personnel

The most important advantage the IDF has over its enemies stems from its retention of high-quality personnel. The most ominous fault line in the IDF, then, is the possible decline of its personnel quality, especially in the permanent (Keva) corps. Manpower quality is, in fact, the key to all the rest—motivation, morale, moral level, decisiveness and military competency.

In the face of almost 1.5 million soldiers comprising the military strength of the surrounding Arab countries, the leading dictum of the IDF, with its half million troops, had always been quality over quantity. This dictum changed markedly after the Yom Kippur War. The surprise assault by the Egyptians and Syrians that caught Israel's standing army off guard on that Day of Atonement in 1973 shocked the IDF hierarchy and brought forth the decision to expand the IDF's size. This expansion almost doubled the size of the IDF. From a pre-Yom Kippur War overall strength of approximately 300,000 troops, the IDF has increased its mobilization capability to about 500,000 troops in 1983. Whereas in 1973 the Army could deploy only ten armored brigades, by 1983 this figure had grown to thirty-three fully mobilized brigades.[26]

This huge expansion brought with it those problems typical to any significant increase in military strength: lower overall quality of recruits, increased centralization and bureaucratization, increased proportions of non-combatants and diminished personal contacts. To an extent, the IDF began to lose some of its unique features and instead began to catch some of the diseases found in other large militaries.

Unfortunately, the Yom Kippur War also had significant losses of experienced officers. Within less than a month the IDF lost (in killed and wounded) more than 1,300 of its front-line officers. Thus, along with postwar expansion in terms of personnel strength, there was the more basic requirement to replace the officers lost in the war. The inevitable result was the lowering of standards for both selection for officer training and commander assignments. Since the IDF is a military driven by personal example in everything, including the area of retention, the mediocrity bred more mediocrity. The vicious cycle inevitably continued.

While the IDF as a whole, regular and reserve forces, still represents the best of Israeli society, there appears to be the beginning of a deteriorating trend in the permanent service corps. Whether it is a result of changes within the IDF itself or simply reflects changes in norms and values in Israeli society in general, this deteriorating trend creates the most dangerous fault line of them all.

Conclusion

Whether all the above are fault lines or afflicted areas, whether these are trends or random fluctuations, only time will tell. However, these issues must be attended to in no time. "The problem in defense is how far you can go without destroying from within that which you are trying to defend from without." These words, spoken half a century ago in reference to the American military, seem to be applicable to the current Israeli military. The IDF, standing victoriously throughout the years as the only force between its country and its enemies, may well be exhausting itself from within. With its frequently repeated engagements in fighting external threats, the IDF has never had enough time to repair its internal cracks. Like a maturing child, the Israeli soldier, swaddled and coddled throughout his infancy and early adolescence, has now reached the point of adulthood. Notwithstanding its strong heritage, and though the current difficulties may be seen as the hardships of coming of age, this phase in the IDF's history may require tough decisions and careful implementation to ensure the strength and uniqueness of the Israeli soldier in future years.

Notes

1. See, for example: Middleton, D. (1985, May 19). Israel's defense: As good as ever? *The New York Times Magazine*, pp. 60 65, 95–97. A number of articles were published in the years 1983–85 in various international magazines addressing, basically, this same theme.
2. Quoted in Gavron, D. (1984). *Israel after Begin*. Boston: Houghton Mifflin Company, p. 82.
3. Ibid., p. 83.
4. The few exceptional cases which have occurred in the history of the IDF only served to accentuate the rule. Glick, for example, reports that between the

Six Day and Yom Kippur wars, there were only nine Israelis who claimed conscientious objector status. Of these, four later changed their minds. When this number is compared to the hundreds of thousands of Israeli youth who enthusiastically sought combat unit assignments during that period, the conscientious objector becomes virtually invisible. Furthermore, following the Yom Kippur War there were even fewer cases than before. Glick, E. B. (1974). *Between Israel and death*. Harrisburg, PA: Stackpole Books.

5. Gavron, *Israel after Begin*, p. 83.

6. A university study of the characteristics of some of these resisters showed that the majority of them were university graduates. Of the thirty-six resisters queried in this study, the average age was thirty, and most of them came from combat units. About three fourths of the study sample had actively served in previous wars including the initial incursion into Lebanon. Tal, Y. (1985, January 25). Most Lebanon resisters—academicians serving in combat units. *Ha'aretz*, p. 3.

7. An attitude survey, conducted in spring of 1984 by the IDF's Department of Behavioral Science, revealed that 17 percent of the 1984 new recruits supported those reservists who demonstratively refused their call-ups to service in Lebanon. *Bamahane* (1985, April). (Special Issue for Israeli Reservists Abroad), 5.

8. Gal, R. (1983). *Unit morale: The secret weapon of the Israeli Defence Forces*. Presented as a major address in the Third International Conference on Psychological Stress and Adjustment in Time of War and Peace, Tel Aviv.

9. Levi, G. (1983, June). The redemption of moral conscience. *Ha'aretz*, pp. 12–13.

10. Stocklin, D. (1984, June 20). The rear interferes! *Bamahane*, 40, 9–11.

11. Accurate numbers regarding signing into the Keva (permanent service corps) are, for security reasons, not available for publication. However, various media reports published in the mid-1980s present a rather gloomy picture regarding the dilution of the Keva ranks. A concern regarding the specific impact of the Lebanon War on the willingness of young officers to remain in the Keva was reported, for example, in an article by Michael Garti in *Ha'aretz* (1984, July 27), The young ones abandon the IDF, p. 7.

12. In a CBS interview conducted in late 1984 in Bahad 1, the IDF's officers' school, the deterioration in the level of quality of officer cadets, all volunteers, was noted. Thus, for example, while five years ago about 40 percent of the cadets came from first class high schools, this percentage has dropped by half in recent times. Rather, D. (1984, September 13). Israeli army losing prestige. CBS Evening News, 7:00 p.m. *Radio-TV Defense Dialog*. Department of Defense, pp. 2–3.

13. "Y." (1983, August 3). Pilots as human beings. *Coterett Rasheet*, p. 14.

14. Quoted in Gavron, *Israel after Begin*, p. 134.

15. Among these sources are Dupuy, T. N., & Martell, P. (1985). *Flawed victory—The 1982 war in Lebanon*. Fairfax, VA: HERO Books; Gabriel, R. (1984). *Operation peace for Galilee: The Israeli-PLO war in Lebanon*. New York: Hill and Wang (A more condensed summary of his critical observations can be found in Gabriel, R. A. [1984, August]. Lessons of war: The IDF in Lebanon. *Military Review*, 64, 47–65.); Schiff, Z., & Ya'ari, E. (1984). *Israel's Lebanon war*. New York: Simon and Schuster.

16. The IDF's official spokesman, Brigadier General Ya'akov Even, in an attempt to dispute these criticisms (voiced especially by Richard Gabriel) claimed that "armored desert warfare tactics.... [in Lebanon were] in fact executed in full awareness and paid maximum dividends in conserving lives." Quoted in Middleton, D. (1984, October 14). Israel in Lebanon: Wrong tactics for terrain? *The New York Times*, p. 23.

17. Gabriel, Lessons of war, pp. 49–50.

18. This criticism, too, is refuted by the argument that the IDF was restrained in its planning in that the political levels never clearly defined the final objectives of the Lebanon incursion. See, for example, Schiff & Ya'ari, *Israel's Lebanon war*.

19. Several examples of such poor utilization of tactical momentum are described in Schiff & Ya'ari, *Israel's Lebanon war*, p. 171.

20. Ibid., pp. 125, 174–179. In a highly debatable article published in *The Washington Times* in August of 1984, facts were presented in a much more critical light. Quoting senior U.S. officials, the article claimed that nearly 20 percent of the Israeli casualties in Lebanon were self-inflicted. The high percentage was attributed by these officials to poor communications, leadership and discipline among Israeli units. The article further cited a high ranking Israeli officer who reportedly said that in one incident alone thirty four soldiers were killed by their own planes. See Sherwood, C. Israeli 'ineptitude' blamed for 'friendly fire' casualties. *The Washington Times*, 1984, August 27, pp. 1 A, 12 A.

21. Thus, for example, a series of articles was published in fall of 1984 in *Ha'aretz* by the Israeli journalist Shlomo Ahronson who quoted documents which had been apparently prepared by "strategic institutes" in San Francisco and Los Angeles and which seriously criticized IDF performance in Lebanon. No detailed references were provided in these articles; consequently, the *Ha'aretz* publication itself ultimately issued a disclaimer regarding the whole series. Similarly the *Washington Times* article (Ibid.) was viewed suspiciously by both Israeli and non-Israeli experts.

22. These include some of the sources mentioned already in this chapter (i.e., Gavron, 1984; Dupuy & Martell, 1985; Gabriel, 1984; and Schiff & Ya'ari, 1984). A more recent study regarding the impact of the Lebanon War on Israel is by Shai Feldman (1985, April). Deception, consensus and war: Israel in Lebanon. In *Middle East Military Balance*. Tel-Aviv: The Jaffee Center for Strategic Studies, Tel-Aviv University.

23. Maroze, T. (1984, March 16). The battle on the IDF. *Ha'aretz* Weekend magazine, pp. 12–13.

24. Hasdai, Y. (1979). *Truth in the shadow of war* (Translated from Hebrew by Moshe Kohn). Tel-Aviv: Zmora, Bitan, Modan Publishers.

25. For example, Pa'il, M. (1975, January). Israeli defence forces: A social aspect. *New Outlook*, 40–44.

26. *The Military Balance, 1973–74*. London: The International Institute for Strategic Studies; *The Military Balance, 1983–84*. London: The International Institute for Strategic Studies.

Bibliography

Allon, Y. (1970). *The making of Israel's army*. New York: Bantam Books.
Alon, N., & Omer, H. Treatment of the chronic post-traumatic syndrome. Unpublished manuscript. Cited by Lieblich, A. (1983). Between strength and toughness. In S. Breznitz (Ed.), *Stress in Israel* (pp. 39–64). New York: Van Nostrand Reinhold.
Amiad, P. (1981, January). *Attitude survey among conscripts regarding service in the IDF* (Research Report). Department of Behavioral Sciences, IDF.
Amikam, Y. (1983, February). They have turned the army into a punching bag. *Yedi'ot Ahronott*, p. 10.
Amir, Y., Kovarski, U., & Sharan, S. (1970). Peer nominations as a predictor of multistage promotions in a ramified organization. *J. of Applied Psychology, 54*, 462–469.
Anderson, J. W. (1984, September). *The warrior spirit* (Working Paper 84–9). Alexandria, VA: U.S. Army Research Institute.
Atzei-Pri, M. (1977). *Response frequencies in officers selection base's files* (Research Report). Classification Branch, IDF, Israel.
Babad, E. Y., & Salomon, G. (1978, September). Professional dilemmas of the psychologist in an organizational emergency. *American Psychologist, 33*(9), 840–846.
Belenky, G., & Kaufman, L. (1984). Staying alive: Knowing what to do until the medic arrives. *Military Review, 64*(1), 28–33.
Belenky, G. L., Tyner, C. F., & Sodetz, F. J. (1983, August). *Israeli battle shock casualties: 1973 and 1982* (WRAIR Report NP 83-4). Washington, DC: Walter Reed Army Institute of Research.
Ben-Gurion, D. (1969). *Medinat Israel Ha-Mithadeshet*. Tel-Aviv: Am Oved.
———. (1970). *Memoirs* (Compiled by Thomas R. Bransten). New York: The World Publishing Company.
Blake, J. A. (1973). The congressional medal of honor in three wars. *Pacific Sociological Review, 16*(2), 166–176.
Blake, J. A., & Butler, S. (1976). The medal of honor, combat orientations and

latent role structure in the United States military. *Sociological Quarterly, 17*(4), 561–567.
Bloom, A. (1982). The women in Israel's military forces. In N. Goldman (Ed.), *Female soldiers: Combatants or non-combatants*. Westport, CT: Greenwood Press.
Bowden, T. (1976). *Army in the service of the state*. Tel-Aviv: University Publishing Projects.
Breznitz, S. (Ed.). (1983). *Stress in Israel*. New York: Van Nostrand Reinhold.
Carlyle, T. (1946). *On heroes, hero-worship and the heroic in history*. London: Oxford University Press.
Chaney, M., & Cannon, M. W. (1981, March-April). Improving combat skills: The National Training Center. *Armor*.
CHEN translates charm: CHEN—the Israel Defence Forces' Women's Corps. (1980, February 27). The Israeli Defence Forces Spokesman.
The Chief of Staff is acting to terminate extreme harassment. (1978, May 22). *Davar*.
The Commander Training Institute of the IDF. (1982, October 24). Commander Training Institute, IDF.
Dickerson, V. (1974, May). *The role of women in the defence force of Israel*. Alexandria, VA: Defense Documentation Center.
Doctoroff, M. (1984, January 26). Col. Dotan and woman's place: At home, in the military. *Washington Jewish Week*, p. 5.
Doering, Z. D., & Grissmer, D. W. (1984, May). What we know and how we know it. A selected review of research and methods for studying active and reserve attrition/retention in the U.S. Armed Forces. *Proceedings of the Second Symposium on Motivation and Morale in the NATO Forces* (pp. 251–299). Brussels: NATO.
Donnelly, C. (1982). The Soviet attitude to stress in battle. *Journal of the Royal Army Medical Corps, 128*, 72–78.
Dupuy, T. (1984). *Elusive victory: The Arab-Israeli wars, 1947–1974*. Fairfax, VA: HERO Books.
Dupuy, T. N., & Martell, P. (1985). *Flawed victory—The 1982 war in Lebanon*. Fairfax, VA: HERO Books.
Effectiveness of preparation program for induction. (1982, February). (Research Report). Department of Behavioral Sciences, IDF.
Egbert, R. L., Meeland, T., Cline, V. B., Forgy, E. W., Spickter, M. W., & Brown, C. (1957, December). *Fighter 1: An analysis of combat fighters and non-fighters* (HumRRO Technical Report #44). Monterey, CA: U.S. Army Leadership Human Research Unit.
Elon, A. (1983). *The Israelis: Founders and sons*. New York: Pelican Books.
Enoch, D., Bar-On, R., Barg, Y., Durst, N., Haran, G., Hovel, S., Israel, A., Reiter, M., Stern, M., & Toubiana, Y. (1983, January). *An indigenous military community as a psychotherapeutic agent: Specific application of forward treatment in combat*. Paper presented at the Third International Conference on Psychological Stress and Adjustment in Time of War and Peace, Tel-Aviv.
Erez, Y. (1983, May 13). Mitzna: Learning from experience. Weekend, the weekend magazine of *Ma'ariv*, p. 23.

Eshet, M. (1985, April). "Peace for Galilee" did not change motivation for service. *Bamahane* (Special issue for reservists abroad), 5.
Ezrahi, Y. (1982, August). *"Operation Peace for Galilee" operation—Main results from the fighting units* (Research Report). Department of Behavioral Sciences, IDF, Israel.
———. (1982). *Morale survey in combat units: Golan Heights, 1982* (Research Report). Department of Behavioral Sciences, IDF, Israel.
Facts about Israel. (1979). Jerusalem: Ministry of Foreign Affairs.
Feldman, O., & Milshtein, A. (1983, May 25). General Moshe Nativ: A farewell interview. *Bamahane, 37,* 12–14.
Feldman, S. (1985, April). Deception, consensus and war: Israel in Lebanon. In *Middle East Military Balance.* Tel-Aviv: The Jaffee Center for Strategic Studies, Tel-Aviv University.
Fiedler, F. (1967). *A theory of leadership effectiveness.* New York: McGraw-Hill.
Gabriel, R. (1982). *To serve with honor.* Westport, CT: Greenwood Press.
Gabriel, R. A. (1982, December). Stress in battle: Coping on the spot. *Army, 32*(12), 36–42.
———. (1984). *Operation peace for Galilee: The Israeli-PLO war in Lebanon.* New York: Hill and Wang.
———. (1984, August). Lessons of war: The IDF in Lebanon. *Military Review, 64,* 47–65.
Gabriel, R., & Gal, R. (1984, January). The IDF officer: Linchpin in unit cohesion. *Army, 34*(1), 42–50.
Gabriel, R., & Savage, P. (1978). *Crisis in command.* New York: Hill and Wang.
Gal, R. (1982, February). *Modes of adjustment and coping with military service in the IDF.* Paper presented at the 18th Conference of the Israeli Psychological Association, Haifa, Israel.
———. (1983, January). *Unit morale: The secret weapon of the Israeli Defence Forces.* Presented as a major address in the Third International Conference on Psychological Stress and Adjustment in Time of War and Peace, Tel-Aviv.
———. (1983). Courage under stress. In S. Breznitz (Ed.), *Stress in Israel* (pp. 65–91). New York: Van Nostrand Reinhold.
———. (in press). Commitment and obedience in the military: An Israeli case study. *Armed Forces and Society.*
———. (in press). Unit morale: From a theoretical puzzle to an empirical illustration—an Israeli example. *Journal of Military Applied Social Psychology.*
Gal, R., & Manning, F. G. (1984). *Correlates of unit cohesion and morale in the U.S. and Israeli armies.* Paper presented at the Annual Convention of the American Psychological Association, Toronto.
Galilli, L. (1984, March 21). IDF veterans complain of emotional difficulties regarding their service. *Ha'aretz.*
Garti, M. (1984, July 27). The young ones abandon the IDF. *Ha'aretz,* p. 7.
Gavron, D. (1984). *Israel after Begin.* Boston: Houghton Mifflin Company.
Glass, A. J. (Ed.). (1973). Lessons learned. In *Neuropsychiatry in World War II, volume II: Overseas theaters.* Washington, DC: U.S. Government Printing Office.
Glick, E. B. (1974). *Between Israel and death.* Harrisburg, PA: Stackpole Books.
Goldman, I. (1982, April). An interview with Colonel Dalia Raz, Commander

of the IDF Women's Corps. *IDF Journal: Israel Defence Forces Spokesman*, 1(1), 43–46.
Goldman, N. L., with Wiegand, K. L. (1984). The Israeli woman in combat. In M. E. Martin & E. S. McCrate (Eds.), *The military, militarism and the polity* (pp. 201–230). New York: The Free Press.
Goldstein, A. (Ed.). (1981). *Toward induction*. Jerusalem: Department of Education, Israel.
Goodman, H. (1984, July 22–28). Face to face. *The Jerusalem Post*, pp. 14, 17.
Greenbaum, C. W. (1979). The small group under the gun. *Journal of Applied Behavioral Science*, 15(3), 392–405.
Greenbaum, C. W., Rogovsky, I., & Shalit, B. (1977). The military psychologists during wartime: A model based on action research and crisis intervention. *Journal of Applied Behavioral Science*, 13(1), 7–21.
Habber, E. (1984, September 26). The general staff 1984: A portrait. In Seven Days, the weekend magazine of *Yedi'ot Ahronott*, 1078, 20–21.
Hackett, J. (1962). *The profession of arms*. London: Times Publishing Company.
Harkabi, Y. (1967, Fall). Basic factors in the Arab collapse. *Orbis*, a Quarterly Journal of World Affairs.
Hasdai, Y. (1979). *Truth in the shadow of war* (Translated from Hebrew by M. Kohn). Tel-Aviv: Zmora, Bitan, Modan Publishers.
Hegel, G.W.F. (1861). *Lectures on the philosophy of history* (Translated from the 3rd German Edition by J. Sibree). London: H. G. Bohn.
Hellman, P. (1985, March). Israel's chariot of fire. *The Atlantic Monthly*, pp. 81–95.
Henderson, W. D. (1985). *Cohesion: The human element in combat*. Washington, DC: National Defense University Press.
Herzog, C. (1975). *The war of atonement: October 1973*. Boston: Little, Brown and Company.
———. (1983). *The Arab-Israeli wars*. Jerusalem: Edanim Publishers.
Hook, S. (1955). *The hero in history*. Boston: Beacon Press.
Huntington, S. P. (1959). *The soldier and the state*. Cambridge, MA: Harvard University Press.
I am not willing to die for nothing: Kibbutznicks, on the eve of their induction, confronting army generals. (1984, June 24). *Ha'aretz*.
IDF Spokesman. (1982). *The unique character of the Israel Defence Forces*. Tel-Aviv: IDF Spokesman's Office.
IDF Spokesman. (1982, March). *The IDF Contribution to the rehabilitation of disadvantaged youth*. Tel-Aviv: IDF Spokesman's Office.
Ingraham, L. H., & Manning, F. J. (1981). Cohesion: Who needs it, what is it, and how do we get it to them? *Military Review*, 61(6), 2–12.
Inspector, Y. (1983). The commander in combat: Part I. *Bamahane*, 13, 17.
Interview with Lt. Gen. Mordechai Gur. (1975, March 12). *Bamahane*.
Interview with Maj. Gen. Moshe Peled, Chief of the Armor Corps. (1978, October). *Bamahane*, 4.
Israelashvilli, M. (1982, April). *The CHEN survey: Attitudes toward conscription, adjustment and satisfaction from service among conscript female soldiers*. Unpublished manuscript, Department of Behavioral Sciences, Israeli Defence

Forces, Israel. Note: Parts of this report were presented at the 18th Conference of the Israeli Psychological Association, Haifa, Israel.
Janowitz, M. (1960). *The professional soldier: A social and political portrait.* Glencoe, IL: Free Press.
Jennings, E. E. (1960). *An anatomy of leadership.* New York: Harper and Brothers.
Johnson, A. W. (1969, December). Combat psychiatry. Part II. The U.S. Army in Vietnam. *Medical Bulletin U.S. Army Europe, 25*(11), 335–339.
Kahalani, A. (1984). *The heights of courage.* Westport, CT: Greenwood Press.
Kahan, Y., Barak, A., & Efrat, Y. (1983). *Final Report of the Commission of Inquiry into the Events at the Refugee Camps in Beirut.* Jerusalem: Government Publication Office.
Kalay, E. (1982, April). *Professional preferences among CHEN basic trainees.* Unpublished manuscript, Department of Behavioral Sciences, Israeli Defence Forces, Israel.
———. (1982, July). *Confidence in commanders* (Research Report). Department of Behavioral Sciences, IDF, Israel. Figures from this report were published in *Skira Hodsheet.* (1983, February-March), *30*(2–3), 82.
Kalman, G. (1977). On combat neuroses. *International Journal Social Psychiatry* (England), *23*(3), 195–203.
Keegan, J. (Ed.). (1979). *World armies.* New York: Facts on File, Inc.
Kellett, A. (1982). *Combat motivation.* Boston: Kluwer Nijhoff Publishing.
Kraus, V. (1981). The perception of occupational structure in Israel. *Megamot, 26*(3), 283–294.
Leadership of the junior leader in the IDF: Principles, methods and means. IDF General Staff publication, Chief, Educational Corps.
Lester, J. T. (1973, June 26). *Israeli military psychology* (ONR Report #R–13–73). London: Office of Naval Research, U.S. Navy, Branch Office.
Lev, I. (1984). *First night without mummy.* Rechovot, Israel: Adar Publishers.
Levav, I., Greenfeld, H., & Baruch, E. (1979, May). Psychiatric combat reactions during the Yom Kippur War. *Am. J. Psychiatry, 136*(5), 637–641.
Levi, G. (1983, June). The redemption of moral conscience. *Ha'aretz,* pp. 12–13.
Lieblich, A. (1978). *Tin soldiers on Jerusalem Beach.* New York: Pantheon.
———. (1983). Between strength and toughness. In S. Breznitz (Ed.), *Stress in Israel* (pp. 39–64). New York: Van Nostrand Reinhold.
Luttwak, E., & Horowitz, D. (1975). *The Israeli army.* London: Allen Lane.
Marcus, J. (1984, June 15). The third Israel. *Ha'aretz.*
Margalit, C., Segal, R., Nardi, C., Wozner, Y., & Goren, Y. (1983, January). *Combat fitness retraining unit (CFRU) for treatment and rehabilitation of combat reactions with poor prognosis in the June 1982 conflict.* Paper presented at the Third International Conference on Psychological Stress and Adjustment in Time of War and Peace, Tel-Aviv.
Marlowe, D., & Ingraham, L. H. (1983, July). Emphasizing cohesion, morale can help prevent battle stress. *Army, 33*(7), 16–17.
Maroze, T. (1984, March 16). The battle on the IDF. *Ha'aretz* Weekend magazine, pp. 12–13.
Marshall, S.L.A. (1957, April). Combat leadership. In *Symposium on Preventive and Social Psychiatry.* Sponsored jointly by the Walter Reed Army Institute

of Research, Walter Reed Army Medical Center and the National Research Council.

Merbaum, M., & Hefez, A. (1976). Some personality characteristics of soldiers exposed to extreme war stress. *Journal of Consulting and Clinical Psychology,* 44(1), 1–6.

Middleton, D. (1984, October 14). Israel in Lebanon: Wrong tactics for terrain? *The New York Times,* p. 23.

———. (1985, May 19). Israel's defense: As good as ever? *The New York Times Magazine,* pp. 60–65, 95–97.

Milgram, S. (1965). Some conditions of obedience and disobedience to authority. *Human Relations,* 18, 57–75.

The Military Balance, 1973–74. London: The International Institute for Strategic Studies.

The Military Balance, 1981–82. London: The International Institute for Strategic Studies.

The Military Balance, 1982–83. London: The International Institute for Strategic Studies.

The Military Balance, 1983–84. London: The International Institute for Strategic Studies.

The Military Balance, 1984–85. London: The International Institute for Strategic Studies.

Milshtein, A. (1983, April 6). What was in the past awardable has become part of combat doctrine. *Bamahane,* 30, 6–7.

Montgomery, V. (1946). *Morale in battle: Analysis.* Germany: British Army of the Rhine.

Moses, R. (1983). Emotional response to stress in Israel: A psychoanalytic perspective. In S. Breznitz (Ed.), *Stress in Israel* (pp. 114–137). New York: Van Nostrand Reinhold.

Nativ, M. (1984, Summer). IDF manpower and Israeli society. *The Jerusalem Quarterly,* 32, 140–144.

Netanyahu, B. (1984, June 26). Statement prepared for the *Jonathan Institute: Second Conference on International Terrorism,* Washington, DC.

Netanyahu, J. (1980). *Self-Portrait of a hero: The letters of Jonathan Netanyahu.* New York: Ballantine Books.

Neumann, M., & Levy, A. (1984, April). A specific military installation for treatment of combat reactions during the war in Lebanon. *Military Medicine,* 149, 196–199.

Newsletter to the soldier in Lebanon. (1982, June 11). Education Corps, Doctrine and Training Branch, IDF, Tel-Aviv.

Noy, S. (1978, June). *Stress and personality as factors in the causality and prognosis of combat reaction.* Paper presented at the Second International Conference on Psychological Stress and Adjustment in Time of War and Peace, Jerusalem.

Noy, S., Nardi, C., & Solomon, Z. (1983, January). *Battle characteristics and the prevalence of combat psychiatric casualties.* Paper presented at the Third International Conference on Psychological Stress and Adjustment in Time of War and Peace, Tel-Aviv.

Nyrop, R. F. (Ed.). (1979). *Israel: A country study.* Washington, DC: American University Press.
Oren, A. (1983, May 11). We may have spoiled our soldiers too much. *Coterett Rasheet, 23,* 20–21, 39.
The "Oxford" of the armor corps. (1983, June 22). *Bamahane, 41,* 18.
Pa'il, M. (1970, August). Combat discipline or purity of arms. *Ma'archot, 209,* 1–11.
———. (1975, January). The Israeli defence forces: A social aspect. *New Outlook: Middle East Monthly,* 40–44.
Peri, Y. (1977). The ideological portrait of the Israeli military elite. *The Jerusalem Quarterly, 3,* 28–41.
———. (1983). *Between battles and ballots: Israeli military in politics.* London: Cambridge University Press.
———. (n. d.). *The professional ethics of the military.* Unpublished manuscript.
Rampton, G. M. (1983). *Visit to Israel.* Visit Report. National Defence Headquarters, Canada.
Rather, D. (1984, September 13). Israeli army losing prestige. CBS Evening News. *Radio-TV Defense Dialog.* Department of Defense, pp. 2–3.
Ravid, Y. (1984, May). Sociometric pilot testing saves time, lives, and money. *Defense Systems Review,* 44–45.
Record, J. (1984, April 15). More medals than we had soldiers: Grenada's decoration glut cheapens honor and valor. *The Washington Post,* p. B5.
Reeb, M. (1968). Construction of a questionnaire to replace a valid structured interview in the Israeli Defence Forces. *Megamot,* Behavioral Sciences Quarterly, *16,* 69–74.
———. (1976). Differential test validity for ethnic groups in the Israeli army and the effect of educational level. *J. of Applied Psychology, 61*(3), 257–261.
Rennie, C. G. (1984, October). *Military motivation and the regimental system in the Israeli army* (Project Report No. PR 258). Ottawa, Canada: Operational Research and Analysis Establishment, Department of National Defence.
Report on the status of women. (1978, August). Jerusalem: Prime Minister's Office.
Rock, S. K., & Schneider, R. J. (1984). Battle stress reactions and the Israeli experience in Lebanon: A brief summary. *Medical Bulletin, 41*(1), 9–11.
Rolbant, S. (1970). *The Israeli soldier: Profile of an army.* New York: Thomas Yoseloff Publishing.
Rosner, A. A. (1944). Neuropsychiatric casualties from Guadalcanal. *American Journal of Medical Science, 207,* 770–776.
Rothenberg, G. E. (1979). *The anatomy of the Israeli army.* New York: Hippocrene Books, Inc.
Sadeh, Y. (1961). Trails of heroism. In *Around the campfire.* Tel-Aviv: Marachot Publications.
Salmon, T. W. (1919). The war neuroses and their lesson. *New York Journal of Medicine, 109,* 993–994.
Sanua, V. D. (1974, May). Psychological effects of the Yom Kippur War. *The Source, 2*(3), 7–8.
Sarason, I. G. (1984, May). *Longitudinal study of Marine Corps drill instructors.* Paper presented at the Second Symposium on Motivation and Morale in NATO Forces, Brussels, Belgium.

Schiff, Z. (1970). *Knafaim Me'al LeSuez* [Wings over Suez]. Tel-Aviv: Ot-Paz.
Schiff, Z., & Ya'ari, E. (1984). *Israel's Lebanon war* (Translated from the Hebrew by Ina Friedman). New York: Simon and Schuster.
Segal, R. (1980, January). *Attitude survey conducted on the August 1979 cohort of conscripts on their day of discharge*. Unpublished manuscript, Unit of Military Psychology, IDF, Israel. Note: Parts of this report were presented at the 18th Conference of the Israeli Psychological Association, Haifa, Israel.
Segal, R., Margalit, C., Reish, M., Zilberman, S., & Friedman, Y. (1983, January). *The contribution of combat physical fitness in a rear unit (CFRU) for the treatment of combat reactions with poor prognosis*. Paper presented at the Third International Conference on Psychological Stress and Adjustment in Time of War and Peace, Tel-Aviv.
Shapira, A. (Ed.). (1970). *The seventh day: Soldiers talk about the Six Day War*. New York: Charles Scribner's Sons.
Sherwood, C. (1984, August 27). Israeli 'ineptitude' blamed for 'friendly fire' casualties. *The Washington Times*, pp. 1-A, 12-A.
Shipler, D. (1983, January 8). The other Israeli casualties: The mentally scarred. *New York Times*, p. 2.
Shirom, A. (1976, September). On some correlates of combat performance. *Administrative Combat Quarterly, 21*, 419–432.
Shurr, R. (1983, September). Back to the valley of tears. *Monitin, 61*, 61–68.
Sohlberg, S. C. (1976). Stress experiences and combat fatigue during the Yom Kippur War—1973. *Psychological Reports, 38*, 523–529.
Solomon, Z., & Noy, S. (1983, January). *Who is at high risk for combat reaction?* Paper presented at the Third International Conference on Psychological Stress and Adjustment in Time of War and Peace, Tel-Aviv.
Special Issue for Israeli Reservists Abroad. (1985, April). *Bamahane*.
Steiner, M., & Neumann, M. (1978). Traumatic neurosis and social support in the Yom Kippur War returnees. *Military Medicine, 143*(12), 866–868.
Stocklin, D. (1984, June 20). The rear interferes! *Bamahane, 40*, 9–11.
Stouffer, S. A., DeVinney, L. C., Star, S. A., & Williams, R. M. (1949). *The American soldier, volume II*. Princeton, NJ: Princeton University Press.
Tal, O. (1984, July 18). General Shomron: Do not wait for orders, take the initiative. *Bamahane, 44*, 7.
Tal, Y. (1985, January 25). Most Lebanon resistors—academicians serving in combat units. *Ha'aretz*, p. 3.
Talshir, R. (1984, November 30). Eve's services. *Ha'aretz*, p. 6.
The "tigers" are back. (1984, May 30). *Bamahane, 37*, 22–23.
To you, the draftee. (1981, June). Division of Manpower, Department of Behavioral Sciences and Chief Education Corps. Tel-Aviv: IDF.
Tubiana, J. H., & Ben-Shakhar, G. (1980). *An objective group questionnaire as a substitute for a personal interview in the prediction of success in military training in Israel*. Unpublished manuscript, Hebrew University of Jerusalem, Jerusalem, Israel.
Tuchman, B. W. (1981). Israel's swift sword. In *Practicing history: Selected essays* (pp. 173–187). New York: Ballantine Books.
Tziner, A., & Eden, D. (1985). Effects of tank crew composition on tank crew

performance: Does the whole equal the sum of its parts? *J. of Applied Psychology, 70*(1), 85–93.
Tziner, A., & Vardi, Y. (1983). Ability as a moderator between cohesiveness and tank crew performance. *J. of Occupational Behavior, 4,* 137–143.
van Creveld, M. (1982, December 12–18). The war: A questioning look. *The Jerusalem Post "International Edition,"* pp. 12–13.
———. (1982). *Fighting power: German and U.S. Army performance 1939–1945.* Westport, CT: Greenwood Press.
———. (1982). Leadership and the officer corps. In *Fighting power: German and U.S. Army performance 1939–1945* (pp. 127–162). Westport, CT: Greenwood Press.
Weisman, G. (1974, June). A psycho-social model for limiting mental reaction during stress. *The Israel Annals of Psychiatry and Related Disciplines, 12*(2), 161.
"Y." (1983, August 3). Pilots as human beings. *Coterett Rasheet,* p. 14.
Yarom, N. (1983). Facing death in war—an existential crisis. In S. Breznitz (Ed.), *Stress in Israel* (pp. 3–38). New York: Van Nostrand Reinhold.
Zinger, Y., & Shorek, U. (1975). *Attitude survey among future conscripts regarding service in the IDF* (Research Report). Unit of Military Psychology, IDF. The main findings of this survey were reported by the author at the 18th Conference of the Israeli Psychological Association, Haifa, Israel, February 1982.
Zusmann, P. (1984). Why is the defence burden so heavy in Israel? In Z. Offer & A. Kober (Eds.), *The price of power* (pp. 17–25). Tel-Aviv: Ministry of Defence Publications.
Zvulun, E. (1974, April). *The reactions of the Israeli soldier in the Yom Kippur War* (Research Report). Unit of Military Psychology, IDF, Israel.

INDEX

Agranat Commission, 28 n.34, 108, 114 n.12, 233
Air Force, 111, 116, 117, 167, 174, 175; Command and Staff School, 125 (see also Poum [Command and Staff School]); as an elite force, 62, 63, 64, 75 n.9; by the end of the British Mandate, 27 n.13; in Lebanon War, 26, 183, 240, 251; in Sinai Campaign, 14; in Six Day War, 15, 16; in War of Attrition, 19–20; women in Air Force, 50 (see also Women's Corps [Chen]); in Yom Kippur War, 160, 161. See also Pilots
Allon, Yigal, 4, 8. See also Palmach
Armored Corps, 63, 65–66, 111, 114 n.18, 125, 174; Armored Divisions ("Ugdot"), 16, 22, 131, 144 (see also IDF, size; structure IDF); assembly of tank crews, 92; bravery awards, 197–98; in Lebanon War, 252, 257 n.16; psychiatric casualties, 213 (see also Psychiatric casualties); in Sinai Campaign, 14; in Six Day War, 16, 18; stability of crews, 40, 154, 157 (see also Cohesion); training, 91, 117–18; trust in commanders, 133, 136, 176 (see also Leadership); women in Armored units, 53 (see also Women's Corps [Chen]); in Yom Kippur War, 160, 237, 238
Artillery, 18, 22, 27 n.13, 40, 91, 133, 144, 197, 213, 240
Awards and medals. See Heroism

Bar-Lev, Haim, 8, 28 n.33, 172, 173, 180, 188 n.29; Bar-Lev Line, 19, 20
Begin, Menachem, 5, 184, 244, 247
Ben-Gal ("Yanoush"), Avigdor, 179, 180, 188 n.29
Ben-Gurion, David, 11, 12, 26 n.1, 27 n.13, 45, 147
Bonding. See Cohesion
Bravery. See Heroism

Chen. See Women's Corps (Chen)
"Chinese Farm," 236–37, 238. See also Yom Kippur War
Cohesion, 69, 135, 149; in basic training, 104, 107, 112 (see also Training); and combat reactions, 214, 216, 218, 219 (see also Psychiatric casualties); and morale, 153–55, 157, 164 n.25, 218, 250; as a norm, 235–39; in the Palmach, 7; in reserve units, 40, 42, 44; among tank crews, 92, 198
Courage. See Heroism

Dayan, Moshe, 8, 13, 27 n.19, 135, 143, 172
Diaspora, 1, 9, 46, 70, 113, 191, 233, 242
Discipline, 231–35; in basic training, 99, 103, 104, 106, 108–9 (*see also* Training); in combat units, 173, 257 n.20 (*see also* Moral standards)
Dotan, Amira, 53, 57 n.18, 57 n.22. See also Women's Corps (Chen)
Druze, 30, 32, 247

Eytan ("Raful"), Rafael, 105, 109–10, 131, 136, 172, 173, 180, 184

"Follow me." *See* Personal example

General Staff, 38, 125, 179, 183, 254; age of members, 168–69, 171–72; casualties, 137, 176; and political career, 187 n.7; as a unified command, 11, 27 n.17. *See also* Leadership
Geva, Eli, 184–85, 188 n.23, 234, 243 n.3. *See also* Leadership; Lebanon War; Moral standards
"Golani" brigade, 65, 102, 235. *See also* Infantry Corps
Gur ("Motta"), Mordechai, 172, 173, 188 n.29, 233

Haganah, 3, 4, 5, 6, 7, 9, 10, 11, 13, 16, 26, 27 n.3, 13, 116; moral standards, 239 (*see also* "Tohar haneshek" [purity of arms]); women in, 46 (*see also* Women's Corps [Chen])
Hasdai, Ya'acov, 182, 253–54
Hashomer, 2, 7, 10, 46, 70, 191
Heroism, 148, 176, 190–208; among officers, 139, 177, 178; awards and medals, 177, 188 n.13, 194–206; awards and medals in Lebanon War, 204–6; awards and medals in Yom Kippur War, 195–204; heritage and ethos, 65, 73, 74, 145, 192–94; quality of medalists, 85, 86; in Yom Kippur War, 21, 154, 160, 195–204
Holocaust, 111, 146, 191, 242, 243

IDF (Israeli Defence Forces): birth of, 9–10, 39, 70, 209–10, 246, 247; doctrines and policy in basic training, 103–4, 105–6, 107–10; leadership, 115–16, 130, 136; manpower, 23, 29 n.37, 35, 76, 83, 86; medical treatment of psychiatric casualties, 222; mobilization, 41; origins of, 1–9, 10, 38, 39, 46, 70, 112, 113, 143, 150, 190–92, 233; POWs, 238; promotion, 166, 170; size of, 9, 15, 16, 22–23, 27 n.13, 32, 34, 36, 131, 173, 178–79, 254; strategy and tactics, 11–12, 17, 19; structure, 11, 14, 30, 35, 40, 94, 125, 129, 144–45, 149, 153, 162, 173; women in combat roles, 46
Infantry Corps, 63, 133, 135, 157, 176, 240; bravery awards, 197; officers, 119, 140 n.6; psychiatric casualties, 213; quality of manpower, 85; reserve units, 40; in Six Day War, 16, 18; size of units, 144; training, 91, 102–3; women in, 53
Intelligence, 21, 33
Irgun ("Irgun Zvai Leumi"), 5, 6, 9, 10, 46

Kaba. *See* Psychological testing/screening
Kahalani, Avigdor, 165, 193. *See also* Seventh brigade
Keva (permanent service), 11, 30, 34–38, 86, 124–26; bravery awards, 196, 199; after Lebanon, 185, 186, 250, 256 n.11; manpower quality, 95 n.13, 181, 182, 254–55; size of, 23, 34; status, 45 n.9; in War of Attrition, 19, 123; women in, 48
Kibbutz (kibbutzniks), 7, 66, 68–69, 75 n.14, 81, 83, 89, 111, 147, 153, 243, 249

Leadership, 35, 115–40, 148, 166–89, 242; and bravery awards, 202, 203, 206, 207 nn.14, 15; kibbutzniks, 69; NCOs, 91, 106–7, 108; origins of, 7, 13; psychiatric casualties, 214, 217, 218; in Six Day War, 15, 16, 17; as a source of combat motivation, 149, 153, 155–57, 158–59, 162, 235. *See also* Officers/Officers Corps; Personal example

Lebanon War, 25–26, 53, 73, 74 n.3, 150, 187, 195, 238, 241, 242; bravery awards, 139, 177, 194, 204–6; casualties, 75 n.13, 105, 137, 138, 177, 210, 240; Col. Geva's case, 184–85, 234 (*see also* Geva, Eli); effects on permanent service, 38, 124, 132, 167, 183 (*see also* Keva); effects on regular service, 61, 68, 69; effects on reserve service, 39, 44, 74 n.2, 123, 247, 248–49, 256 nn.6, 7 (*see also* Reserve Corps); military proficiency, 133, 134, 145, 161, 162, 163 n.3, 176, 252–53; morale, 151, 155; perceived legitimacy, 147, 158–59, 234, 248–49, 251; psychiatric casualties, 211, 219–24, 220, 227 n.6

"Lehi" (Stern gang), 5, 6, 9, 10, 26 n.6, 46

Levi, Moshe, 168–9, 172, 173, 180

Litani operation, 25, 239

Mabal (National Defence College), 170–71

Makam (Center for the Advancement of Special Populations; disadvantaged youth), 78, 81, 84, 94, 95 n.8

Medical screening, 32, 77–78, 87, 128. *See also* Psychological testing/screening

"Merkava" tank, 238

Moral standards: IDF image, 72, 147–48, 185, 242, 250, 254; and legitimacy of war, 158–59, 183, 192, 250–51; before 1948, 3; "tohar haneshek" (purity of arms), 3, 239–41, 243

Morale, 7, 15, 21, 105, 150, 247, 248, 249, 254; as a component of the fighting spirit, 151–53, 155, 157, 236; morale surveys, 151, 158, 163 n.23, 164 n.25; and motivation, 247–50, 251; and psychiatric casualties, 217, 218–19, 224, 228 n.27

Nahal (Fighting Pioneer Youth), 7, 66, 75 n.11, 103, 232

Nativ, Moshe, 56 n.9, 84

Naval officers. *See* Navy

Navy, 63, 64, 65, 85, 111, 116, 117, 125, 157, 176; and bravery awards, 197; elite units, 62, 89; Naval Officers, 80, 89, 117, 121, 127, 140 n.1, 167, 174; in Palmach, 9; in Six Day War, 15; in War of Attrition, 19; in Yom Kippur War, 159–60

NCOs. *See* Leadership

Netanyahu ("Yoni"), Jonathan, 24, 105, 131, 193

Officers/Officers Corps, 11, 30, 98, 106, 115–40, 166–89, 250; bravery awards, 197, 201–2; casualties, 75 n.13, 137–38, 187 n.5; as leaders, 13, 153, 155–57; in Lebanon War, 44, 240 (*see also names of specific wars*); in Palmach, 8; in permanent service, 34–38, 256 n.11; proportion of total strength, 128; psychiatric casualties, 214–15; in reserve service, 43, 44; selection procedures, 80, 81, 83, 85, 90–92, 119, 254, 256 n.12 (*see also* Kaba; Psychological testing/screening); in Sinai Campaign, 14; in Six Day War, 16; special requirements, 33, 67–69; in War of Attrition, 20; in Yom Kippur War, 24, 160. *See also* Navy Pilots

Pa'il, Meir, 36, 182, 188, 239

Palmach, 4, 6, 7–9, 10, 13, 16, 26, 27

n.13, 46, 70, 116, 146, 191–92, 233
Paratroopers, 13, 14, 39, 42, 62, 64–65, 75 n.9, 89, 102–3, 105, 111, 176, 198, 217, 236–37, 239
Personal example, 5, 107, 120, 121, 133, 135–37, 139, 150, 176, 178, 198, 207 n.14. *See also* Leadership
Pilots, 130, 136, 154, 170; bravery awards, 197; POW, 238; selection, 80, 85, 87, 89–90, 93, 140 n.1; training, 43, 104, 126, 176. *See also* Air Force
PLO (Palestine Liberation Organization), 24, 25, 142 n.32, 184, 220, 238, 240, 244 nn.15, 17, 247, 256
Poum (Command and Staff School), 125, 126, 127, 167
POW (Prisoner of War), 53, 238, 239, 240
Psychiatric casualties, 92, 108, 137, 139, 209–30
Psychological testing/screening, 32, 76, 77, 94; and combat reactions, 28 n.19; Kaba, 49, 62, 78–86, 87, 88, 91–93, 116, 117, 118, 201, 215–16, 234; for officers, 90–92, 119; for permanent ("Keva") service, 36; sociometric techniques (peer evaluation), 91–92, 93, 126; for special units, 89–90; for women, 90

Rabin, Yitzhak, 8, 15, 16, 108, 172, 173, 187 n.7, 188 n.29
Raz, Dalia, 49, 56 n.14. *See also* Women's Corps (Chen)
Reserve Corps, 11, 30, 33, 34, 37, 38–44, 88, 147, 233, 255; bravery awards, 196, 198, 199; in Lebanon, 249, 250, 253, 256 n.6; mobilization, 45 n.10, 211, 232; motivation, 86, 226, 247; officers, 68, 121, 122–24; psychiatric casualties, 213, 217, 223; sense of intimacy, 179, 180; in Sinai Campaign, 14; in Six Day War, 28 n.21; strength, 28 n.21, 32; in War of Attrition, 19; in Yom Kippur War, 21, 22, 23, 154

"Rosh Katan" ("small head"), 132, 183, 186

Sabra. *See* Shatilla and Sabra
Sadeh, Yitzhak, 4, 5, 7, 8, 13, 192
Seventh brigade, 160, 165, 179, 179 n.14. *See also* Ben-Gal, ("Yanoush") Avigdor; Kahalani, Avigdor
Sharon, Ariel, 13, 27 n.19, 180, 184, 187 n.7, 239
Shatilla and Sabra, 240, 241, 242, 244 n.15. *See also* Lebanon War
Shomron, Dan, 168–69, 186
Sinai Campaign, 13–14, 28 n.20, 74 n.3, 167, 195, 210, 211
Six Day War, 15–18, 26, 28 n.22, 36, 73, 74 n.3, 145, 146, 147, 150, 161, 167, 171, 175, 186, 194, 195, 210, 211, 238, 239, 246, 250, 252, 256 n.4
SNS (Special Night Squads), 4, 10
Sociometric techniques. *See* Psychological testing/screening

"Tohar haneshek" (purity of arms). *See* Moral standards
Training, 130, 243; basic training, 101–12; leadership, 117, 119–20, 122; Nahal, 66; realistic, 149, 162; reserve units, 42, 43; and screening, 90, 91, 92; women's corps, 50, 54, 90

War of Attrition, 18–20, 123, 150, 210, 246
War of Independence, 1, 9–11, 16, 46, 70, 74 n.3, 141 n.13, 146, 192, 195, 210, 247
Weizmann, Ezer, 175, 187 n.7
Wingate, Orde, 4, 5, 13
Women's Corps (Chen), 23, 32, 46–56, 79, 87, 90, 102, 103, 141 n.13

Yadin, Yigael, 11, 39, 172, 173
Yamit, city of, 232, 248, 251

Yom Kippur War, 20–22, 28 n.34, 29 n.37, 36, 38, 41, 42, 53, 61, 65, 66, 70, 71, 73, 74 n.3, 75 n.13, 78, 85, 86, 99, 105, 108, 111, 114 n.12, 129, 131, 132, 134, 137, 139, 146, 150, 154, 158, 159, 160, 161, 166, 167, 172, 173, 176, 177, 179, 181, 182, 187 n.5, 193, 194, 195–204, 210, 211–18, 221, 233, 235, 236–38, 251, 252, 254, 256 n.4.

Zionism, 1, 2, 3, 4, 46

About the Author

REUVEN GAL, previously Chief Psychologist of the Israeli Defence Forces, has also served as a Research Associate at Walter Reed Army Institute of Research. He has published articles on behavior under stress, military psychology, heroism in combat, and related subjects in such journals as *Journal of Human Stress*, *Journal of Applied Social Psychology*, and *International Social Science Review*.